CAMBRIDGE TEXTS IN THE
HISTORY OF PHILOSOPHY

———

IMMANUEL KANT
Critique of Practical Reason

CAMBRIDGE TEXTS IN THE HISTORY OF PHILOSOPHY

Series editors

KARL AMERIKS
Professor of Philosophy at the University of Notre Dame

DESMOND M. CLARKE
Professor of Philosophy at University College Cork

The main objective of Cambridge Texts in the History of Philosophy is to expand the range, variety and quality of texts in the history of philosophy which are available in English. The series includes texts by familiar names (such as Descartes and Kant) and also by less well-known authors. Wherever possible, texts are published in complete and unabridged form, and translations are specially commissioned for the series. Each volume contains a critical introduction together with a guide to further reading and any necessary glossaries and textual apparatus. The volumes are designed for student use at undergraduate and postgraduate level and will be of interest not only to students of philosophy but also to a wider audience of readers in the history of science, the history of theology and the history of ideas.

For a list of titles published in the series, please see end of book.

IMMANUEL KANT

Critique of Practical Reason

TRANSLATED AND EDITED BY
MARY GREGOR

WITH AN INTRODUCTION BY
ANDREWS REATH
University of California, Riverside

CAMBRIDGE
UNIVERSITY PRESS

PUBLISHED BY THE PRESS SYNDICATE OF THE UNIVERSITY OF CAMBRIDGE
The Pitt Building, Trumpington Street, Cambridge CB2 1RP, United Kingdom

CAMBRIDGE UNIVERSITY PRESS
The Edinburgh Building, Cambridge CB2 2RU, United Kingdom
40 West 20th Street, New York, NY 10011–4211, USA
10 Stamford Road, Oakleigh, Melbourne 3166, Australia

First published 1997

Printed in the United Kingdom at the University Press, Cambridge

Typeset in 10/12 Ehrhardt

A catalogue record for this book is available from the British Library

Library of Congress cataloguing in publication data
Kant, Immanuel, 1724–1804
[Kritik der praktischen Vernunft. English]
Critique of practical reason / Immanuel Kant; translated and
edited by Mary Gregor; with an introduction by Andrews Reath.
p.   cm. – (Cambridge texts in the history of philosophy)
Includes bibliographical references and index.
ISBN 0 521 59051 5 (hardback). – ISBN 0 521 59962 8 (paperback)
1. Ethics.   I. Gregor, Mary J.   II. Title.   III. Series.
B2773.E5B4 1997
170–dc21 97–8913 CIP

ISBN 0 521 59051 5
ISBN 0 521 59962 8

Contents

Introduction

I

The *Critique of Practical Reason*, published in 1788, is the second of Kant's three *Critiques*, falling between the *Critique of Pure Reason* (first edition: 1781, second edition: 1787) and the *Critique of Judgment* (1790). It is also the second of his three major works devoted to moral theory, along with the *Groundwork to the Metaphysics of Morals* (1785) and the *Metaphysics of Morals* (1797). These works develop an account of morality that reacts to those found in both the empiricist and the rationalist traditions, and together they constitute Kant's lasting contribution to moral theory.

Certain remarks in the *Groundwork* suggest that Kant did not originally plan a separate critique of practical reason. He notes that although a critique of practical reason is the only foundation for a metaphysics of morals (i.e. a systematic classification of human duties), the need for critique is less pressing in the case of practical reason than it is for speculative reason, and that an outline of such a critique would suffice for his purposes.[1] In moral thought, ordinary reason is more easily brought "to a high degree of correctness and precision" in that authoritative practical principles are revealed through the workings of ordinary moral consciousness, while in its "pure but theoretical use, reason is wholly dialectical," tending to make illusory and illegitimate metaphysical claims. Furthermore, executing a critique of practical reason would introduce complexities not absolutely necessary to a presentation of the basic principle of duty [*G* 391]. The idea of writing a separate critique of practical reason appears to have occurred to Kant while he was revising the *Critique of Pure Reason* for its second edition.

[1] See Kant's *Groundwork of the Metaphysics of Morals* in the *Practical Philosophy* volume of the Cambridge Edition of the Works of Immanuel Kant, trans. and ed. Mary Gregor (Cambridge University Press, 1996), hereafter *G*, pp. 391, 445. The "outline" is the Third Section of the *Groundwork*, entitled "Transition from a Metaphysics of Morals to a Critique of Pure Practical Reason." References to Kant's works are included in the text and (with the exception of the *Critique of Pure Reason*) give the pages in the German Academy of Sciences edition of Kant's collected works, which are given in the margins of most English translations. Other abbreviations and translations used are as follows:

CPR Critique of Pure Reason, trans. Norman Kemp Smith (New York: St. Martin's Press, 1965).

MM The Metaphysics of Morals, in *Practical Philosophy*, trans. and ed. Mary Gregor (Cambridge University Press, 1996); also in Cambridge Texts in the History of Philosophy (Cambridge University Press, 1996).

References to the *Critique of Practical Reason*, also to the Academy paging, use no abbreviation.

The topics treated in the *Critique of Practical Reason* fall under three main areas: moral theory, freedom of the will, and the doctrine of the "postulates of pure practical reason," in which practical reason provides grounds for assuming the reality of certain metaphysical ideas which could not be established theoretically. The second *Critique* is a work of moral theory. But as this list of topics may indicate, it establishes important connections between themes that had been treated independently in the *Groundwork* and the *Critique of Pure Reason* – in other words, between Kant's moral theory and his epistemology and metaphysics. Or since Kant is never unconcerned with such connections, it is more accurate to say that in the second *Critique* Kant lays these connections out explicitly. In this respect, the second *Critique* makes an essential contribution to the edifice of Kant's critical system. The fact that it is a work of moral theory that puts some of the key elements of Kant's system into place is one aspect of what Kant terms the "primacy of pure practical reason."

Because of the systematic nature of Kant's concerns, it is difficult to appreciate the significance of certain themes in the second *Critique* without some familiarity with the *Groundwork* and the *Critique of Pure Reason*. To provide some orientation to the *Critique*, this section surveys a few of its main themes and provides some, albeit cursory, background from these other works.

Moral theory

The first major division of the *Critique*, its Analytic, presents some of the fundamental ideas of Kant's moral theory. For example, the opening chapter provides an analysis of the moral law as a principle that gives rise to objective requirements on action which are reason-giving simply in virtue of their suitability to serve as laws that any agent can regard as authoritative, without appeal to an agent's desires or interest in happiness, and which accordingly regulates agents' pursuit of their personal ends. The two chapters of the Analytic that follow take up the idea of the good as the "object of practical reason" and respect for the moral law as the motivation to moral conduct. In Chapter 2, Kant explains the "paradox of method" to which his analysis of morality has led him. Traditionally moral theories had accounted for the content of morality by first assuming a conception of the good which seemed self-evident, or which human beings are generally disposed to desire, and then deriving principles of conduct from this antecedent conception of the good. But Kant argues that in order to support the idea that moral requirements apply with rational necessity, a moral theory must first identify a law or principle to which any rational agent is committed simply in virtue of possessing reason and will, and subsequently define the good as that which one wills under the direction of this principle. What is morally good – the actions, ends and states of affairs which are the objects of good willing – is to be specified by the application of this law. Kant holds that any theory that bases morality on a conception of the good that is prior to the fundamental law is a principle of heteronomy in that it subjects the rational will to an external source of authority, and therefore cannot account for the necessity of moral requirements.[2]

Chapter 3 expands upon a long footnote on respect for the moral law in the *Groundwork* [*G* 401n]. Agents who act out of respect for the moral law are motivated to act by their taking moral considerations to be sufficient reasons for action that can override the reasons provided by one's desires and interest in happiness. That is, respect is the immediate recognition of the authority of morality. But it may also be viewed as the feeling produced by our recognition of the authority of morality; or as we might put it, it is how rational agents who are moved by certain kinds of sensible dispositions experience the motivational efficacy of the moral law. Much of this chapter thus explores how moral consciousness effects the human faculty of desire and feeling when it regulates our tendency to regard the claims of self-love as sufficient reasons for action.[3]

While these discussions develop ideas presented in the *Groundwork*, the *Critique of Practical Reason* takes a somewhat different approach to the justification of the moral law. The *Groundwork* separates this task into two stages, and in the second attempts to establish the validity of the moral law by deriving it from a non-moral conception of freedom. The first two chapters of the *Groundwork* use an analysis of the concept of duty to arrive at a statement of the basic principle of duty, but stop short of showing that we ought to endorse this principle. The formal justification of the validity of the moral law, which Kant refers to as its "deduction" [*G* 454], is left to the third chapter. Here Kant tries to show that it is fully rational to accept the moral law as our basic principle of conduct by deriving it from a conception of freedom that we are warranted in attributing to ourselves on grounds

---

[2] Of course, not every interest in an end is heteronomy, and autonomy is not compromised when an end is given by the moral law. Defining the good as the object of practical reason, among other things, allows Kant in the Dialectic to introduce the highest good as the final end of moral conduct. Since the highest good is an end defined by the moral law, its introduction is consistent with Kant's views about autonomy and the priority of the moral law over the concept of the good.

[3] Also worth noting in this survey is the section appended to the second chapter, "Of the Typic of Pure Practical Judgment." Though brief and obscure, it is important to Kant's account of the Categorical Imperative. Kant explains that we judge whether an action is an instance of a universally valid rule of pure practical reason, or what is the same thing, an instance of the moral good, by attempting to conceive of its maxim as a universal law of nature. Our concern in moral evaluation, of course, is whether an action instantiates a valid "law of freedom." Here Kant claims that a law of nature serves as the "type" for a law of freedom, by which he means that a hypothetical law of nature supplies a concrete exemplification of the property of lawfulness, through which we can judge whether an action is a case of a universally valid rule, or has the form of law. This discussion bears on the related formulations of the Categorical Imperative given on *G* 421, the second of which reads: "Act as if the maxim of your action were to become through your will a universal law of nature."

that are independent of morality. The argument is notoriously obscure, but roughly, it employs a set of analytical claims that connect freedom with morality, and rational agency with freedom, and then holds that our possessing theoretical reason, which is a capacity for spontaneous activity, warrants us in regarding ourselves as rational agents in the sense required by his argument.[4] However in the *Critique* Kant argues that the moral law neither allows of nor needs a deduction in his technical sense, but that its authority is firmly established in ordinary moral consciousness as a "fact of reason." [See, e.g. 31, 46–50.] On reflection we do accept the moral law as an authoritative standard of conduct that provides sufficient and overriding reasons for action and we are motivated to act by our judgments of what it requires. We realize that we can do something because we judge that it is our duty, even when it involves setting aside or foregoing substantial desire-based interests, and we are disposed to self-criticism and self-contempt when we fail to. Whether it is reasonable to accept the requirements of morality is not in question in ordinary practical contexts. In claiming that the validity of the moral law is given as a "fact of reason," Kant holds that it cannot and need not be grounded in anything outside of our ordinary moral consciousness, in which we are directly aware of the law-giving activity of reason.

Freedom of the will

The *Critique's* second general area of concern is, in a sense, just another aspect of the first. Kant claims to provide a proof of a strong notion of human freedom – that is, to establish the reality of transcendental freedom, according to which the human will is a capacity for spontaneous activity, or a kind of causal power, which is independent of determination by empirical conditions.

The possibility of transcendental freedom as a causality which is undetermined by antecedent causal conditions had been of concern to Kant in the *Critique of Pure Reason*, and important components of his account of

---

[4] That theoretical reason is a capacity for spontaneous activity is shown by the fact that it formulates ideas that outrun anything given by sensibility, through which it prescribes ends to the understanding that the understanding cannot form for itself. Kant appears to argue here that a rational being who regards himself as possessing this kind of intelligence must regard himself as having the same capacity for spontaneity in his agency. For discussion of different aspects of the argument of *Groundwork*, III, see: Henry E. Allison, *Kant's Theory of Freedom* (Cambridge University Press, 1990), ch. 12; Thomas E. Hill, Jr., *Dignity and Practical Reason* (Ithaca: Cornell University Press, 1992), ch. 6; Christine M. Korsgaard, *Creating the Kingdom of Ends* (Cambridge University Press, 1996), ch. 6. For discussion of the change in Kant's approach to the justification of morality between the *Groundwork* and the second *Critique*, see Dieter Henrich, "Die Deduktion des Sittengesetzes" in *Denken im Schatten des Nihilismus*, Alexander Schwan, ed. (Darmstadt: Wissenschaftliche Buchgesellschaft, 1975); and Karl Ameriks, *Kant's Theory of Mind* (Oxford: Clarendon Press, 1982), ch. VI.

freewill are developed there. Since Kant's theory of freewill draws on the epistemology of the first *Critique*, it will be useful to mention some of its principal doctrines here. First, Kant's transcendental idealism holds that space and time are not mind-independent features of reality, but structural features of experience specific to human cognition; they are the "forms of intuition," or the forms of human perception. The fact that our experience has structural features that are due to our cognitive faculties introduces a distinction between objects as they appear to us ("appearances" or "phenomena") and objects as they are in themselves, considered apart from the conditions under which they appear ("things-in-themselves" or "noumena"). Second, we should recall Kant's view that two different elements of cognition, intuitions and concepts, are required for synthetic knowledge. Intuitions are singular representations through which material is presented to the mind, while concepts are general representations originating in the spontaneous activity of the understanding. The act of bringing intuitions under a concept in a judgment, through which the manifold of intuition is unified and brought to consciousness, is what gives rise to knowledge.

These elements of Kant's epistemology have several important consequences. First, the spatio-temporal properties of objects and the laws governing spatio-temporal events do not characterize things in themselves, but objects as they appear. Since synthetic knowledge presupposes some intuition, which in us is always spatio-temporal, our knowledge is limited to objects as they appear in space and time; there is no knowledge of things in themselves, which cannot be given in intuition. This analysis of the conditions and limits of knowledge entails the impossibility of a certain kind of metaphysics. Traditionally metaphysics had sought a priori demonstrative knowledge of transcendent facts such as the existence of God, the immortality of the soul, and the principles of cosmology. But if these lie beyond the limits of experience (as the tradition agreed), they are beyond human knowledge. Moreover, claims about such transcendent facts are synthetic. Kant argues that metaphysics had been attempting to establish its conclusions through inferences from purely conceptual premises. Since no such deductive argument can establish any synthetic claim, metaphysics could not produce the kind of knowledge which it sought. Finally, while Kant's epistemology undermines traditional metaphysics, it unexpectedly creates the possibility in principle of making assertions about what lies beyond experience, should we find sufficient grounds for doing so. The distinction between appearances and things in themselves, along with the claim that spatio-temporal properties and laws do not represent objects as they are in themselves, creates room for the thought of noumenal objects subject to laws that are different in kind from those governing spatio-temporal events. Merely thinking about noumenal objects is not knowledge, of course, and the fact that we may coherently entertain such thoughts does not license any assertions about noumenal objects. But since nothing can be known about what is not part of the spatio-temporal framework, there can be no disproof of any (purported) noumenal object. Thus, propositions about noumenal objects cannot be contradicted by any valid theoretical knowledge claim. Therefore while transcendental idealism insists that there can be no knowledge of any noumenal entities, it does so in a way that creates room for the thought of such entities and guarantees that propositions about them are not inconsistent with theoretical knowledge.

Returning now to freedom, in the "Antinomy of Pure Reason" Kant had argued that in its theoretical use reason is led to the concept of transcendental freedom by the demand for completeness in explanation. We explain events in nature by tracing them back to their causes – to antecedent conditions that are jointly necessary and sufficient for their occurrence. But since the causes of any given event themselves admit of explanation in terms of antecedent conditions, the demand for explanation sets up the task of reconstructing the chain of antecedent causes. It is natural to think that the search for explanations is only completed when it identifies an event at the beginning of the causal series whose occurrence is not determined by any antecedent conditions and therefore needs no explanation. In this way, the demand for completeness in explanation, which issues from the activity that is constitutive of the theoretical use of reason, leads to the abstract idea of a transcendentally free cause. But Kant had also shown that everything in nature has a cause by arguing that any event that is a possible object of experience for us must stand in causal relations to prior events, which fix its location in a unified spatio-temporal order. The concept of a transcendentally free cause violates one of the conditions of the unity of experience. Thus, the law of natural causality rules out the possibility of encountering instances of transcendental freedom in our experience of the natural world.[5]

In the resolution of the Third Antinomy, Kant argues that transcendental freedom is at least possible in the sense that it is not inconsistent with universal natural causation. The distinction between appearances and things-in-themselves opens up the possibility that events that are subject to causal determination when viewed as phenomena, may, when viewed as noumena, manifest free causality. For example, human actions, viewed as phenomenal events in the natural world, are explained by tracing their occurrence to antecedent conditions from which they follow with necessity. But when considered as noumena, it may be possible to regard them as resulting from transcendentally free causality. By this route Kant's transcendental idealism creates room for the idea of transcendental freedom. However the claim that there is no inconsistency in viewing, say, human actions as the results of free causality falls far short of giving us positive warrant for doing so. The obvious question at this point is whether we have any grounds for regarding human actions as transcendentally free, and no such grounds can be

---

[5] This paragraph draws on Henry E. Allison, *Kant's Theory of Freedom*, pp. 11–28.

supplied by theoretical reason. In its tasks of explaining the natural world and extending empirical knowledge, it is bound to apply the principle of causality to all events. Indeed, since Kant's resolution of the Third Antinomy does not modify the argument for the law of natural causality, the impossibility of encountering any instances of transcendental freedom in our experience of the natural world remains. Thus the *Critique of Pure Reason* leaves theoretical reason in the situation of having demonstrated the consistency of the idea of transcendental freedom, but of being precluded from asserting its reality.

The second *Critique* claims that grounds for ascribing transcendental freedom to ourselves are supplied by the practical use of reason. Since the moral law provides reasons for action that are independent of the content and strength of our desires, and which can require one to set aside or override desire-based reasons, the ability to act from the moral law – the ability to do something simply because we judge that it is a duty – reveals in us an ability to act independently of determination by empirical conditions. But that is to say that the ability to act from the moral law reveals in us a kind of causality that satisfies the definition of transcendental freedom. Thus the fact of reason, in which we recognize the authority of and are aware of our ability to act from the moral law, discloses our freedom. The moral law, as Kant says, "proves not only the possibility but the reality [of freedom] in beings who cognize this law as binding upon them" [47].

There are several points to note here, to which Kant draws our attention in various places. First and most obvious, Kant holds that the practical use of reason is able to give reality to an idea which reason in its theoretical use had to assume as possible, but could not establish. Moreover, practical reason does more than provide grounds for the abstract claim that there is transcendentally free causality; it supplies a determinate statement of the law that governs such causality, namely the moral law [47–50, 105]. Second, the reality that Kant asserts for transcendental freedom is "objective ... though only practical" [49], and is not an illicit extension of theoretical knowledge beyond the limits of possible experience. Since the reality of transcendental freedom is not established through any sensible intuition, it is not an item of empirical or theoretical knowledge that, for example, can enter into the explanation of events. The grounds for ascribing freedom to ourselves come from our recognition of the authority of moral norms, and this ascription is made for practical purposes, as part of our self-conception as rational agents. Third, whereas in the *Groundwork* Kant appears to believe that we must have grounds for ascribing transcendental freedom to ourselves before we can establish the validity of the moral law, the second *Critique* reverses this order: here Kant argues that it is the validity of the moral law that reveals our freedom. Kant notes that "whereas freedom is indeed the *ratio essendi* of the moral law, the moral law is the *ratio cognoscendi* of freedom" [4n]. Finally, the fact that the validity of the moral law establishes the reality of transcendental freedom serves as a further "credential" [*Kreditiv*] for the moral law [48]. That the moral law provides grounds for assuming the reality of an idea that had remained problematic for reason in its theoretical use, and in this way contributes to the construction of Kant's philosophical system, is a further confirmation of its validity that takes the place of a formal deduction.

The postulates of pure practical reason

The Dialectic of the second *Critique* argues that certain necessary moral interests authorize us to assume the existence of God and the immortality of the soul as "postulates of pure practical reason." These postulates are the elements of a "rational faith" or "reasonable faith" [*Vernunftglaube*],[6] to which Kant refers in his remark that he has "found it necessary to destroy knowledge in order to make room for faith." [*CPR* Bxxx]. Kant argues that the moral law generates a duty to do all we can to bring about the highest good in the world, which for now we may understand as the state of affairs in which the ends of morality are realized in their totality. But the only way in which we can regard the highest good as a practical possibility is by assuming the immortality of the soul and the existence of God as a moral author of the universe who has ordered the world so as to support the ends of morality. Since the duty to make the highest good our end is unconditional, it licenses us to postulate the existence of God and the immortality of the soul, as conditions of the practical possibility of the highest good. We consider this argument in more detail in the last section.

As with the idea of freedom, practical reason, in grounding the postulates, resolves questions that reason in its theoretical use raises, but cannot answer. In the first *Critique*, Kant had argued that in its search for the ultimate ground of all items given in experience – a task that is "prescribed by the very nature of reason itself" [*CPR* Avii] – reason is led to the idea of God as the ultimate ground of all that exists and to the idea of the soul as a simple substance that is the real subject of experience, and attempts to infer their reality. The Dialectic of the first *Critique* exposes the purely "dialectical" or illusory nature of these inferences, arguing that they draw synthetic conclusions from purely conceptual premises and that the reality of such objects cannot be established on theoretical grounds since they cannot be given in intuition. By the same token, neither can their reality be disproved.

---

[6] Kant refers to both a "pure rational faith" [*reiner Vernunftglaube*] [126] and a "pure practical rational faith" [144, 146]. *Glaube* maybe translated both as "faith" and as "belief." Mary Gregor renders *Vernunftglaube* as "rational belief" in this translation, while Lewis White Beck uses "rational faith," "faith of pure practical reason," or even "practical faith." John Rawls suggests the term "reasonable faith" to capture the idea of faith supported by reason, in "Themes in Kant's Moral Philosophy," in Eckart Förster, ed., *Kant's Transcendental Deductions* (Stanford: Stanford University Press, 1989), p. 94.

Thus in its theoretical use, reason may inquire into the objective reality of these ideas, but must remain agnostic. As we have seen, Kant's transcendental idealism creates room for the thought of noumenal objects, and the limits on cognition that place such objects beyond knowledge guarantee that assertions of their reality will not contradict any theoretical claim. This permits the argument that practical reason's need to support the rationality of adopting the highest good as our end is a positive ground for assuming the existence of God and the immortality of the soul. Since the warrant for these assertions comes from a need of practical reason rather than from any sensible intuition, they do not extend theoretical knowledge.

II

One might ask how these diverse topics all find their way into a "critique" of practical reason. An answer to this question requires that we lay out the main lines of argument of the *Critique*. To begin, it may help to say something about the idea of "critique" as Kant understands it, and about the distinction between the theoretical and practical uses of reason.

A "critique" is a critical examination of reason by itself, whose purpose is to establish the powers and limits of a use of reason, and in particular to establish the validity and legitimate employment of those a priori concepts and principles which structure a domain of rational activity. The Prefaces of the *Critique of Pure Reason* make clear that its driving concern is with reason's claims to a priori knowledge of the world, and Kant remarks that a critique "will institute a tribunal which will assure to reason its lawful claims and dismiss all groundless pretensions" [*CPR* Axi]. In the process, the first *Critique* examines all the cognitive faculties which claim to be sources of synthetic a priori knowledge – sensibility, understanding and reason in its theoretical use.

The division of the Transcendental Logic into an Analytic and a Dialectic indicates that critique has both a positive, justificatory task and a negative, critical task. The main task of the Analytic is to establish the validity of the pure concepts of the understanding (the categories) in their application to experience and to derive the a priori principles of the understanding, which are rules for the employment of the categories. The Dialectic demonstrates that reason's claims to knowledge of transcendent entities are groundless by exposing the illusory inferences on which they are based, which in the case of the Antinomies lead to apparent contradictions that threaten the coherence of reason. However assigning the task of justification to the Analytic and criticism to the Dialectic oversimplifies. Since the limitations imposed on reason follow directly from the positive epistemological accomplishments of the Analytic, it serves an obvious critical function. And while the Dialectic demonstrates that the ideas of reason provide no speculative knowledge, it also shows that they have a legitimate regulative role in guiding the employment of the understanding. Reason prescribes aims of completeness and systematic unity to the understanding which it cannot form for itself. The ideas of reason set out these ideals, and are the source of maxims and regulative principles that serve as norms for empirical inquiry and the extension of empirical knowledge. Thus, the Dialectic validates the ideas of reason through their role in extending and systematizing empirical knowledge, and shows that the proper theoretical use of reason is its normative function of guiding empirical inquiry.

While the theoretical use of reason is concerned with knowledge of objects, practical reason is concerned with the "determining grounds of the will" [15]. Kant regards the will as the kind of causal power particular to rational agents, and characterizes it variously as the power to produce objects in accordance with representations of those objects, or as the power to act according to the representation of rules or principles.[7] We should be wary of any simple definition of a capacity as complex as "the will," but certainly Kant's characterizations point to two related aspects of rational volition – that it includes a capacity to act intentionally and a capacity to guide one's actions by reasons and principles. One aspect of the will is the ability to act so as to bring about ends, guided by a prior representation of those ends. And agents guide their choices of ends and of actions that are the means to their ends by the application to themselves of principles of various sorts (ranging, for example, from formal principles of rationality to substantive principles of value). In saying that practical reason is concerned with the determining grounds of the will, Kant is saying that it is concerned with the basic principles governing deliberation and choice, through which agents decide what they have most reason to do. Thus, as we will see, one

---

[7] An example of the first is Kant's characterization of the will as

a faculty either of producing objects corresponding to representations or of determining itself to effect such objects (whether the physical power is sufficient or not), that is, of determining its causality ... [15; cf. also 45, 60; *CPR* Bix-x; and Kant's characterization of the capacity for choice [*Willkür*] at *MM* 213.]

For an example of the second, see the reference to the will as

the ability to determine [one's] causality by the representation of rules, hence insofar as they are capable of actions in accordance with principles and consequently in accordance with a priori practical principles ... [32; cf. also 125; and *G* 412, 427.]

The second sort of characterization dominates in the *Groundwork*.

Kant's conception of the will is quite complex, partly because he is not always consistent in his terminology. In the *Metaphysics of Morals* he draws an explicit distinction between "will" [*Wille*] and "the capacity for choice" [*Willkür*]. *Willkür* is the capacity to choose actions or ends as one wishes. *Wille* is "the capacity for desire considered not so much in relation to the action (as *Willkür* is) but rather in relation to the ground determining choice to action" [*MM* 213]. It is, in other words, the capacity to deliberate about and to decide on reasons for action, which are to guide *Willkür* in its choice of actions or ends. So understood *Wille* is just practical reason. Henry Allison observes that "Kant uses the terms *Willkür* and *Wille* to characterize respectively the legislative and executive functions of a unified faculty of volition, which he likewise refers to as *Wille*." [*Kant's Theory of Freedom*, p. 129.] Kant appears to use *Wille* in this broader sense in the *Groundwork* and the second *Critique*. For discussion see Allison, pp. 129–36.

aim of a critique of practical reason is to establish the basic principles of practical reasoning. As the second *Critique* also has an Analytic and a Dialectic, we should expect it to have both justificatory and critical aims, though these aims map onto the division into Analytic and Dialectic even less neatly than they do in the first *Critique*.

The next section outlines the main line of argument in Chapter I of the Analytic, followed in the last section by a sketch of the main themes of the Dialectic.

III

In both the Preface and Introduction, Kant notes that this work is not a critique of *pure* practical reason, but rather a critique of "reason's entire practical faculty" [3] or "only of *practical* reason as such" [15]. Since the practical use of reason is concerned with the principles governing what we have reason to choose, the first question which the *Critique* must answer is "whether pure reason of itself alone suffices to determine the will or whether it can be a determining ground of the will only as empirically conditioned" [15]. What is at stake in this question and why does Kant insist that pure practical reason needs no critique?

At issue is a fundamental question about the nature of practical rationality over which moral theorists have long divided. Hume famously claimed that "Reason is, and ought only to be the slave of the passions, and can pretend to no other office than to serve and obey them."[8] Hume and other empiricists argue for an instrumental conception of practical reason, which comprises a cluster of theses about motivation and the role of reason in deliberation. Empiricists hold that motives and reasons for action must ultimately be based on desires or basic preferences that are not themselves produced by reasoning, which an agent has as a matter of contingent fact. Practical reason has the limited function of prescribing the means to one's ends, seeking consistency among one's desires, forming a conception of one's overall happiness in light of one's desires, and so forth. Desires and actions are subject to rational assessment only in terms of their consistency with other desires and ends, or with one's overall happiness. There are no principles of reason which prescribe the adoption of any final ends or values, nor any rational grounds on which to assess the intrinsic goodness of actions or ends. Practical reason, so conceived, is "empirically conditioned" in Kant's terms, because the reasons that an agent has for acting are based on empirically given desires, which agents may, without irrationality, lack.

To hold that pure reason is practical is to deny that the empirically conditioned use of practical reason is the only form of practical reason, and to

---

[8] Hume, *A Treatise of Human Nature*, ed. L. A. Selby-Bigge, revised by P. H. Nidditch (Oxford: Clarendon Press, 1978), p. 415.

hold that reason by itself provides grounds sufficient to determine choice. Otherwise put, it is to hold that reason prescribes practical principles and values whose normative force is not based on desire, but which apply to any agent simply in virtue of possessing reason and will. These principles provide a basis for evaluating desires, ends and actions for their inherent conformity to reason rather than on instrumental grounds (e.g. in terms of their contribution to an agent's happiness); and they yield reasons for action that may take priority over an agent's given desires and ends. Since they have necessary reason-giving force for all rational agents, Kant terms them "practical laws."

The question, "Does reason by itself provide grounds sufficient to determine the will?" may appear ambiguous between two different questions: (a) Can reason by itself motivate action? and (b) Does reason by itself generate (non-instrumental) practical principles or requirements on conduct? Kant, however, would not allow a sharp separation between these latter questions, and his question includes both. His conception of rational agents is that they are motivated by what they take to be good reasons for action, and that justifying reasons have motivational force for rational agents.[9] If reason generates non-instrumental practical principles, then reason alone can motivate action, and vice versa. Thus to resolve whether reason alone can determine the will it is enough to show that reason by itself generates practical principles, or practical laws. Kant assumes this task at the outset of the Analytic, and proceeds in Chapter 1 to establish the "Fundamental Law of Pure Practical Reason," which he takes to be the basic principle of morality, or Categorical Imperative.

If pure reason is practical, then it is empirical practical reason which needs critique in the negative sense – a critique that is carried out by pure practical reason. Kant notes that it is "incumbent" upon the *Critique* "to prevent empirically conditioned reason from presuming that it, alone and exclusively, furnishes the determining ground of the will" [16]. The "presumption" of empirical practical reason which Kant has in mind may be the natural tendency to give priority to reasons based in one's personal interests – as, for example, is seen in someone who honors his obligations to others, or takes their needs into account, only on the condition that it does not interfere too much with his getting what he wants. This tendency might be reinforced by a view which may initially seem theoretically plausible, that all reasons for action are ultimately desire-based. Implicit in both this tendency

---

[9] This is not to say that rational agents are always motivated by objectively good reasons for action, but only that they are motivated by considerations that they take to provide good reasons (but which may not actually justify). Nor is it to say that sufficient reasons are always effective motives which lead to action, but only that they have some motivational force. For discussion of this aspect of Kant's conception of agency, see Christine M. Korsgaard, *Creating the Kingdom of Ends*, ch. 4, esp. section III; Andrews Reath, "Kant's Theory of Moral Sensibility," *Kant-Studien* 80, no. 3 (1989): 284–302, esp. 295–300; and Henry E. Allison, *Kant's Theory of Freedom*, pp. 85–94, 125–26.

and this theoretical position is the claim that desire-based interests are sources of sufficient reasons – that, for example, the fact that empirical practical reason identifies an action as conducive to one's overall happiness is always a decisive reason in its favor that settles what to do. It is precisely this sort of claim that the moral law deems illegitimate.[10] The moral law sets out a condition of universalizability (specified by the Categorical Imperative) that ends and actions must satisfy to be permissibly adopted. Actions that advance one's desire-based interests are fully choiceworthy only when they conform to the requirements of morality, and respect for the moral law checks the tendency to treat our desire-based interests as sufficient reasons.[11] By establishing the fundamental principle of pure practical reason, the Analytic thus performs the critical task of setting limits to the employment of empirical practical reason. Pure practical reason needs no critique in this sense since it "proves its reality ... by what it does" [3], and since it serves as the final standard for assessing the choiceworthiness of desire-based interests [15].

Let us now turn to the main argument in Chapter 1, which Kant organizes as a series of theorems and corollaries that follow from the definition of a practical law, leading to the claim that pure reason is practical and concluding that the moral law is a principle of autonomy. Kant defines practical laws as principles of conduct that give reasons for action to all agents just insofar as they have reason and will, without depending on any contingent interests that distinguish one rational agent from another. In the ensuing sections, Kant derives from this definition further conditions that a principle must satisfy to qualify as a law.

---

[10] This "presumption" of empirical practical reason is also mentioned in various forms in the *Groundwork*. See, for example the reference to a "natural dialectic, i.e., a propensity to quibble with these strict laws of duty" and to bend them to one's wishes [*G* 405], as well as the tendency to make exceptions to moral principles which one otherwise wills as universal laws "to the advantage of our inclination." [*G* 424] Also relevant are Kant's characterizations of "self-love" and "self-conceit," in Ch. III of the Analytic [73–76]. Self-love is a natural tendency to take one's inclinations as good reasons for action. Self-conceit is the tendency to claim a special worth for your person that does not recognize the limits on what is worthy of choice set by morality, in virtue of which one takes reasons stemming from self-love to be overriding reasons for action. These are tendencies of "our pathologically determinable self, even though it is unfit to give universal law through its maxims, nevertheless striving antecedently to make its claims primary and originally valid, just as if it constituted our entire self" [74]. Worth noting here is Kant's view that we have a tendency to make value claims on behalf of empirical interests, and that when we do so we act as though these interests are all that there are to the self. It is such claims that pure practical reason must limit. For discussion of how respect for morality restricts self-love and self-conceit, see Reath, "Kant's Theory of Moral Sensibility," and Allison, *Kant's Theory of Freedom*, pp. 123–27.
[11] Lest the case be overstated, it is important to bear in mind that Kant regards the satisfaction of desire-based interests as good when certain conditions are fulfilled. For example, note that self-love is called "rational self-love" when limited to conditions of moral permissibility [73]. For discussion of Kant's notion of conditional goodness, see Christine Korsgaard, *Creating the Kingdom of Ends*, chs. 4, 8–9.

"Theorem 1" introduces the concept of a "material practical principle" and claims that no such principles provide practical laws. A material practical principle is a principle that "presupposes an *object* (matter) of the faculty of desire as the determining ground of the will" [21]. This remark deserves some comment. A material practical principle is not simply a principle that directs an agent to some object or end. Since Kant thinks that every action-guiding principle contains an end, the concept would be of no interest if that were all it amounted to.[12] The determining ground of the will is the reason or principle on which one acts. As Kant's explanation indicates, a material practical principle is thus one in which the reason for acting is given by an object for which one has an independently given desire. Simply put, it is a principle which there is reason to accept on the condition that one has an independent desire for (or is antecedently disposed to take satisfaction in) an object. A desire is independent in this context if it is not produced by one's accepting the principle, and if the object of the desire can be described without reference to the principle.[13] Since the "object" or "matter of the faculty of desire" to which Kant refers is presumably an end contained in the principle (either an end prescribed by the principle, or the end to which an action is prescribed as a means), the idea is that there is a reason to act on this principle only if one has an independent desire for this end.

To illustrate, let's take Kant's example of the principle that one should work and save in one's youth so as not to want in one's old age [20]. Individuals normally desire comfort and security, and will have these desires in their old age. Given the fact that one will have these desires when older and that working and saving when younger are necessary means to their satisfaction, there is reason to work and save for this purpose now. The desires for comfort and security are independently given desires: they are not (or will not be) produced by your accepting this principle, and their objects of comfort and security can be specified without referring to the principle. If you know that you will not have these desires – for example, because you know that you will not live that long, are willing to forgo comfort later in life in order to consume more now, and so on – then it would seem that you have no reason to work and save now for that purpose. Since it is a condition of your having reason to work and save now that you will have these independent desires, the principle is a material practical principle. In contrast, consider the principle that one ought to treat others fairly

---

[12] See 34: "Now it is indeed undeniable that every volition must have an object and hence a matter; but the matter is not, just because of this, the determining ground and condition of the maxim ...". See also *MM* 381–85, where Kant claims that every action has an end, that there are objective ends that it is a duty to have, and that objective ends can be the "material ground of choice" [*MM* 381].

[13] Here and in the next paragraph I draw on Rawls's distinction between "object-dependent desires" and "principle-dependent desires." See John Rawls, *Political Liberalism* (New York: Columbia University Press, 1996), pp. 82–86. Also relevant here is Thomas Nagel's distinction between motivated and unmotivated desires; see Nagel, *The Possibility of Altruism* (Princeton: Princeton University Press, 1978), pp. 29–30.

(where fair treatment is prescribed as an end). Someone who accepts this principle will be motivated to treat others fairly, but this desire is not independent of the principle. The desire to treat others fairly is produced by accepting the principle, and the object of the desire (fair treatment of others) can only be specified by a principle; we can't say what it is a desire for until we have a principle defining fair treatment. Because the desire to treat others fairly is a consequence of one's accepting the principle, the presence of this desire is not – in fact, cannot be – a condition of having a reason to accept the principle. Since the reason to accept the principle does not depend on an independently given desire, it is not a material practical principle.

To continue with the argument, one has reason to act on a material practical principle only if one has an independent desire for, or will take satisfaction in, its object. Thus one cannot determine whether an agent has reason to act on such a principle without empirical information about that agent's desires and circumstances. But the validity of a law must be rooted in the basic features of agency, and cannot depend on contingent conditions of this sort that distinguish one agent from another. Such principles therefore cannot provide laws.

Theorem II offers a further generalization about material principles, claiming that they are "of one and the same kind and come under the general principle of self-love or one's own happiness" [22]. This assertion is somewhat puzzling, because other-regarding natural desires such as compassion, or affection for loved ones, could be the basis of principles that are desire-based in Kant's sense, but nonetheless directed at the well-being of others. In what sense do all material principles fall under the principle of happiness? What Kant does here is to make explicit a structural feature shared by material principles. In acting on such a principle, one takes the fact that the object offers prospective satisfaction as a reason for acting, and one decides how to act by asking how much satisfaction it offers – which, of course, is a function of one's current desires and dispositions. Kant defines the principle of happiness or self-love as the principle of making one's overall happiness "the supreme determining ground of choice" [22]. In other words, it is the principle of acting so as to maximize satisfaction over the course of one's life. If this is your fundamental principle of action, you take the contribution of an action to your overall satisfaction as a measure of the reasons in its favor, and decide how to act by asking what will bring you most overall satisfaction. The principle of happiness thus expresses a formal feature which all material principles share, which highlights the way in which such principles provide reasons and the method of choice employed in acting on them.[14] In the Corollary and first Remark to Theorem II, Kant

---

[14] For further discussion of this point, see Andrews Reath, "Hedonism, Heteronomy and Kant's Principle of Happiness," *Pacific Philosophical Quarterly* 70:1, pp. 42–72, esp. 50–59. Remarks in these pages of the *Critique* have led many people to read Kant as a psychological hedonist about non-moral motives. I argue against that interpretation in this paper.

argues that if all practical principles were material, one could draw no interesting distinction between a "higher faculty of desire" and a "lower faculty of desire." This is a distinction between different ways in which the will is determined, or between different models of motivation and choice. Kant's point is that if all practical principles were material principles, there would be no reason to introduce any model of choice other than that captured by the principle of happiness. In fact, it would not be anyone's principle, but just a description of human volition – as most empiricists believe.

Kant now argues in Theorem III that it is the form of a principle that determines whether it can serve as a practical law, and then considers what that form is. Theorems I and II have shown that principles which are reason-giving through their matter (i.e., which there is reason to adopt only if one has an independent desire for the object) fall under the principle of happiness and provide no laws. If we abstract away the matter of a principle as a potential source of reasons, all that remains is its form. Thus if we are to regard a principle or maxim as a practical law, it must determine the will through its form alone – that is, it must be one that there is sufficient reason to accept simply in virtue of its form. Such principles have the "form of law" – the form that enables a principle to serve as a practical law.

The simplicity of Kant's argument masks a number of perplexities and we shall not attempt a complete treatment here. A few things seem relatively clear. First, some practical principles have the form of law while others do not.[15] Whether a principle has the form of law is ascertained by the Categorical Imperative, which yields a formal procedure that assesses a maxim of action by asking whether it can be willed as universal law without inconsistency.[16] Kant gives an example in which one accepts a monetary deposit from someone who subsequently dies. Since no record was made, no one can prove that one has the deposit, and one has only to deny its existence to keep the money. But a maxim of violating the trust of others in order to increase one's wealth does not have the form of law, as we see from the impossibility of willing it as universal law: it would be self-defeating if made a principle from which anyone may act. Second, whether a principle has the form of law can determine whether there is sufficient reason to act on it. Again, there are a number of issues that need sorting out, but we can say this much. The fact that a maxim does *not* have the form of law (as determined by the Categorical Imperative) is a sufficient reason to refrain from certain actions and a sufficient reason to perform certain others. In Kant's example, since the maxim of violating trust to increase one's wealth

---

[15] Here note the first sentence of the Remark to Theorem III.

[16] For some discussions of the procedure based on the universal law formula of the Categorical Imperative (sometimes referred to as the "CI procedure"), see Onora O'Neill, *Constructions of Reason* (Cambridge University Press, 1989), chs. 5–8; John Rawls, "Themes in Kant's Moral Philosophy," pp. 82–90; Christine M. Korsgaard, *Creating the Kingdom of Ends*, chs. 3, 5; Barbara Herman, *The Practice of Moral Judgment*, chs. 3, 6–7 and 10.

cannot be universalized, it is impermissible to deny that the deposit was made (regardless of how much one would benefit from the money), and it is one's duty to reveal its existence. Alternatively, *having* the form of law is a condition that must be satisfied for there to be sufficient reason to act on a principle. For example, an action that contributes to one's overall happiness is reasonably adopted and fully worthy of choice if – but only if – its maxim is universalizable.

Third, Theorem III has stated the condition that a principle must satisfy if it is to serve as a practical law – that there must be sufficient reason to accept it simply in virtue of its form. Clearly this condition is intended to lead (as it does later in §7) to a general principle that is an alternative to the principle of happiness, namely the higher order principle of acting only from maxims that are reason-giving through their form, thus having the form of law. This principle itself must be reason-giving through its form – because, we might say, it is a formal expression of the way in which practical laws provide reasons. And it is a law – the moral law, in fact. Kant takes it to be an abstract statement of the basic principle used by "the most common understanding" [27] to determine whether an action is morally permissible.

Kant argues next that "freedom and unconditional practical law reciprocally imply each other" [29]. His aim is to establish two claims that together establish a deep connection between morality and freedom. They are: (1) If an agent's basic principle is to act only from maxims with the form of law (the moral law), the agent is transcendentally free; and (2) If an agent has a free will, then the moral law is the basic principle of its will. The argument for the first is given as the solution to "Problem I": Assume an agent who finds sufficient reason to act on a maxim only if the maxim has the form of law. Such an agent has the ability to abstract from and, if necessary, set aside reasons taken from its desire-based interests. For example, the weight of the agent's desire-based interests in practical reasoning is not determined by the strength of various desires, but by a judgment issuing from a rational procedure that assesses whether a maxim of acting on some interest has the form of law. One's desire-based interests are ultimately traceable to the empirical conditions which produce these desires. Thus an agent who can act from reasons for action based on the legislative form of a maxim, in abstraction from desire-based interests, can act independently of empirical conditions. An agent with the ability to act on this kind of reason satisfies the definition of transcendental freedom. The other argument solves "Problem II": An agent with a free will can determine itself to act independently of empirical conditions. Since an agent with a will is guided by its conception of what it has reason to do, that is to say: it can act from reasons that are independent of its desire-based interests, or (in Kant's terms) independent of the "matter" of a principle. But a will must act on some principle; otherwise it would display random activity that would not count as volition. What, then, can serve as its basic principle, by which it determines how to act? Since its basic reasons for action do not depend on the matter of a principle, they must be taken from the form. That is to say that a free will must have the basic principle of taking the legislative form of a maxim as a sufficient reason for action.[17]

By this point Kant has, beginning from a definition of a practical law (§1), established the basic condition that a practical law must satisfy (Theorem III) and an analytical connection between freedom and practical law (§§5–6). In §7, Kant states the "Fundamental Law of Pure Practical Reason," which he identifies as the Categorical Imperative. In stating it as an imperative, Kant presents it as a valid law, and he claims here that the moral law is established as a "fact of reason" [*ein Faktum der Vernunft*].[18] In ordinary practical reasoning we do take the moral law as a source of authoritative requirements that limit the weight that we may give to our desire-based interests, and we are able to act on these requirements simply because we ought to. The authority of the moral law is reflected in the standards to which we hold ourselves, the phenomenon of respect for the moral law, the workings of conscience and the moral emotions, and so on. Because of the necessity with which moral requirements present themselves, we presume that they are requirements of reason. Kant's analysis confirms their basis in reason by identifying the features that would be true of a law prescribed by reason and showing that they are present in the basic principle of ordinary moral thought. But the authority of the moral law rests ultimately on the fact that it is firmly rooted in ordinary thought and experience. [Cf. 91–92.]

The fact of reason shows that there are practical laws. It follows that reason by itself provides sufficient determining grounds of the will. Given that laws determine the will through their form (Theorem III), that a will for whom the form of law provides a sufficient reason for action is transcendentally free (Problem I), and that the fundamental principle of morality is a law for us and a determining ground of our will as shown by the fact of reason, it follows that we are transcendentally free.

While Kant sometimes identifies the fact of reason, or consciousness of

[17] Kant develops a more satisfactory version of this argument in the opening sections of *Groundwork*, III [446–47]. For discussion, see the references to Hill and Korsgaard in note 4, and Allison, Kant's *Theory of Freedom*, ch. 11.

[18] On the fact of reason, see Rawls, "Themes in Kant's Moral Philosophy," esp. p. 102: "[the fact of reason] is the fact that in our common moral consciousness we recognize and acknowledge the moral law as supremely authoritative and immediately directive for us." See also Lewis White Beck, *A Commentary on Kant's "Critique of Practical Reason"* (Chicago: University of Chicago Press, 1960), pp. 166–75 and "The Fact of Reason: An Essay on Justification in Ethics," in *Studies in the Philosophy of Kant* (Indianapolis: Bobbs-Merrill, 1965), pp. 200–14 ; and Allison, *Kant's Theory of Freedom*, ch. 13.

The "fact of reason" is an unusual notion, as may be acknowledged in Kant's remark that our consciousness of the moral law is the "sole fact of pure reason" [31]. As Kant stresses, it is certainly not an empirical fact supported by sensible intuition. His choice of this expression signals that the authority of the moral law is given with a kind of immediacy: we are directly aware in an underived way of the authority of the moral law and the law-giving activity of pure practical reason.

the authority of the moral law, with consciousness of freedom,[19] he is clear that it is our recognition of the authority of the moral law that reveals our freedom, and that in the absence of such moral consciousness we would have no reason to ascribe freedom to ourselves [30–1, 47–8]. The sort of causality which a will exercises is a function of the character of the principles by which it is governed. The moral law provides its own sufficient grounds of choice based on the legislative form of one's maxims, which require us to abstract from subjective interests in determining what we have reason to do. A will governed by such a principle thus has the ability to act independently of determination by empirical conditions. The validity of the moral law and the reality of transcendental freedom are, in effect, different aspects of pure practical reason: the moral law is the basic principle, and transcendental freedom is the kind of causality exercised by agents whom it can motivate. But the grounds for attributing such causality to ourselves come from the characteristics of this principle.[20]

One of the most intriguing aspects of Kant's demonstration of freedom is that, as he insists, it does not extend theoretical knowledge, but gives the concept "objective, and though only practical, undoubted *reality*" and that it is introduced "for none other than a practical purpose" [49]. What Kant must substantiate is that the assertion of freedom is rationally based, but not in the way that knowledge claims are. If so, it is not a claim to theoretical knowledge, and therefore complies with the strictures of the first *Critique*. His account includes these elements: That we are transcendentally free is, it would appear, a metaphysical claim about the self of just the sort that reason in its theoretical use attempted, but could not establish. And it is an assertion for which he claims rational and objective grounds: the reality of freedom "is proved by an apodictic law of practical reason ..."; the moral law reveals "that freedom is real" [3–4]. But it is the practical use of reason that, in the ways we have seen, both supplies the grounds for this assertion and gives substance to, or specifies, the abstract idea of freedom.[21] Practical reason supplies a determinate statement of the law that governs the activity of a free will, and our recognition of the validity of the law is the ground for

---

[19] As at 42: "this fact is inseparably connected with, and indeed identical with, consciousness of freedom of the will." Cf. also 29–30, 46.

[20] The freedom revealed by our ability to act from the moral law is a perfectly general capacity to act independently of determination by empirical conditions. It is important for Kant's theory that this capacity underlies *all* choice and action, including those in which one acts from desire-based interests or non-moral motives. In other words, we are free in *all* exercises of agency, not just those in which we act from moral reasons; otherwise (assuming that freedom is a condition of responsibility) we would be responsible for our actions only when we act morally, and could not be held accountable when we act contrary to morality. (Immoral and evil actions are freely chosen – that is why they are evil.) Transcendental freedom is a feature of our will that we would have no reason to ascribe to ourselves in the absence of our moral capacities, and which may be most directly manifested when we act from moral motives. But what our moral consciousness reveals is a feature of volition that it is present in all choice.

ascribing freedom to ourselves. Freedom is manifested in activities in which we acknowledge the authority of this law, such as patterns of reasoning and choice, responses such as respect, and so on. Somewhat oversimplifying, our self-awareness of such activities and capacities is an awareness of freedom. The way in which various elements of moral consciousness give content to the notion of freedom is analogous to the role of intuition in empirical knowledge. But since moral consciousness is not spatio-temporal intuition, the assertion of freedom does not have a theoretical basis. Moreover, this basis is unavailable. Transcendental freedom is not a possible object of intuition, nor is it needed to explain events. The fact that the concept of freedom cannot be determined in the way necessary to enter into empirical knowledge guarantees that it can only be used for practical purposes, as part of our self-conception as agents.

The last "theorem" in Chapter I is Theorem IV. It introduces the central notion of autonomy, claiming among other things (1) that the moral law is a principle of autonomy, in that a will subject to the moral law is bound only to its own fundamental principle, or the principle through which reason is law-giving, and not to any external source of authority; and (2) that only such a principle can ground necessary moral requirements. We cannot do justice to this complex notion here, and must limit ourselves to a brief comment on the first claim. The moral law demands that one base one's reasons on the legislative form of one's maxims, in abstraction from their matter. Kant believes that he has shown that in acting from this principle, one is guided by the will's own principle and is subject only to the authority inherent in one's reason and to nothing external to reason. When one takes one's reasons from the legislative form of one's maxims, one is motivated by that feature of a principle that makes it a law. One thus acts from the principle that is constitutive of practical reason, through which reason is law-giving. But when one bases one's reasons on the matter of a principle, one takes one's reasons from a source external to reason.[22] Perhaps this allows us to see how the requirement expressed by the moral law is simply that of acting from the principle that expresses the nature of pure practical reason, without submitting to any external authority. This is autonomy.

[21] See 56:

the concept [of unconditioned causality] is given significance in the moral law ... thus I have, indeed, no intuition that would determine its objective theoretical reality for it, but it has nonetheless a real application which is exhibited *in concreto* in dispositions or maxims, that is, it has practical reality which can be specified; and this is sufficient to justify it even with regard to noumena.

[22] For example, when one acts on a desire-based interest, one allows one's reasons for action to be determined by one's desires, and ultimately by whatever external factors are responsible for one's desires. However, action that is desire-based in the ordinary sense is not the only form of heteronomy. A principle of submitting to an uncritically accepted social, political or religious authority – for example, of performing an action simply because it is demanded by someone in a position of authority – is a principle of heteronomy, and in

We close this section with two comments about the significance of Kant's doctrine of the fact of reason. First, by claiming that the moral law is given as a fact of reason, Kant adopts a coherentist or non-foundationalist approach to the justification of morality, holding that the authority of morality cannot be derived from theoretical reason, or from a conception of rationality or agency devoid of moral content – indeed that it cannot be based on anything outside of itself.[23] The shape that Kant's theory eventually takes explains in retrospect some of the barriers to producing this kind of "deduction" of the moral law. The moral law is a principle of reason, but of a form of reason that in the practical sphere is revealed primarily through moral consciousness. If so, it is unclear how to give a characterization of this form of practical reason that is independent of morality, which could then be cited as its basis. For the most natural characterization is simply to specify the basic principles of morality. What alternative approaches to justification are there? One can articulate the basic principles that underlie ordinary moral judgments, and show how they express values, attitudes towards persons and conceptions of agency that are firmly rooted in ordinary thought and experience. One can show that the basic principles of morality have the marks of a principle of reason. And one can look for ways in which the different uses of reason form a single coherent system. Kant pursues all these avenues in the *Critique*.

Second, the way in which the fact of reason warrants regarding ourselves as free illustrates a way in which important aspects of our self-conception are rooted in moral consciousness. Kant thinks the moral law provides insight into important deliberative and motivational capacities, including a form of practical reason, that, apart from moral consciousness, we would not understand, much less have any reason to attribute to ourselves. To give an account of these capacities we need to engage in moral theory, because a full description of the relevant capacities presupposes an account of the content and structure of the principles which guide practical reasoning and choice. If so, it is a mistake to allow conceptions of practical reason and motivation that are developed independently of morality to set prior constraints on the content of moral theory – for instance, by insisting that acceptable moral principles must fit into a conception of motivation or rationality derived solely from empirical inquiry. Moral theory must be free

---

precisely the same way: one allows one's actions to be directed by a source of authority external to reason. Kant argues that moral theories that base the principle of right conduct on an antecedent conception of the good are principles of heteronomy because they direct agents to take their reasons for action from a source external to reason. [Cf. 63–65] Indeed, Kant uses the term "heteronomy" mainly to refer to this kind of moral theory, which he thinks incapable of grounding obligation.

[23] For discussion of this point, see Rawls, "Themes in Kant's Moral Philosophy," esp. pp. 102–13. For a discussion of Kant's non-foundationalism in a broader context, see Onora O'Neill, *Constructions of Reason*, chs. 1–3.

to articulate the principles that we actually recognize, and to secure those insights into our nature which they provide.

IV

The Dialectic completes the project of conferring practical reality on the problematic concepts of speculative reason by arguing for the existence of God and the immortality of the soul as "practical postulates" which provide the elements of a "pure practical rational faith" [146]. Kant occasionally refers to freedom as a postulate in the Dialectic, but his considered view stresses an important difference: the (practical) reality of freedom is established directly by the authority of the moral law, while the postulates of God and immortality are introduced as necessary conditions of the practical possibility of the highest good.

The argument for the postulates runs as follows. Kant argues that the moral law generates a duty to do all we can to bring about the highest good in the world, which he specifies as a state of affairs in which all agents have achieved virtue and happiness is distributed in accordance with virtue.[24] As far as we can see, the possibility of the highest good is consistent with the laws of nature, in that it would result if everyone acted from the moral law. Possibility in the minimal sense of consistency with natural laws is a condition of there being a duty to promote the highest good. However, since our experience of human events offers no evidence that such a state of affairs is achievable, and if anything, indicates the contrary, it seems at best an empty possibility. But we cannot rationally and in good faith adopt a state of affairs as our end if we do not believe it to be a real possibility, nor, more to the point, without a conception of the world that shows us how it might occur. Thus is generated a contradiction within practical reason, which Kant refers to as its "antinomy" [113]. For morality creates a duty to promote a state of affairs which our experience suggests is mere fantasy – an "empty imaginary end" [114] – and which, therefore, it seems that we cannot adopt as our end without some kind of irrationality. The only way in which we can conceive of the highest good as a real possibility is by assuming the immortality of the soul and the existence of God as a moral author of the universe who has ordered the laws of nature to support the possibility of moral ends. Thus a "need of pure practical reason" licenses us to postulate the existence of God and the immortality of the soul.

The "antinomy of practical reason" and the idea of a "need of practical reason" deserve further comment. This antinomy results when practical

---

[24] The joint satisfaction of these two conditions would imply that all individuals are virtuous and are able to achieve their permissible ends. How the highest good is introduced or constructed by the moral law, what its content is and what the basis is (if any) of the duty to pursue the highest good are controversial questions. For discussion, see the secondary literature on the Dialectic recommended below in "Further Reading."

reason imposes contradictory demands that threaten its internal coherence: when pure practical reason generates a duty to promote an end which it is either irrational to adopt, or "practically impossible to strive for" [143], given our inability to conceive of its possibility in concrete terms. It is important to Kant's argument that the antinomy affect neither the validity of the moral law, nor the duty to promote the highest good. The latter especially must remain in force as an unconditional requirement, so that we cannot resolve the antinomy by abandoning this duty.

The argument for the postulates turns on the fact that we need to conceive of the possibility of the highest good as a condition of making it our end, and the structure of this need is quite complex. He does not simply claim that we are warranted in postulating the existence of God: "it is morally necessary to assume the existence of God," [125] though he qualifies this necessity as "subjective" rather than "objective," insisting that it is a need, not a duty or a command [125–26, 144–46]. Generally speaking, a need is a condition of satisfying an interest that one in some sense is not free to abandon. Since the duty to promote the highest good is objectively necessary, we may not abandon our interest in it. A condition of making the highest good our end is that we have a way of representing it to ourselves as possible, and this may be done in different ways. The fact that it is not inconsistent with the laws of nature leads to a representation of its possibility, though not one that Kant thinks can sustain our commitment to it. Given our limited perspective on the world and given the way in which our cognitive faculties operate, the only way of representing the possibility of the highest good that enables us to make it our end is through the postulates.[25] This is a "subjective condition of our reason" which makes it necessary for us to represent the possibility of the highest good in this rather than some other way.[26]

[25] Cf. 145: the impossibility of the highest good

is *merely subjective*, that is, our reason finds it *impossible for it* to conceive, in the mere course of nature, a connection so exactly proportioned and so thoroughly purposive between events occurring in the world in accordance with such different laws, although, as with everything else in nature that is purposive, it nevertheless cannot prove ... the impossibility of it in accordance with universal laws of nature.

Assuming a "wise author presiding over nature" is, due to a "subjective condition of reason,"

the only way in which it is theoretically possible for [reason] to think the exact harmony of nature with the realm of morals as the condition of the possibility of the highest good, and at the same time the only way that is conducive to morality ... [145]

[26] So there are at least two components to the need of pure practical reason. We need a way to represent the possibility of the highest good; and because of the "subjective condition of our reason," we need to represent its possibility by postulating a moral author of the universe who has ordered the laws of nature so as to support moral ends. Since different representations of the possibility of the highest good are consistent with (i.e., not contradicted by) theoretical reason, we are free to choose the one that we need.

Kant says more about the idea of a need of reason in "What does it mean to orient oneself in thinking?" trans. by Allen Wood in *Religion and Rational Theology* (Cambridge Edition of the Works of Immanuel Kant), ed. Allen Wood and George di Giovanni (Cambridge University Press, 1996).

There are many points at which one might criticize Kant's argument, but it may be more instructive instead to consider the significance of the notion of a "practical postulate." Kant presents them as rationally grounded beliefs about the world and about ourselves that are justified on other than theoretical grounds – that is, that are grounded in practical interests that we are not free to abandon. The postulates are theoretical or speculative assertions – assertions which "theoretical reason is justified in assuming" [134], or which "speculative reason must concede" [144; cf. 120–21, 135] about the "physical or metaphysical conditions, in a word those which lie in the nature of things, of the possibility of the highest good ..." [143]. Their justification requires special conditions. They must be conceptually coherent and may not contradict any established theoretical claim – a condition secured by transcendental idealism. Accepting these assertions must be a "need of pure practical reason" in the sense that it is a necessary condition of adopting an end which is morally required. Finally, the postulates must not be regarded as extending theoretical knowledge of objects, and, e.g., cited to explain any events in nature. As rationally grounded speculative assertions, they "extend speculative cognition" [132, 134–35] but only "for practical purposes," [133] and they cannot be used for "theoretical purposes" [134]. Since the ground for the postulates is the need of practical reason just described, we may assert only what is necessary to render the possibility of the highest good conceivable. Moreover, since the objects of these assertions are not given in intuition, we are precluded from making synthetic assertions which would determine their nature in any specific way. Thus, somewhat oversimplifying, Kant thinks that we may assert that God exists as a moral author of the universe, or that the soul is a simple eternal substance, but cannot ascribe any determinate properties to these objects. The fact that we are limited in what we may say about these objects guarantees that the postulates are only usable for the purpose of a conception of the world that supports the rationality of adopting the highest good as our end.

The Dialectic clearly has the positive task of justifying the postulates in their restricted practical use. Does it also have a significant critical function? Parallels between the antinomies of the first and second *Critiques* suggest a critical function with similarities to the Analytic's task of prescribing limits to empirical practical reason. The antinomies of pure reason are apparent contradictions threatening the coherence of theoretical reason, which are generated in part by the assumption that the objects given in experience are things-in-themselves, and they are resolved through the distinction between appearances and things-in-themselves. The antinomy of practical reason arises when a view of the course of human events based on our experience of the world leads us to regard the highest good as a practical impossibility. While this view of events is the only one available, conscientious moral agents find themselves in the untenable situation of setting out ideal moral goals that it is our duty to pursue, but which seem to be no more than empty, unachievable ideals, and are therefore not rationally adopted. The distinction between appearances and things-in-themselves points to a way out, in this case by creating room for different estimates about what may be possible within the course of events. If we may assert that the laws of nature have a noumenal ground – for example, that they are the product of a moral author of the universe – we would have a way of envisioning how natural laws could support the possibility of moral ends, and may interpret events in the world as displaying progress toward the achievement of moral goals when this reading is not contradicted by other evident facts. As we have seen, this resolution of the antinomy is made available when the need of practical reason stemming from the duty to pursue the highest good provides the positive warrant for this assertion. The critical task of the Dialectic is thus to show that the contradiction that threatens the coherence of practical reason is only apparent. This it does by blocking an inference from an empirically based conception of events that undermines the possibility of committing ourselves to certain moral ideals, through the claim that they are purely fantastic goals that we have no hope of achieving.

The extent to which all the important conclusions of the *Critique* are in some form a consequence of the fact that pure reason is practical is seen in the way in which the extension of speculative belief represented by the postulates is driven by practical interests and rests on what Kant terms the "primacy of pure practical reason" [119]. When we find that reason in its practical use needs to assert certain propositions that were transcendent for theoretical reason, the question arises as to which use of reason has primacy. If it is reasonable to accept only those assertions that can be established on theoretical grounds, speculative reason has primacy. If practical reason has primacy, it is reasonable to accept speculative propositions that are presupposed by necessary practical interests when the conditions outlined above are satisfied: these propositions contradict no established theoretical claim, accepting them is a need of pure practical reason, and they are not treated as extensions of knowledge but are used only for practical purposes. Kant claims primacy for the practical use of reason because morality places demands on us that are unconditional and have priority over all our other interests, and because "all interest is ultimately practical" [121].[27]

---

[27] I would like to thank Karl Ameriks for his many helpful suggestions during the writing of this introduction.

Chronology

1724	Immanuel Kant born April 22 in Königsberg, East Prussia
1730–2	Attended Vorstädter Hospitalschule (elementary school)
1732–40	Attended the Collegium Fridericianum (parochial–Pietist–school)
1740–46	Attended the University of Königsberg
1747–54	Served as private tutor for families in the vicinity of Königsberg
1755	Completed his dissertation entitled, "Succinct Exposition of Some Meditations on Fire," and received his doctoral degree from the Faculty of Philosophy at the University of Königsberg
1755	*Universal Natural History and Theory of the Heavens*, in which Kant proposed an astronomical theory now known as the Kant–Laplace hypothesis
1755	*New Elucidation of the First Principles of Metaphysical Cognition*, paper presented to the Philosophy Faculty
1756	Three treatises on an earthquake in Lisbon
1762	*The False Subtlety of the Four Syllogistic Figures*
1763	*The Only Possible Argument in Support of a Demonstration of the Existence of God*
1764	*Observations on the Feeling of the Beautiful and the Sublime*
1764	*Inquiry Concerning the Distinctiveness of the Principles of Natural Theology and Morals*
1766	*Dreams of a Spirit-seer elucidated by Dreams of Metaphysics*
1770	Appointed Professor of Logic and Metaphysics at the University of Königsberg; Inaugural Dissertation entitled: *Concerning the Form and Principles of the Sensible and the Intelligible World*
1781	*Critique of Pure Reason*, first (A) edition
1783	*Prolegomena to Any Future Metaphysics*
1784	*Ideas towards a Universal History from a Cosmopolitan Point of View*
1784	*An Answer to the Question: What is Enlightenment?*
1785	Review of Herder's *Ideas for a Philosophy of the History of Mankind*
1785	*Groundwork of the Metaphysics of Morals*
1786	Elected to the Academy of Sciences in Berlin
1786	*Conjectural Beginning of Human History*
1786	*Metaphysical Foundations of Natural Science*

Further reading

The standard German edition of Kant's works is the German Academy of Sciences edition of *Kants gesammelte Schriften* (Berlin: Walter de Gruyter, 1900–). The *Kritik der praktischen Vernunft* is contained in volume 5. Another readily available edition is published by Meiner Verlag (Hamburg, 1990), with an introduction by Karl Vorländer; this edition also has an extensive bibliography of secondary works on the *Critique* (in German, English and French) through 1990. The translation of the *Critique of Practical Reason* used here is, with minor revisions, that found in *Practical Philosophy* (The Cambridge Edition of the Works of Immanuel Kant), trans. and ed. by Mary Gregor (Cambridge University Press, 1996), pp. 133–271. Other English translations include that by Lewis White Beck (Library of Liberal Arts, 1956), which was first published in *Kant's Critique of Practical Reason and other Writings in Moral Philosophy* (Chicago: University of Chicago Press, 1949). An earlier translation was done by Thomas Kingsmill Abbott, in *Kant's Critique of Practical Reason and other Works on the Theory of Ethics* (London: Longman's, Green and Co. Ltd., 1873; sixth edition, 1909).

Lewis White Beck's *A Commentary on Kant's "Critique of Practical Reason"* (Chicago: University of Chicago Press, 1960) is a commentary on the entire *Critique* which provides important background and is useful in sorting out difficult passages. See also his "The Fact of Reason: An Essay on Justification in Ethics," in *Studies in the Philosophy of Kant* (Indianapolis: Bobbs-Merrill, 1965), pp. 200–14. Highly recommended is an essay on Kant's moral theory by John Rawls, "Themes in Kant's Moral Philosophy," in Eckart Förster, ed., *Kant's Transcendental Deductions* (Stanford: Stanford University Press, 1989). Rawls's essay gives a synoptic treatment of several themes, including the fact of reason, Kant's approach to the authentication of the moral law, and his view of the moral law as a law of freedom. Since the second *Critique* relies on many ideas treated in the *Groundwork*, familiarity with Kant's ethical theory is useful in studying this work. The following volumes all contain important essays on a wide range of topics in Kant's normative theory: Onora O'Neill, *Constructions of Reason* (Cambridge University Press, 1989); Thomas E. Hill, Jr., *Dignity and Practical Reason* (Ithaca: Cornell University Press, 1992); Barbara Herman, *The Practice of Moral Judgment* (Cambridge: Harvard University Press, 1993); Christine M. Korsgaard, *Creating the Kingdom of Ends* (Cambridge University Press, 1996).

The Cambridge Companion to Kant, ed. Paul Guyer (Cambridge University Press, 1992), contains introductory essays by noted scholars on several aspects of Kant's philosophy. A general study of Kant's conception of reason which discusses parts of the second *Critique* is Susan Neiman, *The Unity of Reason* (New York/Oxford: Oxford University Press, 1994). An interesting account of developments in German philosophy immediately after Kant is Frederick Beiser, *The Fate of Reason* (Cambridge: Harvard University Press, 1987).

Another important work in which Kant develops his views about freedom, in addition to those referred to above, is Book I of *Religion Within the Boundaries of Mere Reason*, trans. George di Giovanni, in Kant, *Religion and Rational Theology* (Cambridge Edition of the Works of Immanuel Kant), ed. Allen Wood and George di Giovanni (Cambridge University Press, 1996). Treatments of Kant's views about freedom invariably cover parts of the *Critique*. A comprehensive study of this topic, which treats much of the second *Critique*, is Henry E. Allison, *Kant's Theory of Freedom* (Cambridge University Press, 1990). Allison's book also contains an extensive bibliography of the secondary literature. Other studies include: Gerold Prauss, *Kant über Freiheit als Autonomie* (Frankfurt am Main: Vittorio Klosterman, 1983); Allen W. Wood, "Kant's Compatibilism," in *Self and Nature in Kant's Philosophy*, ed. Allen W. Wood (Ithaca: Cornell University Press, 1984); Heiner Klemme, *Kant's Philosophie des Subjekts* (Hamburg: Felix Mèiner, 1996). For a classic criticism of Kant's identification of freedom with acting on the moral law see Henry Sidgwick, "The Kantian Conception of Freewill," appendix to *The Methods of Ethics* (Repr. Indianapolis: Hackett, 1981).

The relation between the argument of *Groundwork*, III and the second *Critique*, and apparent changes in the approach to the deduction of the moral law is treated in various articles by Dieter Henrich. See "Der Begriff der sittlichen Einsicht und Kants Lehre vom Faktum der Vernunft," in *Kant: Zur Deutung seiner Theorie von Erkennen und Handeln*, G. Prauss, ed. (Köln: Kiepenhauer and Witsch, 1973) and "Die Deduktion des Sittengesetzes" in *Denken im Schatten des Nihilismus*, Alexander Schwan, ed. (Darmstadt: Wissenschaftliche Buchgesellschaft, 1975). The first of these is included in a collection of Henrich's translated essays, *The Unity of Reason: Essays on Kant's Philosophy*, ed. Richard Velkley (Cambridge: Harvard University Press, 1994). Another important and often-cited discussion of this topic is Karl Ameriks, *Kant's Theory of Mind* (Oxford: Clarendon Press, 1982), ch. VI.

A discussion of Kant's argument that the moral law is the law of a freewill is given by Christine Korsgaard, in "Morality as Freedom," ch. 6 of *Creating the Kingdom of Ends* (cited above). For discussion of issues in Kant's moral psychology and theory of agency in the second *Critique*, see Terence Irwin, "Morality and Personality: Green and Kant," in *Self and*

Nature in Kant's Philosophy, ed. Allen W. Wood; Andrews Reath, "Hedonism, Heteronomy and Kant's Principle of Happiness," *Pacific Philosophical Quarterly* 70, no. 1 (1989): 42–72 and "Kant's Theory of Moral Sensibility," *Kant-Studien* 80, no. 3 (1989): 284–302. (The latter is a thorough discussion of the account of respect for the moral law in Ch. III of the Analytic.) For discussion of the concept of the good in Ch. II of the Analytic, see John Silber, "The Copernican Revolution in Ethics: The Good Re-examined," *Kant-Studien* 51(1959): 85–101; and Christine Korsgaard, "Kant's Formula of Humanity," ch. 4 of *Creating the Kingdom of Ends* (cited above).

A good treatment of the main themes of the Dialectic, including the arguments for the practical postulates, is Allen W. Wood, *Kant's Moral Religion* (Ithaca: Cornell University Press, 1970). Also of interest as background to the practical postulates are Kant's *Lectures on the Philosophical Doctrine of Religion*, trans. Allen Wood, in *Religion and Rational Theology* (Cambridge Edition of the Works of Immanuel Kant), ed. Allen Wood and George di Giovanni (Cambridge University Press, 1996). The interpretation of Kant's conception of the highest good has been the subject of some controversy. In addition to the above, see Klaus Düsing, "Das Problem des höchsten Gutes in Kants praktischer Philosophie," *Kant-Studien* 62 (1971): 5–42; Yirmiahu Yovel, *Kant and the Philosophy of History* (Princeton: Princeton University Press, 1986); Andrews Reath, "Two Conceptions of the Highest Good in Kant," *Journal of the History of Philosophy* 26 (1988): 593–619; Stephen Engstrom, "The Concept of the Highest Good in Kant's Moral Theory," *Philosophy and Phenomenological Research* 52 (1992): 747–80; and Pauline Kleingeld, "What Do the Virtuous Hope For?: Rereading Kant's Doctrine of the Highest Good," in *Proceedings of the Eighth International Kant-Congress*, Vol. I.1, ed. Hoke Robinson (Milwaukee: Marquette University Press, 1995): 91–112.

Critique
of
Practical Reason

Preface

Why this *Critique*[a] is not entitled a *Critique of Pure Practical Reason* but simply a *Critique of Practical Reason* generally, although its parallelism with the speculative seems to require the first, is sufficiently explained in this treatise. It has merely to show *that there is pure practical reason,* and for this purpose it criticizes reason's entire *practical faculty.* If it succeeds in this it has no need to criticize the *pure faculty itself* in order to see whether reason is merely making a claim in which it presumptuously *oversteps* itself (as does happen with speculative reason). For, if as pure reason it is really practical, it proves its reality and that of its concepts by what it does,[b] and all subtle reasoning against the possibility of its being practical is futile.

With this faculty transcendental *freedom* is also established, taken indeed in that absolute sense in which speculative reason needed it, in its use of the concept of causality, in order to rescue itself from the antinomy into which it unavoidably falls when it wants to think the *unconditioned* in the series of causal connection; this concept, however, it could put forward only problematically, as not impossible to think, without assuring it objective reality, and only lest the supposed impossibility of what it must at least allow to be thinkable call its being into question and plunge it into an abyss of skepticism.

Now, the concept of freedom, insofar as its reality is proved by an apodictic law of practical reason, constitutes the *keystone* of the whole structure of a system of pure reason, even of speculative reason; and all other concepts (those of God and immortality), which as mere ideas remain without support in the latter, now attach themselves to this concept and with it and by means of it get stability and objective reality, that is, their *possibility* is *proved* by this: that freedom is real, for this idea reveals itself through the moral law.

But among all the ideas of speculative reason freedom is also the only one the possibility of which we *know* a priori, though without having

---

[a] *Kritik.* I have adopted the convention of using *Critique* when Kant seems to refer to a book or its content, even if the book does not have the title Kant uses, e.g., "the *Critique* of speculative reason." Otherwise, "critique" or "critical examination" or occasionally "critical philosophy" is used.
[b] *durch die Tat,* possibly "by a deed." See AK 5:98 note r and 5:118 note n.

insight^c into it, because it is the condition* of the moral law, which we do know. The ideas of *God* and *immortality*, however, are not conditions of the moral law but only conditions of the necessary object of a will determined by this law, that is, of the mere practical use of our pure reason; hence with respect to those ideas we cannot affirm that we *cognize* and *have insight into* – I do not merely say the reality but even the possibility of them. But they are, nevertheless, conditions of applying the morally determined will to its object given to it a priori (the highest good). Consequently their possibility in this practical relation can and must be *assumed*, although we cannot theoretically cognize and have insight into them. For practical purposes it is sufficient for this assumption^e that they contain no intrinsic impossibility (contradiction). Here there is a ground of assent that is, in comparison with speculative reason, merely *subjective* but that is yet *objectively* valid for a reason equally pure but practical; by means of the concept of freedom objective reality is given to the ideas of God and

5:5 immortality and a warrant,^{f} indeed a subjective necessity (a need of pure reason) is provided to assume them, although reason is not thereby extended in theoretical cognition and, instead, all that is given is that their possibility, which was hitherto only a *problem*, here becomes an *assertion* and so the practical use of reason is connected with the elements of the theoretical. And this need is not a hypothetical one for some *discretionary* purpose of speculation, where one must assume something if one *wants* to ascend to the completion of the use of reason in speculation, but rather a *need having the force of law*,^{g} to assume something without which that cannot happen which one *ought* to set unfailingly as the aim of one's conduct.

It would certainly be more satisfying to our speculative reason to solve those problems for itself without this circuit and to have put them aside as insight for practical use; but, as matters stand, our faculty of speculation is not so well off. Those who boast of such high cognition should not keep it back but should present it publicly to be tested and esteemed. They want to *prove:* very well, let them prove, and the critical philosophy lays all its

---

*Lest anyone suppose that he finds an *inconsistency* when I now call freedom the condition of the moral law and afterwards, in the treatise, maintain that the moral law is the condition under which we can first *become aware* of freedom, I want only to remark^d that whereas freedom is indeed the *ratio essendi* of the moral law, the moral law is the *ratio cognoscendi* of freedom. For, had not the moral law *already* been distinctly thought in our reason, we should never consider ourselves justified in *assuming* such a thing as freedom (even though it is not self-contradictory). But were there no freedom, the moral law would *not be encountered* at all in ourselves.

^{c} *einzusehen*. See note 9 to *Groundwork of the Metaphysics of Morals* 4:446.
^{d} *erinnern*
^{e} *Für die letztere Forderung*
^{f} Or "authorization," *Befugnis*
^{g} *gesetzliches*

4

weapons at their feet as the victors. *Quid statis? Nolint. Atqui licet esse beatis.*[h] Since they then do not in fact want to, presumably because they cannot, we must take up these weapons again in order to seek in the moral use of reason and to base on it the concepts of *God, freedom,* and *immortality,* for the *possibility* of which speculation does not find sufficient guarantee.

Here, too, the enigma of the critical philosophy is first explained: how one can *deny* objective *reality* to the supersensible *use of the categories* in speculation and yet *grant* them this *reality* with respect to the objects of pure practical reason; for this must previously have seemed *inconsistent,* as long as such a practical use is known only by name. But now one becomes aware, by a thorough analysis of the latter, that the reality thought of here does not aim at any theoretical *determination of the categories* and extension of cognition to the supersensible but that what is meant by it is only that in this respect an *object* belongs to them, because they are either contained in the necessary determination of the will a priori or else are inseparably connected with the object of its determination; hence that inconsistency disappears because one makes a different use of those concepts than speculative reason requires. On the contrary, there is now disclosed a very   5:6 satisfying confirmation of the speculative *Critique*'s *consistent way of thinking* – one which was hardly to be expected before – inasmuch as it insisted on letting objects of experience as such, including even our own subject, hold only as *appearances* but at the same time on putting things in themselves at their basis and hence on not taking everything supersensible as a fiction and its concept as empty of content; now practical reason of itself, without any collusion with speculative reason, furnishes reality to a supersensible object of the category of causality, namely to *freedom* (although, as a practical concept, only for practical use), and hence establishes by means of a fact what could there only be *thought.* By this, the strange though incontestable assertion of the speculative *Critique, that even the thinking subject is* in inner intuition *a mere appearance to itself,* gets its full confirmation in the *Critique of Practical Reason,* and that so thoroughly that one would have to arrive at it even if the former had never proved this proposition at all.*

By this I also understand why the most considerable objections to the *Critique* that have so far come to my attention turn about just these two points: namely, *on the one side* the objective reality of the categories applied

---

*The union of causality as freedom with causality as natural mechanism, the first of which is established by the moral law, the second by the law of nature, and indeed in one and the same subject, the human being, is impossible without representing him with regard to the first as a being in itself but with regard to the second as an appearance, the former in *pure,* the latter in *empirical* consciousness. Otherwise the contradiction of reason with itself is unavoidable.

[h] In Horace *Satires* 1.1.19, a god, having given men the opportunity to change places with each other, says "What are you waiting for? They are not willing. Yet they might be happy."

to noumena, denied in theoretical cognition and affirmed in practical, and *on the other side* the paradoxical requirement to make oneself as subject of freedom a noumenon but at the same, with regard to nature, a phenomenon in one's own empirical consciousness; for, as long as one had as yet formed no determinate concepts of morality and freedom, one could not conjecture, on the one side, what one was to put as a noumenon at the basis of the alleged appearance and, on the other side, whether it was at all possible even to form a concept of it, since all the concepts of the pure understanding in its theoretical use had already been assigned exclusively 5:7 to mere appearances. Only a detailed *Critique of Practical Reason* can remove all this misinterpretation and put in a clear light the consistent way of thinking that constitutes its greatest merit.

So much by way of justifying [the fact] that in this work the concepts and principles^i of pure speculative reason, which have already undergone their special critique, are now and again subjected to examination; although this would not elsewhere be appropriate to the systematic procedure for constructing a science (since matters that have been decided should only be referred to and not raised again), it was *here allowed* and indeed necessary because reason is considered in transition to a quite different use of those concepts from what it made of them *there*. Such a transition makes it necessary to compare the old use with the new, in order to distinguish well the new path from the previous one and at the same time to draw attention to their connection. Accordingly, considerations of this kind, including those that are once more directed to the concept of freedom, though in the practical use of pure reason, should not be regarded as interpolations which might serve only to fill up gaps in the critical system of speculative reason (for this is complete for its purpose), or as like the props and buttresses that are usually added afterwards to a hastily constructed building, but as true members that make the connection of the system plain, so that concepts which could there be represented only problematically can now be seen in their real presentation. This reminder is especially relevant to the concept of freedom, with regard to which one cannot help observing with surprise that so many boast of being quite well able to understand^j it and to explain its possibility while they consider it only in its psychological context, whereas if they had earlier pondered it carefully in its transcendental context they would have cognized its *indispensability* as a problematic concept in the complete use of speculative reason as well as its complete *incomprehensibility*;^{k} and if they afterwards proceeded with it to practical use, they would have had to

---

^{i} *Grundsätze*. Here again, as in the *Groundwork of the Metaphysics of Morals*, Kant draws no consistent distinction between *Grundsatz* and *Prinzip*. *Prinzip* is always, and *Grundsatz* often, translated as "principle."
^{j} *einzusehen*
^{k} *Unbegreiflichkeit*

arrive by themselves at the very same determination of it with respect to its principles that they are now so unwilling to agree to. The concept of freedom is the stumbling block for all *empiricists,* but also the key to the most sublime practical principles for *critical* moralists, who thereby see   5:8 that they must necessarily proceed *rationally.* For this reason I beg the reader not to pass lightly over what is said about this concept at the conclusion of the Analytic.

I must leave it to connoisseurs of a work of this kind to estimate whether such a system of pure practical reason as is here developed from the *Critique* of it has cost much or little trouble, especially so as not to miss the right point of view from which the whole can be correctly traced out. It presupposes, indeed, the *Groundwork of the Metaphysics of Morals,* but only insofar as this constitutes preliminary acquaintance with the principle of duty and provides and justifies a determinate formula of it;* otherwise, it stands on its own. That the *complete classification*[1] of all practical sciences was not added, such as the *Critique* of speculative reason carried out, has a valid ground in the constitution[m] of this practical rational faculty itself. For, the special determination of duties as human duties, with a view to classifying them, is possible only after the subject of this determination (the human being) is cognized as he is really constituted, though only to the extent necessary with reference to duty generally; this, however, does not belong to a *Critique of Practical Reason* as such, which has only to give a complete account of the principles of its possibility, of its extent, and of its limits, without special reference to human nature. Here, accordingly, the classification belongs to the system of science, not to the system of critique.

In the second chapter of the Analytic I have, I hope, dealt adequately with the objection of a certain reviewer[2] of the *Groundwork of the Metaphysics of Morals,* one who is devoted to truth and astute and therefore always worthy of respect: that *there the concept of the good was not established before*   5:9 *the moral principle* (as, in his opinion, was necessary).† I have also taken

---

*A reviewer[1] who wanted to say something censuring this work hit the mark better than he himself may have intended when he said that no new principle of morality is set forth in it but only a *new formula.* But who would even want to introduce a new principle of all morality and, as it were, first invent it? Just as if, before him, the world had been ignorant of what duty is or in thoroughgoing error about it. But whoever knows what a *formula* means to a mathematician, which determines quite precisely what is to be done to solve a problem and does not let him miss it, will not take a formula that does this with respect to all duty in general as something that is insignificant and can be dispensed with.

†The further objection could have been put to me, why have I not previously explicated the concept of the *faculty of desire* or of the *feeling of pleasure,* although this reproach would be unfair because this explication as given in psychology could reasonably be presupposed. However, the definition there could admittedly be so framed that the feeling of pleasure

[1] *Einteilung*

[m] *Beschaffenheit*

7

into consideration many other objections that have reached me from men who show that they have at heart the discovery of truth, and I shall continue to do so (for, those who have only their old system before their eyes and who have already settled what is to be approved or disapproved do not desire any discussion that might stand in the way of their private purpose).

5:10

When it is a matter of determining a particular faculty of the human soul as to its sources, its contents, and its limits, then, from the nature of human cognition, one can begin only with the *parts*, with an accurate and complete presentation of them (complete as far as is possible in the present situation of such elements as we have already acquired). But there is a second thing to be attended to, which is more philosophic and *architectonic:* namely, to grasp correctly the *idea of the whole* and from this idea to see all those parts in their mutual relation by means of their derivation from the concept of that whole in a pure rational faculty. This examination and guarantee is possible only through the most intimate acquaintance with the system; and those who find the first inquiry too irksome and hence do not think it worth their trouble to attain such an acquaintance cannot reach the second stage, namely the overview, which is a synthetic return to what had previously been given analytically; and it is no wonder that they find inconsistencies everywhere, although the gaps they suppose they find are not in the system itself but only in their own incoherent train of thought.

would ground the determination of the faculty of desire (as is in fact commonly done), and thus the supreme principle of practical philosophy would necessarily turn out to be *empirical,* although this has to be settled first and in the present *Critique* is altogether refuted. I will, therefore, give this explication here in the way it must be given in order, as is reasonable, to leave this contested point undecided at the beginning – *Life* is the faculty of a being to act in accordance with laws of the faculty of desire. The *faculty of desire* is a being's *faculty to be by means of its representations the cause of the reality of the objects of these representations. Pleasure* is *the representation of the agreement of an object or of an action with the subjective conditions of life,* i.e., with the faculty of the *causality of a representation with respect to the reality of its object* (or with respect to the determination of the powers of the subject to action in order to produce the object). For the purposes of this *Critique* I have no further need of concepts borrowed from psychology; the *Critique* itself supplies the rest. It is easily seen that the question whether pleasure must always be put at the basis of the faculty of desire or whether under certain conditions pleasure only follows upon its determination, is left undecided by this exposition; for it is composed only of marks belonging to the pure understanding, i.e., categories, which contain nothing empirical. Such a precaution – namely, not to anticipate one's judgments by definitions ventured before complete analysis of the concept, which is often achieved very late – is to be highly recommended throughout philosophy, and yet is often neglected. It may be observed throughout the course of the critical philosophy (of theoretical as well as practical reason) that many opportunities are presented to make up for defects in the old dogmatic procedure of philosophy and to correct errors that are not noticed until one makes such a use of concepts of reason as is directed to the whole.

I have no fear, with respect to this treatise, of the reproach that I want to introduce a *new language*, because here the kind of cognition itself approaches popularity. This reproach with respect to the first *Critique* could also not have occurred to anyone who had thought it through and not merely turned over the pages. To invent new words where the language already has no lack of expressions for given concepts is a childish effort to distinguish oneself from the crowd, if not by new and true thoughts yet by new patches on an old garment. If, therefore, the readers of that work know of more popular expressions that are still just as suitable to the thought as the ones I used seem to me, or if they think they can show the nullity of these thoughts themselves and so too of the expressions signifying them, they would by the first very much oblige me, for I only desire to be understood; but with respect to the second, they would deserve well of philosophy. However, as long as these thoughts stand, I

5:11 very much doubt that expressions suitable for them and yet more common can be found.*

In this way the a priori principles of two faculties of the mind, the   5:12

---

*Here I am less worried (about that unintelligibility) than about occasional misinterpretation with respect to some expressions that I have sought out with the greatest care in order that the concepts to which they point may not be missed. Thus, in the table of categories of *practical* reason under the heading Modality, the *permitted* and the *forbidden* (the practically objectively possible and impossible), have almost the same sense in the common use of language as the immediately following categories, *duty* and *contrary to duty;* here, however, the *first* mean that which harmonizes or conflicts with a merely *possible* practical precept (as, say, the solution of all problems of geometry and mechanics), the *second*, that which is similarly related to a law *actually* present in reason as such; and this distinction in meaning is not altogether foreign even to the common use of language, although it is somewhat unusual. Thus, for example, it is *forbidden* to an orator, as such, to forge new words or constructions; this is to some extent *permitted* to a poet; in neither case is there any thought of duty. For if anyone is willing to forfeit his reputation as an orator, no one can prevent him. We have here to do only with the distinction of *imperatives* under *problematic, assertoric,* and *apodictic* determining grounds. So too, in the note where I compared the moral ideas of practical perfection in different philosophic schools, I distinguished the idea of *wisdom* from that of *holiness,* although I explained them as identical in their ground and objectively. In that place, however, I understood by wisdom only that wisdom to which the human being (the Stoic) lays claim, and thus took it *subjectively,* as an attribute ascribed to the human being. (Perhaps the expression *virtue,* which the Stoic also made much of, could better indicate what is characteristic of his school.) But the expression, a *postulate* of pure practical reason, could most of all occasion misinterpretation if confused with the meaning that postulates of pure mathematics have, which bring with them apodictic certainty. The latter, however, postulate the *possibility of an action,* the object of which has been previously theoretically cognized a priori with complete certitude as *possible.* But the former postulate the possibility of an *object* itself (God and the immortality of the soul) from apodictic *practical* laws, and therefore only on behalf of a practical reason, so that this certainty of the postulated possibility is not at all theoretical, hence also not apodictic, i.e., it is not a necessity cognized with respect to the object but is, instead, an assumption necessary with respect to the subject's observance of its objective but practical laws, hence merely a necessary hypothesis. I could find no better expression for this subjective but nevertheless unconditional rational necessity.

9

faculty of cognition and that of desire, would be found and determined as to the conditions, extent, and boundaries of their use, and a firm basis would thereby be laid for a scientific system of philosophy, both theoretical and practical.

Nothing worse could happen to these labors than that someone should make the unexpected discovery that there is and can be no a priori cognition at all.[3] But there is no danger of this. It would be tantamount to someone's wanting to prove by reason that there is no reason. For, we say that we cognize something by reason only when we are aware that we could have known it even if it had not presented itself to us as it did in experience; hence rational cognition and cognition a priori are one and the same. It is an outright contradiction to want to extract necessity from an empirical proposition (*ex pumice aquam*)[n] and to give a judgment, along with necessity, true universality (without which there is no rational inference and so not even inference from analogy, which is at least a presumed universality and objective necessity and therefore presupposes it). To substitute subjective necessity, that is, custom, for objective necessity, which is to be found only in a priori judgments, is to deny to reason the ability to judge an object, that is, to cognize it and what belongs to it; it is to deny, for example, that when something often or always follows upon a certain prior state one could *infer* it from that (for this would mean objective necessity and the concept of an a priori connection) and to say only that we may expect similar cases (just as animals do), that is, to reject the concept of cause fundamentally as false and a mere delusion of thought. As for wanting to remedy this lack of objective and hence universal validity by saying that one sees no ground for attributing to other rational beings a different way of representing things:[o] if that yielded a valid inference then our ignorance would render us greater service in enlarging our cognition than all our reflection. For, merely because of our not knowing rational beings other than human beings, we would have a right to assume them to be constituted just as we cognize ourselves to be, that is, we would really know them. I do not even mention here that universality of assent does not prove the objective validity of a judgment (i.e., its validity as cognition) but only that, even if universal assent should happen to be correct, it could still not yield a proof of agreement with the object; on the contrary, only objective validity constitutes the ground of a necessary universal agreement.

Hume would be quite content with this system of universal empiricism of principles; for, as is well known, he asked nothing more than that a merely subjective meaning of necessity, namely custom, be assumed in place of any objective meaning of necessity in the concept of cause, so as

---

[n] "water from a pumice stone." Plautus, *The Persians* 1.1.42.
[o] *Vorstellungsart*

to deny to reason any judgment about God, freedom, and immortality: and, if once his principles were granted, he certainly knew very well how to draw conclusions from them with all logical validity. But Hume himself did not make empiricism so universal as to include mathematics.[4] He held its propositions to be analytic, and if this were correct they would in fact be apodictic also: but from this no inference could be drawn to reason's ability to make apodictic judgments in philosophy as well, namely judgments that would be synthetic (as the proposition of causality is). However, if one assumes a *universal* empiricism of principles, then mathematics will be included.

Now, if mathematics comes into conflict with a reason that admits only empirical principles, as inevitably happens in the antinomy where mathematics proves incontestably the infinite divisibility of space, which empiricism cannot allow, then the greatest possible evidence of demonstration is in manifest contradiction with the alleged inferences from empirical principles, and one has to ask, like Cheselden's blind man, "Which deceives me, sight or touch?"[5] (For empiricism is based on a necessity *felt*, but rationalism on a necessity *seen*.)[p] And thus universal empiricism reveals itself as genuine skepticism, which in this unlimited sense has been falsely ascribed to Hume,* since he left at least one certain touchstone of experience in mathematics, whereas genuine skepticism admits no such touchstone at all (which can only be found in a priori principles), although experience consists not of feelings only but also of judgments.

5:14

Since, however, in this philosophic and critical age such empiricism can scarcely be taken seriously, and it is presumably put forward only as an exercise for judgment and in order to put the necessity of rational a priori principles in a clearer light by contrast, one can only be grateful to those who are willing to trouble themselves with this otherwise uninstructive work.

---

*Names that designate the followers of a sect have always been accompanied with a good deal of injustice;[6] this would be much the case if someone said, *N is an idealist*. For, although he not only admits but even insists that real objects, external things, correspond to our representations of external things, he nevertheless holds that the form of intuition of them does not depend on them but only on the human mind.

[p] *eingesehenen*

Introduction
On the idea of a critique of practical reason

The theoretical use of reason was concerned with objects of the cognitive faculty only, and a critique of it with regard to this use really dealt only with the *pure* cognitive faculty, since this raised the suspicion, which was afterwards confirmed, that it might easily lose itself beyond its boundaries, among unattainable objects or even among contradictory concepts. It is quite different with the practical use of reason. In this, reason is concerned with the determining grounds of the will, which is a faculty either of producing objects corresponding to representations or of determining itself to effect such objects (whether the physical power is sufficient or not), that is, of determining its causality. For, in that, reason can at least suffice to determine the will and always has objective reality insofar as volition alone is at issue. The first question here, then, is whether pure reason of itself alone suffices to determine the will or whether it can be a determining ground of the will only as empirically conditioned. Now there enters here a concept of causality justified by the *Critique of Pure Reason* although not capable of being presented empirically, namely that of *freedom;* and if we can now discover grounds for proving that this property does in fact belong to the human will (and so to the will of all rational beings as well), then it will not only be shown that pure reason can be practical but that it alone, and not reason empirically limited, is unconditionally practical. Consequently, we shall not have to do a critique of *pure practical* reason but only of *practical* reason as such. For, pure reason, once it is shown to exist, needs no critique. It is pure reason that itself contains the standard for the critical examination of every use of it. It is therefore incumbent upon the *Critique of Practical Reason* as such to prevent empirically conditioned reason from presuming that it, alone and exclusively, furnishes the determining ground of the will. If it is proved that there is pure reason, its use is alone immanent; the empirically conditioned use, which lays claim to absolute rule,[q] is on the contrary transcendent and expresses itself in demands and commands that go quite beyond its

---

[q] *Alleinherrschaft*

sphere – precisely the opposite relation from what could be said of pure reason in its speculative use.

Since, however, it is still pure reason whose cognition here lies at the basis of its practical use, the division of a *Critique of Practical Reason* must in its general outline be arranged in conformity with that of the speculative. We shall therefore have to have a *Doctrine of Elements*[r] and a *Doctrine of Method* for it; and within the former, an *Analytic,* as the rule of truth, as the first part, and a *Dialectic,* as the exposition and resolution of illusion[s] in the judgments of practical reason. However, the order in the subdivision of the Analytic will be the reverse of that in the *Critique* of pure speculative reason. For, in the present *Critique* we shall begin with *principles* and proceed to *concepts,* and only then, where possible, from them to the senses, whereas in the case of speculative reason we had to begin with the senses and end with principles. The ground for doing so lies, again, in this: that now we have to do with a will and have to consider reason not in its relation to objects but in relation to this will and its causality; thus the principles of empirically unconditioned causality must come first, and only afterward can the attempt be made to establish our concepts of the determining ground of such a will, of their application to objects and finally to the subject and its sensibility. Here the law of causality from freedom, that is, some pure practical rational principle, constitutes the unavoidable beginning and determines the objects to which alone it can be referred.

[r] *Elementarlehre.* On "doctrine" in its strict sense, see the text from the *Critique of Judgment* (5:170) referred to in the note to *The Metaphysics of Morals* (6:205).
[s] *Schein*

The
critique of practical reason
Part one

Doctrine of the elements
of
pure practical reason

Book one
The analytic of pure practical reason

Chapter I
On the Principles of Pure Practical Reason

I.
DEFINITION [t]

Practical *principles* are propositions that contain a general determination of the will, having under it several practical rules. They are subjective, or *maxims*, when the condition is regarded by the subject as holding only for his will; but they are objective, or practical *laws*, when the condition is cognized as objective, that is, as holding for the will of every rational being.

Remark

If it is assumed that *pure* reason can contain within itself a practical ground, that is, one sufficient to determine the will, then there are practical laws; otherwise all practical principles will be mere maxims. Within a pathologically[u] affected will of a rational being there can be found a conflict of maxims with the practical laws cognized by himself. For example, someone can make it his maxim to let no insult pass unavenged and yet at the same time see that this is no practical law but only his maxim – that, on the contrary, as being in one and the same maxim a rule for the will of every rational being it could not harmonize with itself. In cognition of nature[v] the principles of what happens (e.g., the principle of equality of action and reaction in the communication of motion) are at the same time laws of nature; for there the use of reason is theoretical and determined by the constitution of the object. In practical cognition – that is, cognition having to do only with determining grounds of the will – the principles that one makes for oneself are not yet laws to which one is unavoidably

5:20

---

[t] *Erklärung.* See *Critique of Pure Reason* (A:730; B:758), and note *m* to *The Metaphysics of Morals* (6:226).
[u] *pathologisch.* Kant uses "pathological" in the sense of "dependent upon sensibility."
[v] *Naturekenntnis*

subject, because reason, in the practical, has to do with the subject, namely with his faculty of desire, which by its special constitution can make various adjustments to the rule.^w A practical rule is always a product of reason because it prescribes action as a means to an effect, which is its purpose. But for a being in whom reason quite alone is not the determining ground of the will, this rule is an *imperative*, that is, a rule indicated by an "ought," which expresses objective necessitation to the action and signifies that if reason completely determined the will the action would without fail take place in accordance with this rule. Imperatives, therefore, hold objectively and are quite distinct from maxims, which are subjective principles. But the former either determine the conditions of the causality of a rational being as an efficient cause merely with respect to the effect and its adequacy to it or they determine only the will, whether or not it is sufficient for the effect. The first would be hypothetical imperatives and would contain mere precepts of skill; the second, on the contrary, would be categorical and would alone be practical laws. Thus maxims are indeed *principles* but not *imperatives*. But imperatives themselves, when they are conditional – that is, when they do not determine the will simply as will but only with respect to a desired effect, that is, when they are hypothetical imperatives – are indeed practical *precepts* but not *laws*. The latter must sufficiently determine the will as will even before I ask whether I have the ability required for a desired effect or what I am to do in order to produce it, and must thus be categorical: otherwise they are not laws because they lack the necessity which, if it is to be practical, must be independent of conditions that are pathological and therefore only contingently connected with the will. Tell someone, for example, that he must work and save in his youth in order not to want in his old age; this is a correct and also important practical precept of the will. But it is readily seen that here the will is directed to something *else* which it is presupposed that it desires, and as to this desire, it must be left to the agent himself whether he foresees other resources than means acquired by himself, or does not hope to live to old age, or thinks that in case of future need he can make do with little. Reason, from which alone can arise any rule that is to contain necessity, does indeed put necessity even into this precept (for otherwise it would not be an imperative), though it is only a subjectively conditioned necessity and cannot be presupposed in the same degree in all subjects. But it is requisite to reason's lawgiving that it should need to presuppose only *itself*, because a rule is objectively and universally valid only when it holds without the contingent, subjective conditions that distinguish one rational being from another. Now tell someone that he ought never to make a lying promise; this is a rule that has to do only with his will, regardless of whether the purposes the human being may have can be thereby attained; the mere volition is that which is to be determined

---

^w *sich die Regel vielfältig richten kann*

completely a priori by this rule. If, now, it is found that this rule is practically correct, then it is a law because it is a categorical imperative. Thus practical laws refer only to the will, without regard to what is attained by its causality, and one may abstract from this latter (as belonging to the world of sense) so as to have them pure.

2.

THEOREM I

All practical principles that presuppose an *object* (matter) of the faculty of desire as the determining ground of the will are, without exception, empirical and can furnish no practical laws.

By "the matter of the faculty of desire" I understand an object whose reality is desired. Now, when desire for this object precedes the practical rule and is the condition of its becoming a principle, then I say (*first*) that this principle is in that case always empirical. For, the determining ground of choice* is then the representation of an object and that relation of the representation to the subject by which the faculty of desire is determined to realize the object. Such a relation to the subject, however, is called *pleasure* in the reality of an object. This would therefore have to be presupposed as a condition of the possibility of the determination of choice. But it cannot be cognized a priori of any representation of an object, whatever it may be, whether it will be connected with *pleasure* or *displeasure* or be *indifferent*. Hence in such a case the determining ground of choice must always be empirical, and so too must be the practical material principle that presupposes it as a condition.

Now (*second*) a principle that is based only on the subjective condition of receptivity to a pleasure or displeasure (which can always be cognized only empirically and cannot be valid in the same way for all rational beings) can indeed serve as his *maxim* for the subject who possesses this receptivity but not as a *law* even for him (because it is lacking in objective necessity, which must be cognized a priori); such a principle can, accordingly, never furnish a practical law.

5:22

3.

THEOREM II

All material practical principles as such are, without exception, of one and the same kind and come under the general principle of self-love or one's own happiness.

Pleasure arising from the representation of the existence^y of a thing,

---

* *Willkür*. See *The Metaphysics of Morals* (6: 213–14, 226). *Wahl* is translated as "a choice" and *wählen* as "to choose."
^{y} *Existenz*. The word translated as "existence" later in this clause is *Dasein*.

insofar as it is to be a determining ground of desire for this thing, is based on the *receptivity* of the subject, since it *depends* upon the existence of an object; hence it belongs to sense (feeling) and not to the understanding, which expresses a relation of a representation *to an object* by concepts, not to the subject by feelings. It is, then, practical only insofar as the feeling[z] of agreeableness that the subject expects from the reality of an object determines the faculty of desire. Now, a rational being's consciousness of the agreeableness of life uninterruptedly accompanying his whole existence is *happiness,* and the principle of making this the supreme determining ground of choice is the principle of self-love. Thus all material principles, which place the determining ground of choice in the pleasure or displeasure to be felt in the reality of some object, are wholly *of the same kind* insofar as they belong without exception to the principle of self-love or one's own happiness.

Corollary

All *material* practical rules put the determining ground of the will in the *lower faculty of desire,* and were there no *merely formal* laws of the will sufficient to determine it, then neither could *any higher faculty of desire* be admitted.

Remark I

It is surprising that men, otherwise acute, believe they can find a distinction between the *lower* and the *higher* faculty of desire according to whether the *representations* that are connected with the feeling of pleasure have their origin *in the senses* or in the *understanding.* For when one inquires about the determining grounds of desire and puts them in the agreeableness expected from something or other, it does not matter at all where the *representation* of this pleasing object comes from but only how much it *pleases.* If a representation, even though it may have its seat and origin in the understanding, can determine choice only by presupposing a feeling of pleasure in the subject, its being a determining ground of choice is wholly dependent upon the nature of inner sense, namely that this can be agreeably affected by the representation. However dissimilar representations of objects may be – they may be representations of the understanding or even of reason, in contrast to representations of sense – the feeling

5:23

---

[z] *Empfindung.* On Kant's use of *Empfindung* and *Gefühl,* see note k to the *Groundwork of the Metaphysics of Morals,* (4:399). In order to avoid excessive annotation, in the present context "feeling" is used for both *Empfindung* and *Gefühl* unless the sense of *Empfindung* seems doubtful.

of pleasure by which alone they properly constitute the determining ground of the will (the agreeableness, the gratification[a] expected from the object, which impels activity to produce it) is nevertheless of one and the same kind not only insofar as it can always be cognized only empirically but also insofar as it affects one and the same vital force that is manifested in the faculty of desire, and in this respect can differ only in degree from any other determining ground. Otherwise, how could one make a comparison in *magnitude* between two determining grounds quite different as to the kind of representation, so as to prefer the one that most affects the faculty of desire? The same human being can return unread an instructive book that he cannot again obtain, in order not to miss a hunt; he can leave in the middle of a fine speech in order not to be late for a meal; he can leave an intellectual conversation, such as he otherwise values highly, in order to take his place at the gaming table; he can even repulse a poor man whom at other times it is a joy for him to benefit because he now has only enough money in his pocket to pay for his admission to the theater. If the determination of his will rests on the feeling of agreeableness or disagreeableness that he expects from some cause, it is all the same to him by what kind of representation he is affected. The only thing that concerns him, in order to decide upon a choice, is how intense, how long, how easily acquired, and how often repeated this agreeableness is. Just as, to someone who wants money to spend it is all the same whether the material in it, the gold, was dug out of a mountain or washed out of sand provided it is accepted everywhere at the same value, so no one asks, when he is concerned only with the agreeableness of life, whether representations belong to the understanding or to the senses but only *how much* and *how great* satisfaction they will furnish him for the longest time. Only those who would like to deny to pure reason the ability to determine the will without some feeling being presupposed could deviate so far from their own definition[b] as to explain[c] as quite heterogeneous what they have themselves previously brought under one and the same principle. Thus it is found, for example, that we can find satisfaction in the mere *exercise of our powers*, in consciousness of our strength of soul in overcoming obstacles opposed to our plans, in cultivating our talents of spirit, and so forth, and we correctly call these joys and delights *more refined* because they are more under our control than others, do not wear out but rather strengthen feeling for further enjoyment of them, and while they delight they at the

5:24

---

[a] See note v to the *Groundwork of the Metaphysics of Morals* (4:393). In the following pages Kant again uses a variety of words for "pleasure," and no attempt has been made to distinguish, in particular, between *Zufriedenheit* and *Vergnügen*.
[b] *Erklärung*
[c] *erklären*

same time cultivate. But as for passing them off, on this account, as a different way of determining the will than merely through sense, even though they presuppose for the possibility of that satisfaction a feeling for it implanted in us as the first condition of this pleasure: this is just as when ignorant people who would like to dabble in metaphysics think of matter so refined, so superrefined, that they make themselves giddy with it and then believe that in this way they have devised a *spiritual* and yet extended being. If, with Epicurus, we have virtue determine the will only by means of the gratification it promises, we cannot afterward find fault with him for holding that this is of exactly the same kind as those of the coarsest senses; for we have no ground at all to charge him with ascribing the representations by which this feeling is excited in us to the bodily senses only. As far as can be conjectured, he sought the source of many of them in the use of the higher cognitive faculty; but this did not and could not prevent him from holding, in accordance with the principle mentioned above, that the satisfaction itself which those intellectual representations afford us and by which alone they can be determining grounds of the will is of exactly the same kind. *Consistency* is the greatest obligation*[d]* of a philosopher and yet the most rarely found. The ancient Greek schools give us more examples of it than we find in our *syncretistic* age, in which a certain *coalition system* of contradictory principles, replete with dishonesty and shallowness, is contrived, because it commends itself better to a public that is satisfied with knowing something of everything and nothing as a whole, so that it can turn its hand to anything. The principle of one's own happiness, however much understanding and reason may be used in it, still contains no determining ground for the will other than such as is suitable to the *lower* faculty of desire; and thus either there is no higher faculty of desire at all or else *pure reason* must be practical of itself and alone, that is, it must be able to determine the will by the mere form of a practical rule without presupposing any feeling and hence without any representation of the agreeable or disagreeable as the matter of the faculty of desire, which is always an empirical condition of principles. Then only, insofar as reason

5:25 of itself (not in the service of the inclinations) determines the will, is reason a true *higher* faculty of desire, to which the pathologically determinable is subordinate, and then only is reason really, and indeed *specifically*, distinct from the latter, so that even the least admixture of the latter's impulses infringes upon its strength and superiority, just as anything at all empirical as a condition in a mathematical demonstration degrades and destroys its dignity and force. In a practical law reason determines the will immediately, not by means of an intervening feeling of pleasure or displeasure, not even in this law; and that it can as pure reason be practical is what alone makes it possible for it to *be lawgiving.*

[d] *Obliegenheit*

22

Remark II

To be happy is necessarily the demand of every rational but finite being and therefore an unavoidable determining ground of its faculty of desire. For, satisfaction with one's whole existence is not, as it were, an original possession and a beatitude,ᶜ which would presuppose a consciousness of one's independent self-sufficiency, but is instead a problem imposed upon him by his finite nature itself, because he is needy and this need is directed to the matter of his faculty of desire, that is, something related to a subjective feeling of pleasure or displeasure underlying it by which is determined what he needs in order to be satisfied with his condition. But just because this material determining ground can be cognized only empirically by the subject, it is impossible to regard this problem as law, since a law, as objective, must contain the *very same determining ground* of the will in all cases and for all rational beings. For, although the concept of happiness *everywhere* underlies the practical relation of *objects* to the faculty of desire, it is still only the general name for subjective determining grounds, and it determines nothing specific about it although this is all that matters in this practical problem and without such determination the problem cannot be solved at all. That is to say, where each has to put his happiness comes down to the particular feeling of pleasure and displeasure in each and, even within one and the same subject, to needs that differ as this feeling changes; and a law that is *subjectively necessary* (as a law of nature) is thus *objectively* a very *contingent* practical principle, which can and must be very different in different subjects, and hence can never yield a law because, in the desire for happiness, it is not the form of lawfulness that counts but simply the matter, namely whether I am to expect satisfaction from following the law, and how much. Principles of self-love can indeed contain universal rules of skill (for finding means to one's purposes), but in that case they are only theoretical principles* (such as, e.g., how someone who would like to eat bread has to construct a mill). But practical precepts based on them can never be universal because the determining ground of the faculty of desire is based on the feeling of pleasure or displeasure, which can never be assumed to be universally directed to the same objects. 5:26

But suppose that finite rational beings were thoroughly agreed with respect to what they had to take as objects of their feelings of pleasure and

---

*Propositions that in mathematics or physics are called *practical* should properly be called *technical.* For in these teachings it is not at all a question of the determination of the will; they only point out the manifold of the possible action that is sufficient to produce a certain effect, and are thus as theoretical as any proposition that asserts the connection of a cause with an effect. Whoever approves the effect must also be willing to approve the cause.
ᶜ *eine Seligkeit*

pain and even with respect to the means they must use to obtain the first and avoid the other; even then they could by no means pass off the *principle of self-love* as *a practical law;* for, this unanimity itself would still be only contingent. The determining ground would still be only subjectively valid and merely empirical and would not have that necessity which is thought in every law, namely objective necessity from a priori grounds, unless one had to say that this necessity is not practical at all but only physical, namely that the action is as unavoidably forced from us by our inclination as is yawning when we see others yawn. It would be better to maintain that there are no practical laws at all but only *counsels* on behalf of our desires than to raise merely subjective principles to the rank of practical laws, which absolutely must have objective and not merely subjective necessity and which must be cognized a priori by reason, not by experience (however empirically universal this may be). Even the rules of uniform appearances are called laws of nature (e.g., mechanical laws) only when they are either cognized really a priori or (as in the case of chemical laws) when it is assumed that they would be cognized a priori from objective grounds if our insight went deeper. But in the case of merely subjective practical principles it is expressly made a condition that they must have as their basis not objective but subjective conditions of choice, and hence that they must always be represented as mere maxims, never as practical laws. This latter remark seems at first glance to be mere cavilling at words; but it defines the terms*ᶠ* of the most important distinction that can ever be considered in practical investigations.

5:27

4.
THEOREM III

If a rational being is to think of his maxims as practical universal laws, he can think of them only as principles that contain the determining ground of the will not by their matter but only by their form.

The matter of a practical principle is the object of the will. This is either the determining ground of the will or it is not. If it is the determining ground of the will, then the rule of the will is subject to an empirical condition (to the relation of the determining representation to the feeling of pleasure or displeasure), and so is not a practical law. Now, all that remains of a law if one separates from it everything material, that is, every object of the will (as its determining ground), is the mere *form* of giving universal law. Therefore, either a rational being cannot think of *his* subjectively practical principles, that is, his maxims, as being at the same time universal laws or he must assume that their mere form, by which *they are fit for a giving of universal law*, of itself and alone makes them practical laws.

ᶠ sie ist die Wortbestimmung

Remark

The most common understanding can distinguish without instruction what form in a maxim makes it fit for a giving of universal law and what does not. I have, for example, made it my maxim to increase my wealth by every safe means. Now I have a *deposit* in my hands, the owner of which has died and left no record of it. This is, naturally, a case for my maxim. Now I want only to know whether that maxim could also hold as a universal practical law. I therefore apply the maxim to the present case and ask whether it could indeed take the form of a law, and consequently whether I could through my maxim at the same time give such a law as this: that everyone may deny a deposit which no one can prove has been made. I at once become aware that such a principle, as a law, would annihilate itself since it would bring it about that there would be no deposits at all. A practical law that I cognize as such must qualify for a giving of universal law: this is an identical proposition and therefore self-evident. Now, if I say that my will is subject to a practical *law*, I cannot cite my inclination (e.g., in the present case my avarice) as the determining ground of my will appropriate to a universal practical law; for this is so far from being qualified for a giving of universal law that in the form of a universal law it must instead destroy itself.

5:28

It is, therefore, strange that intelligent men · could have thought of passing off the desire for happiness as a universal *practical law* on the ground that the desire, and so too the *maxim* by which each makes this desire the determining ground of his will, is universal. For whereas elsewhere a universal law of nature makes everything harmonious, here, if one wanted to give the maxim the universality of a law, the most extreme opposite of harmony would follow, the worst conflict, and the complete annihilation of the maxim itself and its purpose. For then the will of all has not one and the same object but each has his own (his own welfare), which can indeed happen to accord with the purposes of others who are likewise pursuing their own but which is far from sufficing for a law because the exceptions that one is warranted in making upon occasion are endless and cannot be determinately embraced in a universal rule. In this way there results a harmony like that which a certain satirical poem depicts in the unanimity between a married couple bent on going to ruin: "*O marvellous harmony, what he wants she wants too*" and so forth, or like what is said of the pledge of King Francis I to the Emperor Charles V: "What my brother Charles would have (Milan), that I would also have." Empirical determining grounds are not fit for any universal external legislation[g] and are no more fit for internal lawgiving; for each person puts at the basis of inclination his subject – another person, another subject – and even within each

[g] *allgemeinen äußern Gesetzgebung*

25

subject now the influence of one inclination has priority and now that of another. To discover a law that under this condition would govern them all – that is to say, with omnilateral concord – is quite impossible.

5.
PROBLEM I

Supposing that the mere lawgiving form of maxims is the only sufficient determining ground of a will: to find the constitution of a will that is determinable by it alone.

Since the mere form of a law can be represented only by reason and is therefore not an object of the senses and consequently does not belong among appearances, the representation of this form as the determining ground of the will is distinct from all determining grounds of events in nature in accordance with the law of causality, because in their case the determining grounds must themselves be appearances. But if no determining ground of the will other than that universal lawgiving form can serve as a law for it, such a will must be thought as altogether independent of the natural law of appearances in their relations to one another, namely the law of causality. But such independence is called *freedom* in the strictest, that is, in the transcendental, sense. Therefore, a will for which the mere lawgiving form of a maxim can alone serve as a law is a free will.

5:29

6.
PROBLEM II

Supposing that a will *is free:* to find the law that alone is competent to determine it necessarily.

Since the matter of a practical law, that is, an object of maxim, can never be given otherwise than empirically whereas a free will, as independent of empirical conditions (i.e., conditions belonging to the sensible world), must nevertheless be determinable, a free will must find a determining ground in the law but independently of the *matter* of the law. But, besides the matter of the law, nothing further is contained in it than the lawgiving form. The lawgiving form, insofar as this is contained in the maxim, is therefore the only thing that can constitute a determining ground of the will.

Remark

Thus freedom and unconditional practical law reciprocally imply each other.[h] Now I do not ask here whether they are in fact different or whether

---

[h] *weisen . . . wechselsweise auf einander zurück.* In the *Groundwork of the Metaphysics of Morals* (4:450), Kant said that freedom and the lawgiving of one's own will are both autonomy and hence *Wechselbegriffe.*

it is not much rather the case that an unconditional law is merely the self-consciousness of a pure practical reason, this being identical with the positive concept of freedom; I ask instead from what our *cognition* of the unconditionally practical *starts*, whether from freedom or from the practical law. It cannot start from freedom, for we can neither be immediately conscious of this, since the first concept of it is negative, nor can we conclude to it from experience, since experience lets us cognize only the law of appearances and hence the mechanism of nature, the direct opposite of freedom. It is therefore the *moral law*, of which we become immediately conscious (as soon as we draw up maxims of the will for ourselves), that *first* offers itself to us and, inasmuch as reason presents it as a determining ground not to be outweighed by any sensible conditions and indeed quite independent of them, leads directly to the concept of freedom. But how is consciousness of that moral law possible? We can become aware of pure practical laws just as we are aware of pure theoretical principles, by attending to the necessity with which reason prescribes them to us and to the setting aside of all empirical conditions to which reason directs us. The concept of a pure will arises from the first, as consciousness of a pure understanding arises from the latter. That this is the true subordination of our concepts and that morality first discloses to us the concept of freedom, so that it is *practical reason* which first poses to speculative reason, with this concept, the most insoluble problem so as to put it in the greatest perplexity, is clear from the following: that, since nothing in appearances can be explained by the concept of freedom and there the mechanism of nature must instead constitute the only guide; since, moreover, the antinomy of pure reason when it wants to ascend to the unconditioned in the series of causes gets it entangled in incomprehensibilities on one side as much as on the other, whereas the latter (mechanism) is at least useful in the explanation of appearances, one would never have ventured to introduce freedom into science had not the moral law, and with it practical reason, come in and forced this concept upon us. But experience also confirms this order of concepts in us. Suppose someone asserts of his lustful inclination that, when the desired object and the opportunity are present, it is quite irresistible to him; ask him whether, if a gallows were erected in front of the house where he finds this opportunity and he would be hanged on it immediately after gratifying his lust, he would not then control his inclination. One need not conjecture very long what he would reply. But ask him whether, if his prince demanded, on pain of the same immediate execution, that he give false testimony against an honorable man whom the prince would like to destroy under a plausible pretext, he would consider it possible to overcome his love of life, however great it may be. He would perhaps not venture to assert whether he would do it or not, but he must admit without hesitation that it would be possible for him. He judges, therefore, that he can do something

5:30

27

because he is aware that he ought to do it and cognizes freedom within him, which, without the moral law, would have remained unknown to him.

7.

FUNDAMENTAL LAW OF PURE PRACTICAL REASON

So act that the maxim of your will could always hold at the same time as a principle in a giving of universal law.

5:31

Remark

Pure geometry has postulates as practical propositions which, however, contain nothing further than the presupposition that one *could* do something if it were required that one should do it, and these are the only propositions of pure geometry that concern an existing thing.[i] They are thus practical rules under a problematic condition of the will. Here, however, the rule says: one ought absolutely to proceed in a certain way. The practical rule is therefore unconditional and so is represented a priori as a categorical practical proposition by which the will is objectively determined absolutely and immediately (by the practical rule itself, which accordingly is here a law). For, pure reason, *practical of itself,* is here immediately lawgiving. The will is thought as independent of empirical conditions and hence, as a pure will, as determined *by the mere form of law,* and this determining ground is regarded as the supreme condition of all maxims. The thing is strange enough, and has nothing like it in all the rest of our practical cognition. For, the a priori thought of a possible giving of universal law, which is thus merely problematic, is unconditionally commanded as a law without borrowing anything from experience or from some external will. But it is also not a precept in accordance with which an action by which a desired effect is possible should be done (for then the rule would always be physically conditioned); it is instead a rule that determines the will a priori only with respect to the form of its maxims; and so it is at least not impossible to think of a law that serves only for the *subjective* form of principles as yet a determining ground through the *objective* form of a law as such. Consciousness of this fundamental law may be called a fact of reason because one cannot reason it out from antecedent data of reason, for example, from consciousness of freedom (since this is not antecedently given to us) and because it instead forces itself upon us of itself as a synthetic a priori proposition that is not based on any intuition, either pure or empirical, although it would be analytic if the freedom of the will were presupposed; but for this, as a positive concept, an intellectual intuition

[i] *ein Dasein*

would be required, which certainly cannot be assumed here. However, in order to avoid misinterpretation in regarding this law as *given*, it must be noted carefully that it is not an empirical fact but the sole fact of pure reason which, by it, announces itself as originally lawgiving (*sic volo, sic jubeo*).[j]

Corollary

Pure reason is practical of itself alone and gives (to the human being) a universal law which we call the *moral law*.

Remark   5:32

The fact mentioned above is undeniable. One need only analyze the judgment that people pass on the lawfulness of their actions in order to find that, whatever inclination may say to the contrary, their reason, incorruptible and self-constrained, always holds the maxim of the will in an action up to the pure will, that is, to itself inasmuch as it regards itself as a priori practical. Now this principle of morality, just on account of the universality of the lawgiving that makes it the formal supreme determining ground of the will regardless of all subjective differences, is declared by reason to be at the same time a law for all rational beings insofar as they have a will, that is, the ability[k] to determine their causality by the representation of rules, hence insofar as they are capable of actions in accordance with principles and consequently also in accordance with a priori practical principles (for these alone have that necessity which reason requires for a principle). It is, therefore, not limited to human beings only but applies to all finite beings that have reason and will and even includes the infinite being as the supreme intelligence. In the first case, however, the law has the form of an imperative, because in them, as rational beings, one can presuppose a *pure* will but, insofar as they are beings affected by needs and sensible motives, not a *holy* will, that is, such a will as would not be capable of any maxim conflicting with the moral law. Accordingly the moral law is for them an *imperative* that commands categorically because the law is unconditional; the relation of such a will to this law is *dependence* under the name of obligation, which signifies a *necessitation*, though only by reason and its objective law, to an action which is called *duty* because a choice that is pathologically affected (though not thereby determined, hence still free) brings with it a wish arising from *subjective* causes, because of which it can often be opposed to the pure objective determining ground and thus needs a resistance of practical reason which, as moral necessita-

[j]What I will, I command. Juvenal *Satire* 6.
[k] *Vermögen*

tion, may be called an internal but intellectual constraint. In the supremely self-sufficient intelligence, choice is rightly represented as incapable of any maxim that could not at the same time be objectively a law, and the concept of *holiness*, which on that account belongs to it, puts it, not indeed above all practical laws, but rather above all practically restrictive laws and so above obligation and duty. This holiness of will is nevertheless a practical *idea*, which must necessarily serve as a *model* to which all finite rational beings can only approximate without end and which the pure moral law, itself called holy because of this, constantly and rightly holds before their eyes; the utmost that finite practical reason can effect is to make sure

5:33 of this unending progress of one's maxims toward this model and of their constancy in continual progress, that is, virtue; and virtue itself, in turn, at least as a naturally acquired ability, can never be completed, because assurance in such a case never becomes apodictic certainty and, as persuasion, is very dangerous.

8.

THEOREM IV

Autonomy of the will is the sole principle of all moral laws and of duties in keeping with them; *heteronomy* of choice, on the other hand, not only does not ground any obligation at all but is instead opposed to the principle of obligation and to the morality of the will. That is to say, the sole principle of morality consists in independence from all matter of the law (namely, from a desired object) and at the same time in the determination of choice through the mere form of giving universal law that a maxim must be capable of. That *independence*, however, is freedom in the *negative* sense, whereas this *lawgiving of its own*[1] on the part of pure and, as such, practical reason is freedom in the *positive* sense. Thus the moral law expresses nothing other than the *autonomy* of pure practical reason, that is, freedom, and this is itself the formal condition of all maxims, under which alone they can accord with the supreme practical law. If, therefore, the matter of volition, which can be nothing other than the object of a desire that is connected with the law, enters into the practical law *as a condition of its possibility*, there results heteronomy of choice, namely dependence upon the natural law of following some impulse or inclination, and the will does not give itself the law but only the precept for rationally following pathological law; but a maxim which, in this way, can never contain within it the form of giving universal law not only establishes no obligation but is itself opposed to the principle of a *pure* practical reason and so also to the moral disposition, even though the action arising from it may be in conformity with the law.

[1] *diese eigene Gesetzgebung*

Thus a practical precept that brings with it a material (hence empirical) condition must never be reckoned a practical law. For, the law of the pure will, which is free, puts the will in a sphere quite different from the empirical, and the necessity that the law expresses, since it is not to be a natural necessity, can therefore consist only in the formal conditions of the possibility of a law in general. All the matter of practical rules rests always on subjective conditions, which afford it no universality for rational beings other than a merely conditional one (in case I *desire* this or that, what I would then have to do in order to make it real), and they all turn on the principle *of one's own happiness*. Now it is indeed undeniable that every volition must also have an object and hence a matter; but the matter is not, just because of this, the determining ground and condition of the maxim; for if it is, then the maxim cannot be presented in the form of giving universal law, since expectation of the existence of the object would then be the determining cause of choice, and the dependence of the faculty of desire upon the existence of some thing would have to be put at the basis of volition; and since this dependence can be sought only in empirical conditions, it can never furnish the basis for a necessary and universal rule. Thus, the happiness of other beings can be the object of the will of a rational being. But if it were the determining ground of the maxim, one would have to presuppose that we find not only a natural satisfaction in the well-being of others but also a need, such as a sympathetic sensibility[m] brings with it in human beings. But I cannot presuppose this need in every rational being (not at all in God). Thus the matter of the maxim can indeed remain, but it must not be the condition of the maxim since the maxim would then not be fit for a law. Hence the mere form of a law, which limits the matter, must at the same time be a ground for adding this matter to the will but not for presupposing it. Let the matter be, for example, my own happiness. This, if I attribute it to each (as, in the case of finite beings, I may in fact do), can become an *objective* practical law only if I include in it the happiness of others. Thus the law to promote the happiness of others arises not from the presupposition that this is an object of everyone's choice but merely from this: that the form of universality, which reason requires as the condition of giving to a maxim of self-love the objective validity of a law, becomes the determining ground of the will; and so the object (the happiness of others) was not the determining ground of the pure will; this was, instead, the mere lawful form alone, by which I limited my maxim based on inclination in order to afford it the   5:35
universality of a law and in this way to make it suitable for pure practical reason; only from this limitation, and not from the addition of an external

[m] *Sinnesart*

31

incentive," could there arise the concept of *obligation* to extend the maxim
of my self-love to the happiness of others as well.

Remark II

The direct opposite of the principle of morality is the principle of *one's
own* happiness made the determining ground of the will; and, as I have
shown above, whatever puts the determining ground that is to serve as a
law anywhere else than in the lawgiving form of the maxim must be
counted in this. This conflict, however, is not merely logical, like that
between empirically conditioned rules that one might nevertheless want to
raise to necessary principles of cognition; it is instead practical and would
ruin morality altogether were not the voice of reason in reference to the
will so distinct, so irrepressible, and so audible even to the most common
human beings; thus it can maintain itself only in the perplexing specula-
tions of the schools, which are brazen enough to shut their ears to that
heavenly voice in order to support a theory they need not break their
heads over.

Suppose that an acquaintance whom you otherwise liked tried to justify
to you his having given false testimony by first pleading what he asserts to
be the sacred duty of his own happiness and then by recounting all the
advantages he had acquired by doing so, pointing out the prudence he had
observed in order to be secure from discovery even by yourself, to whom
he reveals the secret only because he can deny it at any time; and suppose
he were then to affirm, in all seriousness, that he has fulfilled a true
human duty: you would either laugh in his face or shrink back from him
with disgust, even though, if someone has directed his principles solely to
his own advantage, you would not have the least objection to bring against
these measures. Or suppose that someone recommends to you as steward
a man to whom you could blindly trust all your affairs and, in order to
inspire you with confidence, extols him as a prudent human being with
masterly understanding of his own advantage and also as an indefatigably
active one, who lets pass no opportunity to advance it; and finally, lest any
concern about a vulgar selfishness in him stand in the way, the recommender praises his understanding of how to live with refinement, seeking
his satisfaction not in making money or in coarse luxury but in enlarging
his knowledge, in select and instructive society, and even in beneficence to
the needy, while as to the means (which of course derive all their worth or
lack of it from the end) he is not particular and is ready to use other
5:36   people's money and goods for his end as if they were his own, provided he
knows that he can do so without being discovered or thwarted; you would

---

" *Triebfeder*. It subsequently becomes clear that Kant does not maintain the distinction drawn
between *Triebfeder* and *Bewegungsgrund* in the *Groundwork of the Metaphysics of Morals* (4:427).

believe either that the recommender was making a fool of you or that he had lost his mind. So distinctly and sharply drawn are the boundaries of morality and self-love that even the most common eye cannot fail to distinguish whether something belongs to the one or the other. The few remarks that follow may seem superfluous where the truth is so evident, but they may serve at least to afford the judgement of common human reason somewhat greater distinctness.

The principle of happiness can indeed furnish maxims, but never such as would be fit for laws of the will, even if *universal* happiness were made the object. For, because cognition of this rests on sheer data of experience, each judgement about it depending very much upon the opinion of each which is itself very changeable, it can indeed give *general* rules but never *universal* rules, that is, it can give rules that on the average are most often correct but not rules that must hold always and necessarily; hence no practical *laws* can be based on it. Just because an object of choice is here put at the basis of its rule and must therefore precede it, the rule can be referred to and can be based upon nothing other than what one approves,^o and so it refers to and is based upon experience, and then the variety of judgment must be endless. This principle, therefore, does not prescribe the very same practical rules to all rational beings, even though the rules come under a common heading,^p namely that of happiness. The moral law, however, is thought as objectively necessary only because it is to hold for everyone having reason and will.

The maxim of self-love (prudence) merely *advises;* the law of morality *commands.* But there is a great difference between that which we are *advised* to do and that to which we are *obligated.*

What is to be done in accordance with the principle of the autonomy of choice is seen quite easily and without hesitation by the most common understanding; what is to be done on the presupposition of heteronomy of choice is difficult to see and requires knowledge of the world; in other words, what *duty* is, is plain of itself to everyone, but what brings true lasting advantage, if this is to extend to the whole of one's existence, is always veiled in impenetrable obscurity, and much prudence is required to adapt the practical rule in accordance with it to the ends of life even tolerably, by making appropriate exceptions. But the moral law commands compliance from everyone, and indeed the most exact compliance. Appraising what is to be done in accordance with it must, therefore, not be so difficult that the most common and unpracticed understanding should not know how to go about it, even without worldly prudence.

To satisfy the categorical command of morality is within everyone's power at all times; to satisfy the empirically conditioned precept of happi-   5:37

---

^o *empfiehlt.* Hartenstein reads *empfindet* (feels).
^p *Titel*

ness is but seldom possible and is far from being possible for everyone even with respect to only a single purpose. The reason is that in the first case it is a question only of the maxim, which must be genuine and pure, whereas in the latter case it is also a question of one's powers and one's physical ability to make a desired object real. A command that everyone should seek to make himself happy would be foolish, for one never commands of someone what he unavoidably wants already. One would have to command of him only the measures – or, better, provide him with them, since he cannot do all that he wants to do. But to command morality under the name of duty is quite reasonable; for, first, it is not the case that everyone willingly obeys its precept when it is in conflict with his inclinations; and as for the measures – how he can comply with it – here these need not be taught; for in regard to this, what he wills to do, that he also can do.

He who has *lost* at play can indeed be *chagrined* with himself and his imprudence; but if he is conscious of having *cheated* at play (although he has gained by it), he must *despise* himself as soon as he compares himself with the moral law. This must, therefore, be something other than the principle of one's own happiness. For, to have to say to himself "I am a *worthless* man*q* although I have filled my purse," he must have a different criterion of judgment from that by which he commends himself and says "I am a *prudent* man,*r* for I have enriched my cash box."

Finally there is in the idea of our practical reason something further that accompanies the transgression of a moral law, namely its *deserving punishment*. Now, becoming a partaker in happiness cannot be combined with the concept of a punishment as such. For, although he who punishes can at the same time have the kindly intention of directing the punishment to this end as well, yet it must first be justified in itself as punishment, that is, as mere harm,*s* so that he who is punished, if it stopped there and he could see no kindness hidden behind this harshness, must himself admit that justice was done to him*t* and that what was allotted him was perfectly suited to his conduct. In every punishment as such there must first be justice,*u* and this constitutes what is essential in this concept. Kindness can, indeed, be connected with it, but the one who deserves punishment for his conduct has not the least cause to count on this. Thus punishment is a physical harm that, even if it is not connected with moral wickedness as a *natural* consequence, would still have to be connected with it as a

---

q *Unwürdiger*
r *Mensch*
s Or "ill-being," *Übel*. In the following passage *Böse* is translated as "wickedness." On the distinction between *Übel* and *Böse* see AK5:59–60.
t *es sei ihm Recht geschehen*
u *Gerechtigkeit*

consequence in accordance with the principles of a moral lawgiving. Now if every crime, even without regard to the physical consequence with respect to the agent, is of itself punishable – that is, forfeits happiness (at least in part) – it would obviously be absurd to say that the crime consisted just in his having brought a punishment upon himself and thereby in-   5:38 fringed upon his own happiness (which, in accordance with the principle of self-love, would have to be the proper concept of all crime). The punishment would in this way be the ground for calling something a crime, and justice would have to consist instead in omitting all punish- ment and even warding off that which is natural; for then there would no longer be any wickedness in the action, since the harm that would other- wise follow upon it and on account of which alone the action would be called wicked would now be prevented. But to look upon all punishments and rewards as mere machinery in the hands of a higher power, serving only to put rational beings into activity toward their final purpose (happi- ness) is so patently a mechanism which does away with the freedom of their will that it need not detain us here.

More refined, though equally untrue, is the pretense of those who assume a certain special moral sense which, instead of reason, determines the moral law and in accordance with which consciousness of virtue is immediately connected with satisfaction and pleasure, and consciousness of vice with mental unease and pain, so that everything is still reduced to desire for one's own happiness. Without repeating what has been said above, I want only to note the deception[v] going on here. In order to represent someone vicious as tormented with mental unease by conscious- ness of his offenses they must first represent him as morally good, at least to some degree, in what is most basic to his character, just as they must represent someone who is delighted by consciousness of his dutiful ac- tions as already virtuous. The concept of morality and duty would there- fore have to precede any regard for this satisfaction and cannot be derived from it. Now, one must first value the importance of what we call duty, the authority of the moral law, and the immediate worth that compliance with it gives a person in his own eyes, in order to feel that satisfaction in consciousness of one's conformity with it and bitter remorse if one can reproach oneself with having transgressed it. Thus one cannot feel such satisfaction or mental unease prior to cognition of obligation and cannot make it the basis of the latter. Someone must be at least half way toward being an honest man even to frame for himself a representation of those feelings. For the rest, as the human will is by virtue of its freedom immedi- ately determinable by the moral law, I certainly do not deny that frequent practice in conformity with this determining ground can finally produce subjectively a feeling of satisfaction with oneself; on the contrary, to estab-

[v] *Täuschung*

lish and to cultivate this feeling, which alone deserves to be called moral feeling strictly speaking, itself belongs to duty; but the concept of duty cannot be derived from it – otherwise we should have to think of a feeling

5:39 of a law as such*w* and make what can only be thought by reason an object of sensation;*x* and this, if it is not to be a flat contradiction, would quite do away with any concept of duty and put in its place merely a mechanical play of refined inclinations sometimes contending with the coarser.

If we now compare our *formal* supreme principle of pure practical reason (as that of an autonomy of the will) with all previous *material* principles of morality, we can set forth all the rest, as such, in a table in which all possible cases are actually exhausted, except the one formal principle; and thus we can prove visually that it is futile to look around for any other principle than that now presented. That is to say, all possible determining grounds of the will are either merely *subjective* and therefore empirical or also *objective* and rational; and both are either *external* or *internal.*

5:40

Practical Material Determining Grounds[7]	
in the principle of morality are	
Subjective	
External	*Internal*
Of education	Of physical feeling
(according to Montaigne)	(according to Epicurus)
Of the civil constitution	Of moral feeling
(according to Mandeville)	(according to Hutcheson)
Objective	
Internal	*External*
Of perfection	Of the will of God
(according to Wolff	(according to Crusius and other theo-
and the Stoics)	logical moralists)

5:41 Those in the first group*y* are without exception empirical and obviously not at all qualified for the universal principle of morality. But those in the second group are based on reason (for, perfection as a *characteristic*z* of things, and the supreme perfection represented in *substance,* i.e. God, are both to be thought only by means of rational concepts). However, the first concept, namely that of *perfection,* can be taken either in the *theoretical* sense, and then it signifies nothing other than the completeness of each thing in its kind (transcendental perfection) or of a thing merely as a thing in general (metaphysical perfection), and we are not concerned with that here. But the concept of perfection in the *practical* sense is the fitness or

w *ein Gefühl eines Gesetzes als eines solchen*

x *Empfindung*

y "on the left side," as the table is set up in the Academy edition, i.e., the "subjective principles."

z *Beschaffenheit*

adequacy of a thing for all sorts of ends. This perfection, as a *characteristic* of the human being and so as internal is nothing other than *talent* and what strengthens or completes this, *skill.* The supreme perfection in *substance* – that is, God – and so as external (from a practical point of view) is the adequacy of this being to all ends in general. Now, if ends must first be given to us, in relation to which alone the concept of *perfection* (whether internal in ourselves or external in God) can be the determining ground of the will; and if an end as an *object* which must precede the determination of the will by a practical rule and contain the ground of the possibility of such a determination – hence as the *matter* of the will taken as its determining ground – is always empirical; then it can serve as the Epicurean principle of the doctrine of happiness but never as the pure rational principle of the doctrine of morals and of duty (so too, talents and their development only because they contribute to the advantages of life, or the will of God if agreement with it is taken as the object of the will without an antecedent practical principle independent of this idea, can become motives of the will only by means of the happiness we expect from them); from this it follows, *first,* that all the principles exhibited here are *material*; *second,* that they include all possible material principles; and, finally, the conclusion from this, that since material principles are quite unfit to be the supreme moral law (as has been proved), the *formal practical principle* of pure reason (in accordance with which the mere form of a possible giving of universal law through our maxims must constitute the supreme and immediate determining ground of the will) is the *sole* principle that can *possibly* be fit for categorical imperatives, that is, practical laws (which make actions duties), and in general for the principle of morality, whether in appraisals or in application to the human will in determining it.

I.

ON THE DEDUCTION OF THE PRINCIPLES OF PURE PRACTICAL REASON

This Analytic shows that pure reason can be practical – that is, can of itself, independently of anything empirical, determine the will – and it does so by a fact in which pure reason in us proves itself actually practical, namely autonomy in the principle of morality by which reason determines the will to deeds. At the same time it shows that this fact is inseparably connected with, and indeed identical with, consciousness of freedom of the will, whereby the will of a rational being that, as belonging to the sensible world cognizes itself as, like other efficient causes, necessarily subject to laws of causality, yet in the practical is also conscious of itself on another side, namely as a being in itself, conscious of its existence as determinable in an intelligible order of things – conscious of this not, indeed, by a special intuition of itself but according to certain dynamic laws that can determine its causality in the sensible world; for it has been sufficiently proved elsewhere[8] that freedom, if it is attributed to us, transfers us into an intelligible order of things.

If we compare with this Analytic the analytical part of the *Critique* of pure speculative reason, we see a contrast between them worth noting. Not principles but instead pure sensible *intuition* (space and time) was there the first datum that made a priori cognition possible and, indeed, only for objects of the senses. Synthetic principles from mere concepts without intuition were impossible; instead, such principles could be had only with reference to intuition, which was sensible, and so only with reference to objects of possible experience, since the concepts of the understanding joined with such intuition alone make possible that cognition which we call experience. Speculative reason was quite rightly denied anything positive for *cognition* beyond objects of experience, hence of things as noumena. Nevertheless, speculative reason went so far as to secure the concept of noumena – that is, the possibility and indeed the necessity of thinking them – and, for example, to preserve against all objections the assumption of freedom, regarded negatively, as quite compatible with those principles and limitations of pure theoretical reason, 5:43 though without letting us cognize anything determinate and enlarging about such objects, inasmuch as it instead cut off altogether any prospect of that.

On the other hand, the moral law, even though it gives no such *prospect*, nevertheless provides a fact absolutely inexplicable from any data of the sensible world and from the whole compass of our theoretical use of reason, a fact that points to a pure world of the understanding and, indeed, even *determines* it *positively* and lets us cognize something of it, namely a law.

This law is to furnish the sensible world, as a *sensible nature* (in what concerns rational beings), with the form of a world of the understanding, that is, of a *supersensible* nature, though without infringing upon the mechanism of the former. Now, nature in the most general sense is the existence of things under laws. The sensible nature of rational beings in general is their existence under empirically conditioned laws and is thus, for reason, *heteronomy*. The supersensible nature of the same beings, on the other hand, is their existence in accordance with laws that are independent of any empirical condition and thus belong to the *autonomy* of pure reason. And since the laws by which the existence of things depends on cognition are practical, supersensible nature, so far as we can make for ourselves a concept of it, is nothing other than *a nature under the autonomy of pure practical reason*. The law of this autonomy, however, is the moral law, which is therefore the fundamental law of a supersensible nature and of a pure world of the understanding, the counterpart of which is to exist in the sensible world but without infringing upon its laws. The former could be called the *archetypal world (natura archetypa)* which we cognize only in reason, whereas the latter could be called the *ectypal world (natura ectypa)* because it contains the possible effect of the idea of the former as the determining ground of the will. For, the moral law in fact transfers us, in idea,^{*a*} into a nature in which pure reason, if it were accompanied with suitable physical power, would produce the highest good, and it determines our will to confer on the sensible world the form of a whole of rational beings.

The most ordinary attention to oneself confirms that this idea is really, as it were, the pattern for the determinations of our will.

When the maxim on which I intend to give testimony is tested by 5:44 practical reason, I always consider what it would be if it were to hold as a universal law of nature. It is obvious that in this way everyone would be necessitated to truthfulness. For it cannot hold with the universality of a law of nature that statements should be allowed as proof and yet be intentionally untrue. Similarly, the maxim that I adopt with respect to disposing freely of my life is at once determined when I ask myself what it would have to be in order that a nature should maintain itself in accordance with such a law. It is obvious that in such a nature no one could end his life *at will,*^{*b*} for such an arrangement would not be an enduring natural order. And so in all other cases. But in actual nature, insofar as it is an object of experience, the free will is not of itself determined to such maxims as could of themselves establish a nature in accordance with universal laws, or even to such maxims as could of themselves fit into a nature arranged in accordance with them; they are, instead, private inclinations which do constitute a natural whole in accordance with pathological (physical) laws but not a nature that would be possible only through our will in accordance with pure practical laws. Yet we are conscious through reason of a law to which all our maxims are subject, as if a natural order must at the same time arise from our will. This law must therefore be the idea of a nature not given empirically and yet possible through freedom, hence a supersensible nature to which we give objective reality at least in a practical respect, since we regard it as an object of our will as pure rational beings.

Hence the difference between the laws of a nature to which *the will is subject* and of a *nature which* is subject *to a will* (as far as the relation of the will to its free actions is concerned) rests on this: that in the former the objects must be the causes of the representations that determine the will, whereas in the latter the will is to be the cause of the objects, so that its causality has its determining ground solely in the pure faculty of reason, which can therefore also be called a pure practical reason.

There are, accordingly, two very different problems: how, *on the one*

^{*a*} *der Idee nach*
^{*b*} *willkürlich*

39

side, pure reason can *cognize* objects a priori and how, *on the other side,* it
5:45 can be an immediate determining ground of the will, that is, of the causality of a rational being with respect to the reality of objects (merely through
the thought of the universal validity of its own maxims as law).

The first, as belonging to the *Critique* of pure speculative reason,
requires that it first be explained how intuitions, without which no object
at all can be given and without which, therefore, none can be cognized
synthetically, are possible a priori; and its solution turns out to be that
these are without exception sensible only and therefore do not make
possible any speculative cognition that would go further than possible
experience reaches and, consequently, that all principles of that pure
speculative reason do no more than make experience possible, either of
given objects or of those that may be given to us ad infinitum but are never
completely given.

The second, which belongs to the *Critique of Practical Reason,* requires
no explanation of how objects of the faculty of desire are possible, for that,
as a problem of theoretical cognition of nature, is left to the *Critique* of
speculative reason, but only how reason can determine maxims of the will,
whether this takes place only by means of empirical representations as
determining grounds of whether pure reason might also be practical and
might be a law of a possible order of nature not empirically cognizable.
The possibility of such a supersensible nature, the concept of which can
also be the ground of its reality through our free will, requires no a priori
intuition (of an intelligible world), which in this case, as supersensible,
would also have to be impossible for us. For it is a question only of the
determining ground or volition in maxims of volition, whether it is empirical or whether it is a concept of pure reason (of its lawfulness in general),
and how it can be the latter. Whether the causality of the will is adequate
for the reality of the objects or not is left to the theoretical principles of
reason to estimate, this being an investigation into the possibility of objects of volition, the intuition of which is accordingly no component of the
practical problem. It is here a question only of the determination of the
will and of the determining ground of its maxims as a free will, not of its
result. For, provided that the will conforms to the law of pure reason, then
5:46 its power in execution*ᶜ* may be as it may, and a nature may or may not
actually arise in accordance with these maxims of giving law for a possible
nature; the *Critique* which investigates whether and how reason can be
practical, that is, whether and how it can determine the will immediately,
does not trouble itself with this.

In this undertaking the *Critique* can therefore not be censured for
beginning with pure practical laws and their reality, and it must begin
there. Instead of intuition, however, it takes as its basis those laws, the

ᶜ Vermögen . . . in der Ausführung

40

concept of their existence in the intelligible world, namely the concept of freedom. For this concept means nothing else, and those laws are possible only in relation to the freedom of the will; but on the presupposition of freedom they are necessary or, conversely, freedom is necessary because those laws are necessary, as practical postulates. How this consciousness of moral laws or, what is the same thing, this consciousness of freedom is possible cannot be further explained; its admissibility can, however, be defended in the theoretical *Critique*.

The *exposition* of the supreme principle of practical reason is now finished, that is, it has been shown, first, what it contains, that it stands of itself*d* altogether a priori and independently of empirical principles, and then what distinguishes it from all other practical principles. With the *deduction*, that is, the justification of its objective and universal validity and the discernment*e* of the possibility of such a synthetic proposition a priori, one cannot hope to get on so well as was the case with the principles of the pure theoretical understanding. For, these referred to objects of possible experience, namely appearances, and it could be proved that these appearances could be *cognized* as objects of experience only by being brought under the categories in accordance with these laws and consequently that all possible experience must conform to these laws. But I cannot not take such a course in the deduction of the moral law. For, the moral law is not concerned with cognition of the constitution of objects that may be given to reason from elsewhere but rather with a cognition insofar as it can itself become the ground of the existence of objects and insofar as reason, by this cognition, has causality in a rational being, that is, pure reason, which can be regarded as a faculty immediately determining the will.

But all human insight is at an end as soon as we have arrived at basic powers or basic faculties;*f* for there is nothing through which their possibil- 5:47 ity can be conceived, and yet it may not be invented and assumed at one's discretion. Therefore, in the theoretical use of reason only experience can justify us in assuming them. But this substitute, adducing empirical proofs in place of a deduction from sources of cognition a priori, is also denied us here with respect to the pure practical faculty of reason. For, whatever needs to draw the evidence for its reality from experience must be dependent for the grounds of its possibility upon principles of experience, whereas pure but practical reason, by its very concept, cannot possibly be held to be dependent in this way. Moreover the moral law is given, as it were, as a fact of pure reason of which we are a priori conscious and which is apodictically certain, though it be granted that no example of exact observance of it can be found in experience. Hence the objective reality of

d *für sich bestehe*
e *Einsicht*
f *Grundkräften oder Grundvermögen*

41

the moral law cannot be proved by any deduction, by any efforts of theoretical reason, speculative or empirically supported, so that, even if one were willing to renounce its apodictic certainty, it could not be confirmed by experience and thus proved a posteriori; and it is nevertheless firmly established of itself.

But something different and quite paradoxical[g] takes the place of this vainly sought deduction of the moral principle, namely that the moral principle, conversely itself serves as the principle of the deduction of an inscrutable faculty which no experience could prove but which speculative reason had to assume as at least possible (in order to find among its cosmological ideas what is unconditioned in its causality, so as not to contradict itself), namely the faculty of freedom, of which the moral law, which itself has no need of justifying grounds, proves not only the possibility but the reality in beings who cognize this law as binding upon them. The moral law is, in fact, a law of causality through freedom and hence a law of the possibility of a supersensible nature, just as the metaphysical law of events in the sensible world was a law of the causality of sensible nature; and the moral law thus determines that which speculative philosophy had to leave undetermined, namely the law for a causality the concept of which was only negative in the latter, and thus for the first time provides objective reality to this concept.

5:48   This kind of credential of the moral law – that it is itself laid down as a principle of the deduction of freedom as a causality of pure reason – is fully sufficient in place of any a priori justification, since theoretical reason was forced *to assume* at least the possibility of freedom in order to fill a need of its own. For, the moral law proves its reality, so as even to satisfy the *Critique* of speculative reason, by adding a positive determination to a causality thought only negatively, the possibility of which was incomprehensible to speculative reason, which was nevertheless forced to assume it; it adds, namely, the concept of a reason determining the will immediately (by the condition of a universal lawful form of its maxims), and thus is able for the first time to give objective though only practical reality to reason, which always became extravagant when it wanted to proceed speculatively with its ideas, and changes its *transcendent* use into an *immanent* use (in which reason is by means of ideas itself an efficient cause in the field of experience).

The determination of the causality of beings in the sensible world can as such never be unconditioned, and yet for every series of conditions there must necessarily be something unconditioned and so too a causality that is altogether self-determining. Hence the idea of freedom as a faculty of absolute spontaneity was not a need but, *as far as its possibility is concerned,* an analytic principle of pure speculative reason. It is, however,

[g] *Widersinnisches*

absolutely impossible to give anywhere in experience an example of it, since among the causes of things as appearances no determination of causality that would be absolutely unconditioned can be found; hence we could *defend* the *thought* of a freely acting cause, when we apply this to a being in the sensible world, only insofar as this being is also regarded on the other side as a noumenon, by showing that it is not self-contradictory to regard all its actions as physically conditioned insofar as they are appearances and yet also to regard their causality as physically unconditioned insofar as the acting being is a being of the understanding,[h] and thus making the concept of freedom a regulative principle of reason; by it I do not cognize at all the object to which such causality is attributed – what the object may be – but I nevertheless remove the obstacle inasmuch as on the one side, in the explanation of events in the world and so too of the actions of rational beings, I grant the mechanism of natural necessity the justice of going back from the conditioned to the condition ad infinitum, while on the other side I keep open for speculative reason the place which for it is vacant, namely the intelligible, in order to transfer the unconditioned into it. But I could not *realize* this *thought*, that is, could not convert it into *cognition* of a being acting in this way, not even of its mere possibility. Pure practical reason now fills this vacant place with a determinate law of causality in an intelligible world (with freedom), namely the moral law. By this, speculative reason does not gain anything with respect to its insight but it still gains something only with respect to the *security* of its problematic concept of freedom, which is here afforded *objective* and, though only practical, undoubted *reality*. Even the concept of causality, which has application and so too significance strictly speaking[i] only in reference to appearances, in order to connect them into experiences (as the *Critique of Pure Reason* proves) is not enlarged in such a way as to extend its use beyond the boundaries mentioned. For, if reason sought to do this it would have to try to show how the logical relation of ground and consequence could be used synthetically with a kind of intuition different from the sensible, that is, how a *causa noumenon* is possible; this it cannot do, but as practical reason it does not even concern itself with this inasmuch as it only puts the *determining ground* of the causality of the human being as a sensible being (which is given) *in pure reason* (which is therefore called practical), and accordingly uses the concept of cause itself – from whose application to objects for theoretical cognition it can here abstract altogether (since this concept is always found a priori in the understanding, even independently of any intuition) – not in order to cognize objects but to determine causality with respect to objects in general, and so for none other than a practical purpose; and thus it can transfer the determin-

5:49

---

[h] *Verstandeswesen*
[i] *dessen Anwendung, mithin auch Bedeutung eigentlich nur . . . stattfindet*

ing ground of the will into the intelligible order of things inasmuch as it readily admits at the same time that it does not understand how the concept of cause might be determined for cognition of these things. It must, of course, cognize in a determinate way causality with respect to the actions of the will in the sensible world, since otherwise practical reason could not actually produce any deed. But as for the concept which it makes of its own causality as noumenon, it need not determine it theoretically with a view to cognition of its supersensible existence and so need not be able to give it significance in this way. For, the concept receives significance apart from this – though only for practical use – namely, through the moral law. Even regarded theoretically it always remains a pure concept of the understanding given a priori, which can be applied to objects whether they are given sensibly or not sensibly, although in the latter case it has not determinate theoretical significance or application but is merely the understanding's formal though still essential thought of an object in general. The significance which reason furnishes it through the moral law is solely practical, namely that the idea of the law of a causality (of the will) itself has causality or is its determining ground.

II.
ON THE WARRANT OF PURE REASON IN ITS PRACTICAL USE TO AN EXTENSION WHICH IS NOT POSSIBLE TO IT IN ITS SPECULATIVE USE

In the moral principle we have presented a law of causality which puts the determining ground of the latter above all conditions of the sensible world; and as for the will and hence the subject of this will (the human being),[j] we have not merely *thought* it, as it is determinable inasmuch as it belongs to an intelligible world, as belonging to a world of pure understanding though in this relation unknown to us (as can happen according to the *Critique* of speculative reason): we have also *determined* it with respect to its causality by means of a law that cannot be counted as any natural law of the sensible world; and thus we have *extended* our cognition beyond the boundaries of the latter, a claim that the *Critique of Pure Reason* declared void in all speculation. How, then, is the practical use of pure reason here to be united[k] with its theoretical use with respect to determining the boundaries of its competence?[l]

David Hume, who can be said to have really begun all the assaults on the rights of pure reason which made a thorough investigation of them

---

[j] I take the pronouns in the rest of this sentence to refer to "the will," although "the human being" is a possible referent.
[k] *vereinigt, perhaps "reconciled"*
[l] *ihres Vermögens*

necessary, concluded as follows. The concept of *cause* is a concept that contains the *necessity* of the connection of the existence of what is different 5:51 just insofar as it is different, so that if A is posited I cognize that something altogether different from it, B, must necessarily also exist. But necessity can be attributed to a connection only insofar as the connection is cognized a priori; for, experience would enable us to cognize of such a conjunction*ᵐ* only that it is, not that it is necessarily so. Now it is impossible, he says, to cognize a priori and as necessary the connection between one thing and *another* (or between one determination and another altogether different from it) if they are not given in perception. Therefore the concept of a cause is itself fraudulent and deceptive and, to speak of it in the mildest way, an illusion to be excused insofar as the *custom*ⁿ (a *subjective* necessity) of perceiving certain things or their determinations as often associated along with or after one another in their existence is insensibly taken for an *objective* necessity of putting such a connection in the objects themselves; and thus the concept of a cause is acquired surreptitiously and not rightfully – indeed, it can never be acquired or certified because it demands a connection in itself void, chimerical, and untenable before reason, one to which no object can ever correspond. So, with respect to all cognition having to do with the existence of things (mathematics thus remaining excepted) *empiricism* was first introduced as the sole source of principles, but along with it the most rigorous *skepticism* with respect to the whole of natural science (as philosophy). For, on such principles we can never *infer* a consequence from the given determinations of things as existing (since for this the concept of a cause, which contains the necessity of such a connection, would be required) but can only expect, by the rule of imagination, cases similar to preceding ones, though this expectation is never secure however often it is fulfilled. Of no event could one say: something *must* have preceded it, upon which it *necessarily followed, that is, it must have a cause;* and thus, however frequent the cases one knew of in which there was such an antecedent, so that a rule could be derived from them, one could still not, on account of this, assume it as always and necessarily happening in this way, and one would also have to give blind chance its right, with which all use of reason ceases; and this firmly grounds and makes irrefutable skepticism with respect to inferences rising 5:52 from effects to causes.

Mathematics escaped well so far because Hume held that its propositions were all analytic, that is, proceeded from one determination to another by virtue of identity and consequently by the principle*ᵒ* of contradiction (but this is false since they are instead all synthetic; and although,

---

ᵐ *Verbindung*
ⁿ Or "habit," *Gewohnheit*
ᵒ *Satze*

e.g., geometry does not have to do with the existence of things but only with their determination a priori in a possible intuition, it nevertheless passes, just as through the causal concept, from one determination (A) to another altogether different one (B) as still necessarily connected with the former). But in the end that science, so highly esteemed for its apodictic certainty, must also succumb to *empiricism in principles* on the same ground on which Hume put custom in the place of objective necessity in the concept of cause; despite all its pride, it must consent to lower its bold claims commanding a priori assent and expect approval of the universal validity of its propositions from the kindness of observers who, as witnesses, would not refuse to admit that what the geometer propounds as principles they have always perceived as well, and who would therefore allow it to be expected in the future even though it is not necessary. In this way Hume's empiricism in principles also leads unavoidably to skepticism even with respect to mathematics and consequently in every *scientific* theoretical use of reason (for this belongs either to philosophy or to mathematics). I leave each to appraise for himself whether (in view of such a terrible downfall of the chief branches of cognition) the common use of reason will come through any better and will not instead become irretrievably entangled in this same destruction of all science, so that from the same principles a *universal* skepticism will have to follow (though it would, admittedly, concern only the learned).

As for my labor in the *Critique of Pure Reason,* which was occasioned by that Humean skeptical teaching but went much further and included the whole field of pure theoretical reason in its synthetic use and so too the field of what is generally called metaphysics, I proceeded as follows with respect to the doubt of the Scottish philosopher concerning the concept of causality. When Hume took objects of experience as things in themselves (as is done almost everywhere) he was quite correct in declaring the concept of cause to be deceptive and a false illusion; for, as to things in themselves and the determinations of them as such, it cannot be seen why, because something, A, is posited, something else, B, must necessarily be posited also, and thus he could certainly not admit such an a priori cognition of things in themselves. Still less could this acute man grant an empirical origin of this concept, since this directly contradicts the necessity of the connection that constitutes what is essential in the concept of causality; hence the concept was proscribed and into its place stepped custom in observation of the course of perceptions.

From my investigations, however, it resulted that the objects with which we have to do in experience are by no means things in themselves but only appearances and that, although in the case of things in themselves it is not to be understood and is indeed impossible to see[p] how, if A

5:53

---

[p] *nicht abzusehen ist, ja unmöglilch ist einzusehen*

is posited it should be *contradictory* not to posit B which is quite different from A (the necessity of the connection between A as cause and B as effect), yet it can very well be thought that as appearances they must necessarily be connected *in one experience* in a certain way (e.g., with respect to temporal relations) and cannot be separated without *contradicting* that connection by means of which this experience is possible, in which they are objects and in which alone they are cognizable by us. And it was found to be so in fact as well; and thus I was able not only to prove the objective reality of the concept of cause with respect to objects of experience but also to *deduce* it as an a priori concept because of the necessity of the connection that it brings with it, that is, to show its possibility from pure understanding without empirical sources; and thus, after removing empiricism from its origin, I was able to overthrow the unavoidable consequence of empiricism, namely skepticism first with respect to natural science and then, because skepticism in mathematics follows from just the same grounds, with respect to mathematics as well, both of which sciences have reference to objects of possible experience; in this way I was able to eradicate total doubt of whatever theoretical reason professes to have insight into. 5:54

But how is it with the application of this category of causality (and so too of all the others, for without them no cognition can be had of what exists) to things that are not objects of possible experience but lie beyond its boundaries? For I was able to deduce the objective reality of these concepts only with respect to *objects of possible experience.* But what gives them a place in the pure understanding, from which they are referred to objects in general (whether sensible or not) is just this: that I also saved them only in case I proved that objects may nevertheless be *thought* through them although not determined a priori. If anything is still wanting, it is the condition *for the application* of these categories and especially that of causality to objects, namely intuition; where this is not given, application with *a view to theoretical cognition* of an object as a noumenon is made impossible, so that such cognition, when someone ventures upon it, is altogether forbidden (as also happens in the *Critique of Pure Reason*), while the objective reality of the concept (of causality) nevertheless remains and can be used even of noumena, although this concept cannot be theoretically determined in the least and thereby produce a cognition. For, that this concept, even in relation to an object, contains nothing impossible was proved by this: that in any application to objects of the senses, its seat in the pure understanding was secured; and even though, when it might subsequently be referred to things in themselves (which cannot be objects of experience), it is not capable of being determined so as to represent *a determinate object* for the sake of theoretical cognition, yet for the sake of something else (the practical, perhaps) it could be capable of being determined for its application; and this would not be the case if, as

47

Hume maintained, this concept of causality contained something that it is always impossible to think.

In order now to discover this condition of the application of the concept in question to noumena, we need only recall *why we are not satisfied with its application to objects of experience* but would like to use it of things in themselves as well. For then it soon becomes apparent that it is not a theoretical but a practical purpose that makes this a necessity for us. Even if we were successful in this application we would still have made no true acquisition for speculation, in cognition of nature or, in general, with respect to any objects that might be given to us; instead we would at most have taken a long step from the sensibly conditioned (and we already have enough to do to remain in it and diligently go through the chain of causes) to the supersensible, in order to complete our cognition on the side of grounds and to fix its boundary, although an infinite gulf between that boundary and what we know remains always unfilled and we would have listened to a frivolous curiosity rather than a solid desire for knowledge.

However, besides the relation in which the *understanding* stands to object (in theoretical cognition) it has also a relation to the faculty of desire, which is therefore called the will and is called the pure will insofar as the pure understanding (which in this case is called reason) is practical through the mere representation of a law. The objective reality of a pure will or, what is the same thing, of a pure practical reason is given a priori in the moral law, as it were by a fact – for so we may call a determination of the will that is unavoidable even though it does not rest upon empirical principles. In the concept of a will, however, the concept of causality is already contained, and thus in the concept of a pure will there is contained the concept of a causality with freedom, that is, a causality that is not determinable in accordance with laws of nature and hence not capable of any empirical intuition as proof of its reality, but that nevertheless perfectly justifies its objective reality a priori in the pure practical law, though not (as is easily seen) with a view to the theoretical use of reason but only to its practical use. Now, the concept of a being that has free will is the concept of a *causa noumenon;* and one is already assured that this concept does not contradict itself since the concept of a cause, as having arisen wholly from the pure understanding, also has its objective reality with respect to objects in general assured by the deduction inasmuch as, being in its origin independent of all sensible conditions and so of itself not restricted to phenomena (unless one should want to make a determinate theoretical use of it), the concept could certainly be applied to things as beings of the pure understanding. But because no intuition, which can only be sensible, can be put under this application, *causa noumenon* with respect to the theoretical use of reason is, though a possible, thinkable concept, nevertheless an empty one. But I do not now claim *to know theoretically* by this concept the

5:55

5:56

constitution of a being *insofar as* it has a *pure* will; it is enough for me to thereby only designate it as such a being and hence only to connect the concept of causality with that of freedom (and with what is inseparable from it, the moral law as its determining ground); and I am certainly authorized to do so by virtue of the pure, not empirical origin of the concept of cause, inasmuch as I consider myself authorized to make no other use of it than with regard to the moral law which determines its reality, that is, only a practical use.

Had I, with Hume, deprived the concept of causality of objective reality in its practical[q] use not only with respect to things in themselves (the supersensible) but also with respect to objects of the senses, it would be declared devoid of all meaning and, as a theoretically impossible concept, quite unusable; and since no use at all can be made of what is nothing,[r] the practical use of a concept *theoretically null* would have been absurd. Now, however, the concept of an empirically unconditioned causality is indeed theoretically empty (without any intuition appropriate to it) but it is nevertheless possible and refers to an undetermined object; in place of that, however, the concept is given significance in the moral law and consequently in its practical reference; thus I have, indeed, no intuition that would determine its objective theoretical reality for it, but it has nonetheless a real application which is exhibited *in concreto* in dispositions or maxims, that is, it has practical reality which can be specified; and this is sufficient to justify it even with regard to noumena.

But this objective reality of a pure concept of the understanding in the field of the supersensible, once introduced, gives all the other categories objective reality as well, though only insofar as they stand in *necessary* connection with the determining ground of the pure will (the moral law) – an objective reality which is, however, of only practical applicability and has not the least influence on theoretical cognition of these objects, as insight into their nature by pure reason, so as to extend this. As we shall also find in the sequel, these categories have reference only to beings as *intelligences,* and in them only to the relation of *reason* to the *will* and consequently always to the *practical* only, and beyond this they lay claim to no cognition of these beings; as for whatever other properties, belonging to the theoretical way of representing such supersensible things, may be brought forward in connection with these categories, these are without exception to be counted not as knowledge but only as a warrant (for practical purposes, however, a necessity) to admit and presuppose them, even where supersensible beings (such as God) are assumed by analogy, that is, by a purely rational relation of which we make a practical use with respect to what is sensible; and so, by this application to the supersensible

5:57

---

[q] Vorländer amends this to read *im theoretischen Gebrauche,* "in its theoretical use."
[r] *von Nichts*

but only for practical purposes, pure theoretical reason is not given the least encouragement to fly into the transcendent.[s]

The analytic of practical reason
Chapter II
On the concept of an object of pure practical reason

By a concept of an object of practical reason I understand the representation of an object as an effect possible through freedom. To be an object of practical cognition so understood signifies, therefore, only the relation of the will to the action by which it or its opposite would be made real, and to appraise whether or not something is an object of *pure* practical reason is only to distinguish the possibility or impossibility of *willing* the action by which, if we had the ability to do so (and experience must judge about this), a certain object would be made real. If the object is taken as the determining ground of our faculty of desire, the *physical possibility* of it by the free use of our powers must precede our appraisal of whether it is an object of practical reason or not. On the other hand, if the a priori law can be regarded as the determining ground of the action, and this, accordingly, can be regarded as determined by pure practical reason, then the judgment whether or not something is an object of pure practical reason is quite independent of this comparison with our physical ability, and the question is only whether we could *will* an action which is directed to the existence of an object if the object were within our power;[t] hence the *moral possibility* of the action must come first, since in this case the determining ground of the will is not the object but the law of the will.

5:58

The only objects of a practical reason are therefore those of the *good* and the *evil*. For by the first is understood a necessary object of the faculty of desire, by the second, of the faculty of aversion,[u] both, however, in accordance with a principle of reason.

If the concept of the good is not to be derived from an antecedent practical law but, instead, is to serve as its basis, it can be only the concept of something whose existence promises pleasure and thus determines the causality of the subject, that is, the faculty of desire, to produce it. Now because it is impossible to see a priori which representation will be accompanied with *pleasure* and which with *displeasure*, it would be up to experience alone to make out what is immediately good or evil. The property of the

[s] *zum Schwärmen ins Überschwengliche*
[t] *in unserer Gewalt*
[u] *des Begehrungs- . . . des Verabscheuungsvermögen*

subject, with reference to which alone this experience can be had, is the *feeling*[v] of pleasure and displeasure, as a receptivity belonging to inner sense, and thus the concept of that which is immediately good would be directed only to that with which the feeling of *gratification*[w] is immediately connected, and the concept of the simply evil would have to be referred only to that which immediately excites *pain.* But since this is opposed even to the use of language, which distinguishes the *agreeable* from the *good* and the *disagreeable* from the *evil* and requires that good and evil always be appraised by reason and hence through concepts, which can be universally communicated, not through mere feeling, which is restricted to individual subjects and their receptivity; and since, nevertheless, pleasure or displeasure cannot of themselves be connected a priori with any representation of an object, a philosopher who believed that he had to put a feeling of pleasure at the basis of his practical appraisal would have to call *good* that which is a *means* to the agreeable, and *evil* that which is a cause of disagreeableness and of pain; for, appraisal of the relation of means to ends certainly belongs to reason. But, although reason alone is capable of discerning the connection of means with their purposes (so that the will could also be defined as the faculty of ends, inasmuch as these are always determining grounds of the faculty of desire in accordance with principles), the practical maxims that would follow from the above concept of the good merely as a means would never contain as the object of the will anything good in itself, but always only good *for something;* the good would always be merely the useful, and that for which it is useful would always have to lie outside the will, in feeling. Now if the latter, as agreeable feeling, had to be distinguished from the concept of the good, then there would be nothing at all immediately good, and the good would have to be sought, instead, only in the means to something else, namely some agreeableness. 5:59

There is an old formula of the schools, *nihil appetimus, nisi sub ratione boni; nihil aversamur, nisi sub ratione mali;*[x] and it has a use which is often correct but also often very detrimental to philosophy, because the expressions *boni* and *mali* contain an ambiguity,[y] owing to the poverty of the language, by which they are capable of a double sense and thus unavoidably involve practical laws in ambiguities;[z] and the philosophy which, in using them, becomes aware of the difference of concepts in the same word but can still find no special expressions for them is forced into

---

[v] *Gefühl*

[w] *Empfindung des Vergnügens.* Throughout this paragraph, in which *Gefühl* and *Empfindung* are both translated as "feeling," Kant uses the two words interchangeably.

[x] We desire nothing except under the form of the good; nothing is avoided except under the form of the bad.

[y] *Zweideutigkeit*

[z] *auf Schrauben stellen*

subtle distinctions about which there is subsequently no agreement inasmuch as the difference cannot be directly indicated by any suitable expression.*

The German language has the good fortune to possess expressions which do not allow this difference to be overlooked. For that which the Latins denominate with a single word, *bonum*, it has two very different concepts and equally different expressions as well: for *bonum* it has *das Gute*[a] and *das Wohl*,[b] for *malum* it has *das Böse*[c] and *das Übel*[d] (or *Weh*),[e] so that there are two very different appraisals of an action depending upon whether we take into consideration the *good* and *evil* of it or our *well-being* and *woe* (ill-being). From this it already follows that the above psychological proposition is at least very doubtful if it is translated: we desire nothing except with a view to our *well-being* or *woe*, whereas if it is rendered: we will nothing under the direction of reason except insofar as we hold it to be good or evil, it is indubitably certain and at the same time quite clearly expressed.

5:60

Well-being or *ill-being* always signifies only a reference to our state of *agreeableness* or *disagreeableness*, of gratification or pain, and if we desire or avoid an object on this account we do so only insofar as it is referred to our sensibility and to the feeling of pleasure or displeasure it causes. But *good* or *evil* always signifies a reference to the *will* insofar as it is determined by the *law of reason* to make something its object; for, it is never determined directly by the object and the representation of it, but is instead a faculty of making a rule of reason the motive of an action (by which an object can become real). Thus good or evil is, strictly speaking, referred to actions, not to the person's state of feeling, and if anything is to be good or evil absolutely (and in every respect and without any further condition), or is to be held to be such, it would be only the way of acting, the maxim of the will, and consequently the acting person himself as a good or evil human being, that could be so called, but not a thing.

Thus one may always laugh at the Stoic who in the most intense pains

---

*Moreover, the expression *sub ratione boni* is also ambiguous. For it may mean: we represent to ourselves something as good when and *because we desire* (will) *it*, or also: we desire something *because we represent it to ourselves as good*, so that either desire is the determining ground of the concept of the object as a good, or the concept of the good is the determining ground of desire (of the will); so in the first case *sub ratione boni* would mean, we will something *under the idea* of the good; in the second, we will something *in consequence of this idea*, which must precede volition as its determining ground.

[a] good
[b] well-being
[c] evil
[d] ill-being
[e] woe

of gout cried out: Pain, however you torment me I will still never admit that you are something evil (κακov, *malum*)!; nevertheless, he was correct. He felt that the pain was an ill, and his cry betrayed that; but he had no cause whatever to grant that any evil attached to him because of it, for the pain did not in the least diminish the worth of his person but only the worth of his condition. A single lie of which he had been aware would have had to strike down his pride,*f* but the pain served only as an occasion to raise it when he was aware that he had not incurred it by any wrongful action and thereby made himself deserving of punishment.

What we are to call good must be an object of the faculty of desire in the judgment of every reasonable human being, and evil an object of aversion in the eyes of everyone; hence for this appraisal reason is needed, in addition to sense. So it is with truthfulness as opposed to lying, with justice as opposed to violence, and so forth. But we can call something an ill which everyone must yet at the same time pronounce good, sometimes mediately but sometimes even immediately. Someone who submits to a surgical operation feels it no doubt as an ill, but through reason he and everyone else pronounce it good. But if someone who likes to vex and disturb peace-loving people finally gets a sound thrashing for one of his provocations, this is certainly an ill, yet everyone would approve of it and take it as good in itself even if nothing further resulted from it; indeed, even the one who received it must in his reason recognize that justice was done to him,*g* because he sees the proportion between well-being and acting well, which reason unavoidably holds before him, here put into practice exactly.

5:61

Certainly, our well-being and woe count for a *very great deal* in the appraisal of our practical reason and, as far as our nature as sensible beings is concerned, *all* that counts is our *happiness* if this is appraised, as reason especially requires, not in terms of transitory feeling but of the influence this contingency has on our whole existence and our satisfaction with it; but happiness is not *the only thing* that counts. The human being is a being with needs, insofar as he belongs to the sensible world, and to this extent his reason certainly has a commission from the side of his sensibility which it cannot refuse, to attend to its interest and to form practical maxims with a view to happiness in this life and, where possible, in a future life as well. But he is nevertheless not so completely an animal as to be indifferent to all that reason says on its own and to use reason merely as a tool for the satisfaction of his needs as a sensible being. For, that he has reason does not at all raise him in worth above mere animality if reason is to serve him only for the sake of what instinct accomplishes

f Mut
g das ihm Recht geschehe

5:62 for animals; reason would in that case be only a particular mode[h] nature had used to equip the human being for the same end to which it has destined[i] animals, without destining him to a higher end. No doubt once this arrangement of nature has been made for him he needs reason in order to take into consideration at all times his well-being and woe; but besides this he has it for a higher purpose:[j] namely, not only to reflect upon what is good or evil in itself as well – about which only pure reason, not sensibly interested at all, can judge – but also to distinguish the latter appraisal altogether from the former and to make it the supreme condition of the former.

In this appraisal of what is good and evil in itself, as distinguished from what can be called so only with reference to well-being or ill-being, it is a question of the following points. Either a rational principle is already thought as in itself the determining ground of the will without regard to possible objects of the faculty of desire (hence through the mere lawful form of the maxim), in which case that principle is a practical law a priori and pure reason is taken to be practical of itself. In that case the law determines the will *immediately*, the action in conformity with it is *in itself good*, and a will whose maxim always conforms with this law is *good absolutely*, *good in every respect* and the *supreme condition of all good*. Or else a determining ground of the faculty of desire precedes the maxim of the will, which presupposes an object of pleasure or displeasure and hence something that *gratifies* or *pains*, and the maxim of reason to pursue the former and avoid the latter determines actions which are good with reference to our inclination and hence good only mediately (relatively to a further end, as means to it), and such maxims can in that case never be called laws but can still be called rational practical precepts. The end itself, the gratification that we seek, is in the latter case not a *good* but a *well-being*, not a concept of reason but an empirical concept of an object of feeling; but the use of means to it, that is, the action, is nevertheless called good (because rational reflection is required for it), not, however, good absolutely but only with reference to our sensibility, with respect to its feeling of pleasure and displeasure; but the will whose maxim is affected by it is not a pure will, which is directed only to that by which pure reason can of itself be practical.

This is the place to explain the paradox of method in a *Critique of*
5:63 *Practical Reason, namely, that the concept of good and evil must not be determined before the moral law (for which, as it would seem, this concept would have to be made the basis) but only (as was done here) after it and by means of it.* That is to say: even if we did not know that the principle of morality is a pure

[h] *Manier*
[i] *bestimmt hat*
[j] *Behuf*

law determining the will a priori, we would at least have to leave it *unde-cided* in the beginning whether the will has only empirical or also pure determining grounds a priori, in order not to assume principles quite gratuitously (*gratis*); for, it it is contrary to all basic rules of philosophic procedure to assume as already decided the foremost question to be decided. Suppose that we wanted to begin with the concept of the good in order to derive from it laws of the will: then this concept of an object (as a good object) would at the same time supply this as the sole determining ground of the will. Now, since this concept had no practical a priori law for its standard, the criterion of good or evil could be placed in nothing other than the agreement of the object with our feeling of pleasure or displeasure, and the use of reason could only consist partly in determining this pleasure or displeasure in connection with all the feelings of my existence and partly in determining the means for providing myself with the object of such feelings. Now, since what is in keeping with the feeling of pleasure can be made out only through experience, and since the practical law is nevertheless, by hypothesis, to be based on this as its condition, the possibility of a priori practical laws would be at once excluded, because it was thought to be necessary first of all to find an object for the will, the concept of which, as that of a good, would have to constitute the universal though empirical determining ground of the will. But what it was necessary to investigate first was whether there is not also an a priori determining ground of the will (which could never be found elsewhere than in a pure practical law, and indeed insofar as it prescribes to maxims only their lawful form without regard to an object). Since, however, an object in accordance with concepts of the good and evil had already been made the basis of all practical laws, while the former, without a law preceding it, could be thought only by empirical concepts, the possibility of even thinking of a pure practical law was already removed in advance; on the other hand, if the latter had first been investigated analyti- 5:64 cally it would have been found that, instead of the concept of the good as an object determining and making possible the moral law, it is on the contrary the moral law that first determines and makes possible the concept of the good, insofar as it deserves this name absolutely.

This remark, which concerns only the method of ultimate moral investigations, is important. It explains at once the occasioning ground of all the errors of philosophers with respect to the supreme principle of morals. For they sought an object of the will in order to make it into the matter and the ground of a law (which was thus to be the determining ground of the will not immediately but rather by means of that object referred to the feeling of pleasure or displeasure), whereas they should first have searched for a law that determined the will a priori and immediately, and only then determined the object conformable to the will. Now, whether they placed this object of pleasure, which was to yield the supreme concept of good, in happiness, in perfection, in moral feeling, or in the will of God, their principle was in every case heteronomy and they had to come unavoidably upon empirical conditions for a moral law, since they could call their object, as the immediate determining ground of the will, good or evil only by its immediate relation to feeling, which is always empirical. Only a formal law, that is, one that prescribes to reason nothing more than the form of its universal lawgiving as the supreme condition of maxims, can be a priori a determining ground of practical reason. The ancients revealed this error openly by directing their moral investigation entirely to the determination of the concept of the *highest good*, and so of an object which they intended afterwards to make the determining ground of the will in the moral law, an object which can much later – when the moral law has first been established by itself and justified as the immediate determining ground of the will – be represented as object to the will, now determined a priori in its form; and this we will undertake in the Dialectic of pure practical reason. The moderns, with whom the question of the highest good seems to have gone out of use or at least to have become a secondary matter, hide the above error (as in many other cases) behind

5:65 indeterminate words; but one can still see it showing through their systems, since it always reveals heteronomy of practical reason, from which an a priori moral law commanding universally can never arise.

Now, since the concepts of good and evil, as consequences of the a priori determination of the will, presuppose also a pure practical principle and hence a causality of pure reason, they do not refer originally to objects (as, say, determinations of the synthetic unity of the manifold of given intuitions in one consciousness), as do the pure concepts of the understanding or categories of reason used theoretically; instead, they presuppose these objects as given; they are rather, without exception, *modi* of a single category, namely that of causality, insofar as the determining ground of causality consists in reason's representation of a law of causality which, as the law of freedom, reason gives to itself and thereby proves itself a priori to be practical. However, since actions *on the one side* indeed belong under a law which is no law of nature but a law of freedom, and consequently belong to the conduct of intelligible beings, but *on the other side* as also events in the sensible world yet belong to appearances, the determinations of a practical reason can take place only with reference to the latter and therefore, indeed, conformably with the categories of the understanding, but not with a view to a theoretical use of the understanding, in order to bring a priori the manifold of (sensible) *intuition* under one consciousness, but only in order to subject a priori the manifold of *desires* to the unity of consciousness of a practical reason commanding in the moral law, or of a pure will.

These *categories of freedom* – for this is what we are going to call them in

CRITIQUE OF PRACTICAL REASON

contrast to those theoretical concepts which are categories of nature – have an obvious advantage over the latter inasmuch as the latter are only forms of thought which, by means of universal concepts, designate only indeterminately objects in general for every intuition possible for us; the former, on the contrary, are directed to the determination of a free choice[k] (to which indeed no fully corresponding intuition can be given but which – as does not happen in the case of any concepts of the theoretical use of our cognitive faculty – has as its basis a pure practical law a priori); hence, instead of the form of intuition (space and time), which does not lie in reason itself but must be drawn from elsewhere, namely from sensibility, these, as practical elementary concepts, have as their basis the *form of a pure will* as given within reason and therefore within the thinking faculty itself; by this it happens that, since all precepts of pure practical reason have to do only with the *determination of the will*, not with the natural conditions (of practical ability) for *carrying out its purpose*, the practical a priori concepts in relation to the supreme principle of freedom at once become cognitions and do not have to wait for intuitions in order to receive meaning; and this happens for the noteworthy reason that they themselves produce the reality of that to which they refer (the disposition of the will), which is not the business of theoretical concepts. But one must note well that these categories concern only practical reason in general and so proceed in their order from those which are as yet morally undetermined and sensibly conditioned to those which, being sensibly unconditioned, are determined only by the moral law.

5:66

TABLE
of the categories of freedom with respect to the concepts of the good and evil

1.
Of quantity

Subjective, in accordance with maxims (*intentions of the will*[l] of the individual)
Objective, in accordance with principles (*precepts*)
A priori objective as well as subjective principles of freedom (*laws*)

2.	3
Of quality	Of relation
Practical rules of *commission*	To *personality*
(*praeceptivae*)	To the *condition*[m] of the person

[k] *freien Willkür*
[l] *Willensmeinungen*
[m] or "state," *Zustand*

57

Practical rules of *omission*	*Reciprocally*, of one person
(*prohibitivae*)	to the condition of others
Practical rules of *exceptions*	
(*exceptivae*)	

4.

Of modality

The *permitted* and the *forbidden*

Duty and what is *contrary to duty*

Perfect and *imperfect* duty

5:67   One quickly sees that in this table freedom is regarded as a kind of causality – which, however, is not subject to empirical grounds of determination – with respect to actions possible through it as appearances in the sensible world, and that consequently it is referred to the categories of their natural possibility," while yet each category is taken so universally that the determining ground of that causality can be taken to be also outside the sensible world in freedom as the property of an intelligible being, until the categories of modality introduce, but only *problematically*, the transition from practical principles in general to those of morality, which can only afterwards be presented *dogmatically* through the moral law.

    I add nothing further here to elucidate the present table, since it is intelligible enough in itself. A division of this kind, drawn up in accordance with principles, is very useful in any science, for the sake of thoroughness as well as intelligibility. Thus, for example, one knows at once from the above table and its first number where one has to set out from in practical considerations: from the maxims that each bases on his inclination, from the precepts that hold for a species° of rational beings insofar as they agree in certain inclinations, and finally from the law that holds for all without regard for their inclinations, and so forth. In this way one surveys the whole plan of what has to be done, every question of practical philosophy that has to be answered, and also the order that is to be followed.

OF THE TYPIC OF PURE PRACTICAL JUDGMENT ^p

The concepts of good and evil first determine an object for the will. They themselves, however, stand under a practical rule of reason which, if it is pure reason, determines the will a priori with respect to its object. Now, whether an action possible for us in sensibility is or is not a case that

---

" *ihrer Naturmöglichkeit.* Abbot translates the phrase as "its [freedom's] physical possibility."
° *Gattung*
ᵖ *Urteilskraft,* i.e., "the faculty of judgment"

stands under the rule requires practical judgment, by which what is said in the rule universally (*in abstracto*) is applied to an action *in concreto*. But a practical rule of pure reason *first*, as *practical*, concerns the existence of an object, and *second*, as a *practical rule* of pure reason, brings with it necessity with respect to the existence of an action and is thus a practical law, not a natural law through empirical grounds of determination but a law of   5:68 freedom in accordance with which the will is to be determinable independently of anything empirical (merely through the representation of a law in general and its form); however, all cases of possible actions that occur can be only empirical, that is, belong to experience and nature; hence, it seems absurd to want to find in the sensible world a case which, though as such it stands only under the law of nature, yet admits of the application to it of a law of freedom and to which there could be applied the supersensible idea of the morally good, which is to be exhibited in it *in concreto*. Thus the judgment of pure practical reason is subject to the very same difficulties as that of pure theoretical reason, though the latter had means at hand of escaping from these difficulties, namely that with respect to its theoretical use it depended upon intuitions to which pure concepts of the understanding could be applied, and such intuitions (though only of objects of the senses) can be given a priori and thus, as far as the connection of the manifold in them is concerned, given a priori (as *schemata*) conformably with pure concepts of the understanding. On the other hand, the morally good as an object is something supersensible, so that nothing corresponding to it can be found in any sensible intuition; and judgment under laws of pure practical reason seems, therefore, to be subject to special difficulties having their source in this: that a law of freedom is to applied to actions as events that take place in the sensible world and so, to this extent, belong to nature.

But here again a favorable prospect opens for pure practical judgment. Subsumption of an action possible to me in the sensible world under a *pure practical law* does not concern the possibility of the *action* as an event in the sensible world; for, it belongs to the theoretical use of reason to appraise that possibility in accordance with the law of causality, a pure concept of the understanding for which reason has a *schema* in sensible intuition. Physical causality, or the condition under which it takes place, belongs among concepts of nature, whose schema transcendental imagination sketches. Here, however, we have to do not with the schema of a case in accordance with laws but with the schema of a law itself (if the word schema is appropriate here), since the *determination of the will* (not the   5:69 action with reference to its result) through the law alone without any other determining ground connects the concept of causality to conditions quite other than those which constitute natural connection.

To a natural law, as a law to which objects of sensible intuition as such are subject, there must correspond a schema, that is, a universal procedure of the imagination (by which it presents a priori to the senses the pure concept of the understanding which the law determines). But no intuition can be put under the law of freedom (as that of a causality not sensibly conditioned) – and hence under the concept of the unconditioned good as well – and hence no schema on behalf of its application *in concreto*. Thus the moral law has no cognitive faculty other than the understanding (not the imagination) by means of which it can be applied to objects of nature, and what the understanding can put under an idea of reason is not a *schema* of sensibility but a law, such a law, however, as can be presented *in concreto* in objects of the senses and hence a law of nature, though only as to its form; this law is what the understanding can put under an idea of reason on behalf of judgment, and we can, accordingly, call it the *type* of the moral law.

The rule of judgment under laws of pure practical reason is this: ask yourself whether, if the action you propose were to take place by a law of the nature of which you were yourself a part, you could indeed regard it as possible through your will. Everyone does, in fact, appraise actions as morally good or evil by this rule. Thus one says: if *everyone* permitted himself to deceive when he believed it to be to his advantage, or considered himself authorized to shorten his life as soon as he was thoroughly weary of it, or looked with complete indifference on the need of others, and if you belonged to such an order of things, would you be in it with the assent of your will? Now everyone knows very well that if he permits himself to deceive secretly it does not follow that everyone else does so, or that if, unobserved, he is hard-hearted[q] everyone would not straightaway be so toward him; accordingly, this comparison of the maxim of his actions with a universal law of nature is also not the determining ground of his will. Such a law is, nevertheless, a *type* for the appraisal of maxims in accordance with moral principles. If the maxim of the action is not so constituted that it can stand the test as to the form of a law of nature in general, then it is morally impossible. This is how even the most common understanding judges; for the law of nature always lies at the basis of its most ordinary judgments, even those of experience. Thus it has the law of nature always at hand, only that in cases where causality from freedom is to be appraised it makes that *law of nature* merely the type of a *law of freedom*, because without having at hand something which it could make an example in a case of experience, it could not provide use in application for the law of a pure practical reason.

Hence it is also permitted to use *the nature of the sensible world* as the *type* of an *intelligible nature*, provided that I do not carry over into the latter

5:70

---

[q] *lieblos*

intuitions and what depends upon them but refer to it only the *form of lawfulness* in general (the concept of which occurs even in the most common use of reason, although it cannot be determinately cognized a priori for any purpose other than the pure practical use of reason). For to this extent laws as such are the same, no matter from what they derive their determining grounds.

Furthermore, since of all the intelligible absolutely nothing [is cognized] except freedom (by means of the moral law), and even this only insofar as it is a presupposition inseparable from that law; and since, moreover, all intelligible objects to which reason might lead us under the guidance of that law have in turn no reality for us except on behalf of that law and of the use of pure practical reason, although reason is entitled and even required to use nature (in the understanding's pure form of nature) as the *type* of judgment; the present remark will serve to prevent reckoning among concepts themselves that which belongs only to the *typic* of concepts. This, then, as the typic of judgment, guards against *empiricism* of practical reason, which places the practical concepts of good and evil merely in experiential consequences (so-called happiness), although happiness and the endless useful consequences of a will determined by self-love, if this will at the same time made itself into a universal law of nature, can certainly serve as a quite suitable type for the morally good but is still not identical with it. The same typic also guards against *mysticism* of practical reason, which makes what served only as a *symbol* into a *schema*, that is, puts under the application 5:71 of moral concepts real but not sensible intuitions (of an invisible kingdom of God) and strays into the transcendent. Only *rationalism* of judgment is suitable for the use of moral concepts, since it takes from sensible nature nothing more than what pure reason can also think for itself, that is, conformity with law, and transfers into the supersensible nothing but what can, conversely, be really exhibited by actions in the sensible world in accordance with the formal rule of a law of nature in general. However, it is much more important and advisable to guard against *empiricism* of practical reason, since *mysticism* is still compatible with the purity and sublimity of the moral law and, besides, it is not natural and not in keeping with the common way of thinking to strain one's imagination to supersensible intuitions, so that the danger from this side is not so general; empiricism, on the contrary, destroys at its roots the morality of dispositions (in which, and not merely in actions, consists the high worth that humanity can and ought to procure for itself through morality), and substitutes for it something quite different, namely in place of duty an empirical interest, with which the inclinations generally are secretly leagued; and empiricism, moreover, being on this account allied with all the inclinations, which (no matter what fashion they put on) degrade humanity when they are raised to the dignity of a supreme practical principle and which are, nevertheless, so favorable to everyone's way of feeling,^r is for that reason much more dangerous than any enthusiasm, which can never constitute a lasting condition of any great number of people.^s

Chapter III
On the incentives of pure practical reason

What is essential to any moral worth of actions is *that the moral law determine the will immediately*. If the determination of the will takes place *conformably* with the moral law but only by means of a feeling, of whatever kind, that has to be presupposed in order for the law to become a sufficient determining ground of the will, so that the action is not done *for the sake of the law*, then the action will contain *legality* indeed but not *morality*. 5:72 Now, if by *incentive (elater animi)* is understood the subjective determining ground of the will of a being whose reason does not by its nature necessarily conform with the objective law, then it will follow: first; that no incentives at all can be attributed to the divine will but that the incentive of the human will (and of the will of every created rational being) can never be anything other than the moral law; and thus that the objective determining ground must always and quite alone be also the subjectively sufficient determining ground of action if this is not merely to fulfill the *letter* of the law without containing its *spirit*.*

For the sake of the law and in order to give it influence on the will one must not, then, look for some other incentive by which that of the moral law itself might be dispensed with, because this would produce sheer hypocrisy without substance,^t and it is even hazardous to let any other incentive (such as that of advantage) so much as cooperate *alongside* the moral law; so nothing further remains than to determine carefully in what way the moral law becomes the incentive and, inasmuch as it is, what happens to the human faculty of desire as an effect of that determining ground upon it. For, how a law can be of itself and immediately a determining ground of the will (though this is what is essential in all morality) is for human reason an insoluble problem and identical with that of how a free will is possible. What we shall have to show a priori is, therefore, not the ground from which^u the moral law in itself supplies an incentive but rather

---

*Of every action that conforms to the law but is not done for the sake of the law, one can say that it is morally good only in accordance with the *letter* but not the *spirit* (the disposition).
^r *Sinnesart*
^s The construction of the last part of this sentence is, as Natorp remarks, "difficult, but with Kant perhaps still possible." With minor changes I have reproduced Abbott's construction.
^t *ohne Bestand*
^u *woher*

what it effects (or, to put it better, must effect) in the mind insofar as it is an incentive.

What is essential in every determination of the will by the moral law is that, as a free will – and so not only without the cooperation of sensible impulses but even with rejection of all of them and with infringement upon all inclinations insofar as they could be opposed to that law – it is determined solely by the law. So far, then, the effect of the moral law as incentive is only negative, and as such this incentive can be cognized a priori. For, all inclination and every sensible impulse is based on feeling, and the negative effect on feeling (by the infringement upon the inclina-   5:73
tions that takes place) is itself feeling. Hence we can see a priori that the moral law, as the determining ground of the will, must by thwarting all our inclinations produce a feeling that can be called pain; and here we have the first and perhaps the only case in which we can determine a priori from concepts the relation of a cognition (here the cognition of a pure practical reason) to the feeling of pleasure or displeasure. All the inclinations together (which can be brought into a tolerable system and the satisfaction of which is then called one's own happiness) constitute regard for oneself^v (*solipsismus*). This is either the self-regard of *love for oneself*, a predominant *benevolence* toward oneself (*Philautia*), or that of *satisfaction with oneself* (*Arrogantia*). The former is called, in particular, *self-love;*^{w} the latter, *self-conceit.*^{x} Pure practical reason merely *infringes upon* self-love, inasmuch as it only restricts it, as natural and active in us even prior to the moral law, to the condition of agreement with this law, and then it is called *rational self-love.* But it *strikes down* self-conceit altogether, since all claims to esteem for oneself that precede accord with the moral law are null and quite unwarranted because certainty of a disposition in accord with this law is the first condition of any worth of a person (we shall soon make this more distinct), and any presumption prior to this is false and opposed to the law. Now, the propensity to self-esteem, so long as it rests only on sensibility, belongs with the inclinations which the moral law infringes upon. So the moral law strikes down self-conceit. But since this law is still something in itself positive – namely the form of an intellectual causality, that is, of freedom – it is at the same time an object of *respect* inasmuch as, in opposition to its subjective antagonist, namely the inclinations in us, it *weakens* self-conceit; and inasmuch as it even *strikes down* self-conceit, that is, humiliates it, it is an object of the greatest *respect* and so too the ground of a positive feeling that is not of empirical origin and is cognized a priori. Consequently, respect for the moral law is a feeling that is produced by

^{v} *Selbstsucht*
^{w} *Eigenliebe*
^{x} *Eigendünkel*

an intellectual ground, and this feeling is the only one that we can cognize completely a priori and the necessity of which we can have insight into.

5:74   In the preceding chapter we have seen that anything which presents itself as an object of the will *prior to* the moral law is excluded from the determining grounds of the will called the unconditionally good by that law itself as the supreme condition of practical reason, and that the mere practical form, which consists in the fitness of maxims for giving universal law, first determines what is good in itself and absolutely and grounds the maxims of a pure will, which alone is good in every respect. Now, however, we find our nature as sensible beings so constituted that the matter of the faculty of desire (objects of inclination, whether of hope or fear) first forces itself upon us, and we find our pathologically determinable self, even though it is quite unfit to give universal law through its maxims, nevertheless striving antecedently to make its claims primary and originally valid, just as if it constituted our entire self. This propensity to make oneself as having subjective determining grounds of choice[y] into the objective determining ground of the will in general can be called *self-love;* and if self-love makes itself lawgiving and the unconditional practical principle, it can be called *self-conceit.* Now the moral law, which alone is truly objective (namely objective in every respect), excludes altogether the influence of self-love on the supreme practical principle and infringes without end upon self-conceit, which prescribes as laws the subjective conditions of self-love. Now, what in our own judgment infringes upon our self-conceit humiliates. Hence the moral law unavoidably humiliates every human being when he compares with it the sensible propensity of his nature. If something represented *as a determining ground of our will* humiliates us in our self-consciousness, it awakens *respect* for itself insofar as it is positive and a determining ground. Therefore the moral law is even subjectively a ground of respect. Now, all that is found in self-love belongs to inclination, while all inclination rests on feeling, so that what infringes upon all the inclinations in self-love has, just by this, a necessary influence on feeling; thus we conceive how it is possible to see a priori that the moral law can exercise an effect on feeling, inasmuch as it excludes the inclinations and the propensity to make them the supreme practical condition, that is, self-love, from all participation in the supreme lawgiving – an effect which on the one side is merely *negative* but on the other side, and indeed with respect to the restrict-

5:75   ing ground of pure practical reason, is *positive;* and for this no special kind of feeling need be assumed, under the name of a practical or moral feeling preceding the moral law and serving as its basis.

The negative effect upon feeling (disagreeableness) is *pathological,* as is every influence on feeling and every feeling in general. As the effect of

---

[y] *sich selbst nach den subjectiven Bestimmungsgründen seiner Willkür*

consciousness of the moral law, and consequently in relation to an intelligible cause, namely the subject of pure practical reason as the supreme lawgiver, this feeling of a rational subject affected by inclinations is indeed called humiliation (intellectual contempt); but in relation to its positive ground, the law, it is at the same time called respect for the law; there is indeed no feeling for this law, but inasmuch as it moves resistance out of the way, in the judgment of reason this removal of a hindrance is esteemed equivalent to a positive furthering of its causality. Because of this, this feeling can now also be called a feeling of respect for the moral law, while on both grounds together it can be called a *moral feeling*.

Thus the moral law, since it is a formal determining ground of action through practical pure reason and since it is also a material but only objective determining ground of the objects of action under the name of good and evil, is also a subjective determining ground – that is, an incentive – to this action inasmuch as it has influence on the sensibility of the subject and effects a feeling conducive to the influence of the law upon the will. There is here no *antecedent* feeling in the subject that would be attuned to morality: that is impossible, since all feeling is sensible whereas the incentive of the moral disposition must be free from any sensible condition. Instead, sensible feeling, which underlies all our inclinations, is indeed the condition of that feeling we call respect, but the cause determining it lies in pure practical reason; and so this feeling, on account of its origin, cannot be called pathologically effected but must be called *practically effected,* and is effected as follows: the representation of the moral law deprives self-love of its influence and self-conceit of its illusion, and thereby the hindrance to pure practical reason is lessened and the representation of the superiority of its objective law to the impulses of sensibility, and with it the relative weightiness of the law (with regard to a will affected by impulses), is produced in the judgment of reason through the removal of the counterweight. And so respect for the law is not the incentive to morality; instead it is morality itself subjectively considered as an incentive inasmuch as pure practical reason, by rejecting all the claims of self-love in opposition with its own, supplies authority to the law, which now alone has influence. With regard to this it should be noted that, since respect is an effect on feeling and hence on the sensibility of a rational being, it presupposes this sensibility and so too the finitude of such beings on whom the moral law imposes respect, and that respect for the *law* cannot be attributed to a supreme being or even to one free from all sensibility, in whom this cannot be an obstacle to practical reason.

5:76

This feeling (under the name of moral feeling) is therefore produced solely by reason. It does not serve for appraising actions and certainly not for grounding the objective moral law itself, but only as an incentive to make this law its maxim. But what name could one more suitably apply to this singular feeling which cannot be compared to any pathological feeling? It is of such a peculiar kind that it seems to be at the disposal^z only of reason, and indeed of practical pure reason.

Respect is always directed only to persons, never to things. The latter can awaken in us *inclination* and even *love* if they are animals (e.g., horses, dogs, and so forth), or also *fear*, like the sea, a volcano, a beast of prey, but never *respect*. Something that comes nearer to this feeling is *admiration*, and this as an affect, amazement, can be directed to things also, for example, lofty mountains, the magnitude, number, and distance of the heavenly bodies, the strength and swiftness of many animals, and so forth. But none of this is respect. A human being can also be an object of my love, fear, or admiration even to amazement and yet not be an object of respect. His jocular humor, his courage and strength, the power he has by his rank among others, could inspire me with feelings of this kind even though inner respect toward him is lacking. Fontenelle [9] says, "*I bow before an eminent man, but my spirit does not bow.*" I can add: before a humble common man^a in whom I perceive uprightness of character in a higher degree than I am aware of in myself *my spirit bows*, whether I want it or whether I do not and hold my head ever so high, that he may not overlook my superior position. Why is this? His example holds before me a law that strikes down my self-conceit when I compare it with my conduct, and I see observance of that law and hence its *practicability* proved before me in fact. Now, I may even be aware of a like degree of uprightness in myself, and yet the respect remains. For, since in human beings all good is defective, the law made intuitive by an example still strikes down my pride, the standard being furnished by the man I see before me whose impurity,^b such as it may be, is not so well known to me as is my own who therefore appears to me in a purer light. *Respect* is a *tribute* that we cannot refuse to pay to merit, whether we want to or not; we may indeed withhold it outwardly but we still cannot help feeling it inwardly.

So little is respect a feeling of *pleasure* that we give way to it only reluctantly with regard to a human being. We try to discover something that could lighten the burden of it for us, some fault in him to compensate us for the humiliation that comes upon us through such an example. Even the dead are not always safe from this critical examination, especially if their example appears inimitable. Even the moral law itself in its *solemn majesty* is exposed to this striving to resist respect for it. Can it be thought that any other cause can be assigned for our being so ready to demean it to our familiar inclination, or that there is any other cause of our taking such trouble to make it out to be the popular precept of our own advantage well

5:77

---

^z *zu Gebote*

^a *niedrigen, bürgerlich gemeinen Mann*

^b *Unlauterkeit.* See *Religion within the Boundaries of Mere Reason* (6:29–30). Later in the sentence "purer" is used to translate *reinerem.*

understood, than that we want to be free from the intimidating respect that shows us our own unworthiness with such severity? But, in turn, *so little displeasure* is there in it that, once one has laid self-conceit aside and allowed practical influence to that respect, one can in turn never get enough of contemplating the majesty of this law, and the soul believes itself elevated in proportion as it sees the holy elevated above itself and its frail nature. No doubt, great talents and activity proportioned to them can also produce respect or a feeling analogous to it, and it is also quite proper to offer it; and then it seems as if admiration were the same as that feeling. But if one looks more closely one will notice that, since it always remains uncertain how much was contributed to someone's competence by native talent and how much by his industry in cultivating it, reason represents it to us as presumably the fruit of cultivation and so as merit, and this noticeably reduces our self-conceit and either casts a reproach on us or imposes on us the following of such an example in the way suitable to us. This respect, then, which we show to such a person (strictly speaking to the law that his example holds before us) is not mere admiration, as is also confirmed by this: that when the common run of admirers believes it has somehow learned the badness of character of such a man (such as Voltaire) it gives up all respect for him, whereas the true scholar still feels it at least with regard to his talents, because he is himself engaged in a business and a calling that make imitation of such a man to some extent a law for him. 5:78

Respect for the moral law is therefore the sole and also the undoubted moral incentive, and this feeling is also directed to no object except on this basis. First, the moral law determines the will objectively and immediately in the judgment of reason; but freedom, the causality of which is determinable only through the law, consists just in this: that it restricts all inclinations, and consequently the esteem of the person himself, to the condition of compliance with its pure law. This restriction now has an effect on feeling and produces the feeling of displeasure which can be cognized a priori from the moral law. It is, however, so far a *negative* effect which, as arising from the influence of a pure practical reason, mainly infringes upon the activity of the subject so far as inclinations are his determining grounds and hence upon the opinion of his personal worth (which, in the absence of agreement with the moral law, is reduced to nothing), so that the effect of this law on feeling is merely humiliation, which we can thus discern a priori though we cannot cognize in it the force of the pure practical law as incentive but only the resistance to incentives of sensibility. But the same law is yet objectively – that is, in the representation of pure reason – an immediate determining ground of the will, so that this humiliation takes place only relatively to the purity of the law; accordingly, the lowering of pretensions to moral self-esteem – that is, humiliation on the sensible side – is an elevation of the moral – that is, practical – esteem 5:79

for the law itself on the intellectual side; in a word, it is respect for the law, and so also a feeling that is positive in its intellectual cause, which is known a priori. For, whatever diminishes the hindrances to an activity is a furthering of this activity itself. Recognition of the moral law is, however, consciousness of an activity of practical reason from objective grounds, which fails to express its effect in actions only because subjective (pathological) causes hinder it. Therefore respect for the moral law must be regarded as also a positive though indirect effect of the moral law on feeling insofar as the law weakens the hindering influence of the inclinations by humiliating self-conceit, and must therefore be regarded as a subjective ground of activity – that is, as the incentive to compliance with the law – and as the ground for maxims of a course of life in conformity with it. From the concept of an incentive arises that of an *interest*, which can never be attributed to any being unless it has reason and which signifies an *incentive* of the will insofar as it is *represented by reason*. Since in a morally good will the law itself must be the incentive, the *moral interest* is a pure sense-free interest of practical reason alone. On the concept of an interest is based that of a *maxim*. A maxim is therefore morally genuine only if it rests solely on the interest one takes in compliance with the law. All three concepts, however – that of an *incentive*, of an *interest* and of a *maxim* – can be applied only to finite beings. For they all presuppose a limitation of the nature of a being, in that the subjective constitution of its choice does not of itself accord with the objective law of a practical reason; they presuppose a need to be impelled to activity by something because an internal obstacle is opposed to it. Thus they cannot be applied to the divine will.

There is something so singular in the boundless esteem for the pure moral law stripped of all advantage – as practical reason, whose voice makes even the boldest evildoer tremble and forces him to hide from its 5:80 sight, presents it to us for obedience – that one cannot wonder at finding this influence of a mere intellectual idea on feeling quite impenetrable for speculative reason and at having to be satisfied that one can yet see a priori this much: that such a feeling is inseparably connected with the representation of the moral law in every finite rational being. If this feeling of respect were pathological and hence a feeling of *pleasure* based on the inner *sense*, it would be futile to [try to] discover a priori a connection of it with any idea. But it is a feeling which is directed only to the practical and which depends on the representation of a law only as to its form and not on account of any object of the law; thus it cannot be reckoned either as enjoyment or as pain, and yet it produces an *interest* in compliance with the law which we call *moral* interest, just as the capacity to take such an interest in the law (or respect for the moral law itself) is *the moral feeling* properly speaking.

The consciousness of a *free* submission of the will to the law, yet as combined with an unavoidable constraint put on all inclinations though only by one's own reason, is respect for the law. The law that demands this respect and also inspires it is, as one sees, none other than the moral law (for no other excludes all inclinations from immediate influence on the will). An action that is objectively practical in accordance with this law, with the exclusion of every determining ground of inclination, is called *duty*, which, because of that exclusion, contains in its concept practical *necessitation*, that is, determination to actions however *reluctantly* they may be done. The feeling that arises from consciousness of this necessitation is not pathological, as would be a feeling produced by an object of the senses, but practical only, that is, possible through a preceding (objective) determination of the will and causality of reason. As *submission* to a law, that is, as a command (indicating constraint for the sensibly affected subject), it therefore contains in it no pleasure but instead, so far, displeasure in the action. On the other hand, however, since this constraint is exercised only by the lawgiving of his *own* reason, it also contains something *elevating*, and the subjective effect on feeling, inasmuch as pure practical reason is the sole cause of it,ᶜ can thus be called *self-approbation* with reference to pure practical reason, inasmuch as he cognized himself as determined to it solely by the law and without any interest, and now becomes conscious of an altogether different interest subjectively produced by the law, which is purely practical and *free;* and his taking this interest in a dutiful action is not advised by any inclination; instead, reason through the practical law absolutely commands it and also actually produces it, because of which it has a quite special name, that of respect.   5:81

The concept of duty, therefore, requires of the action *objective* accord with the law but requires of the maxim of the action *subjective* respect for the law, as the sole way of determining the will by the law. And on this rests the distinction between consciousness of having acted in *conformity with duty* and *from duty*, that is, respect for the law, the first of which (legality) is possible even if the inclinations alone have been the determining grounds of the will whereas the second (*morality*), moral worth, must be placed solely in this: that the action takes place from duty, that is, for the sake of the law alone.*

It is of the greatest importance in all moral appraisals to attend with the utmost exactness to the subjective principle of all maxims, so that all the

---

*If one examines accurately the concept of respect for persons, as it has already been set forth, one becomes aware that it always rests on consciousness of a duty which an example holds before us, and that, accordingly, respect can never have any but a moral ground; and it is very good and even, from a psychological point of view, very useful for knowledge of human beings that whenever we use this expression we should attend to the hidden and wonderful, yet often recurring, regard which the human being in his appraisals has for the moral law.

ᶜ *der letzteren.* "Something elevating" (literally, "elevation") is grammatically possible.

morality of actions is placed in their necessity *from duty* and from respect for the law, not from love and liking[d] for what the actions are to produce. For human beings and all created rational beings moral necessity is necessitation, that is, obligation, and every action based on it is to be represented as duty, not as a kind of conduct which we already favor of our own accord or could come to favor – as if we could ever bring it about that without respect for the law, which is connected with fear or at least apprehension of transgressing it, we of ourselves, like the Deity raised beyond all dependence, could come into possession of *holiness* of will by an accord of will with the pure moral law becoming, as it were, our nature, an accord never to be disturbed (in which case the law would finally cease to be a command for us, since we could never be tempted to be unfaithful to it).

5:82

The moral law is, in other words, for the will of a perfect being a law of *holiness*, but for the will of every finite rational being a law of *duty*, of moral necessitation and of the determination of his actions through *respect* for this law and *reverence*[e] for his duty. No other subjective principle must be assumed as incentive, for then the action can indeed turn out as the law prescribes, but since, though in conformity with duty it was not done from duty, the disposition to the action is not moral; and in this lawgiving it is really the disposition that matters.

It is very beautiful to do good to human beings from love for them and from sympathetic benevolence, or to be just from love of order; but this is not yet the genuine moral maxim of our conduct, the maxim befitting our position among rational beings as *human beings*, when we presume with proud conceit, like volunteers, not to trouble ourselves about the thought of duty and, as independent of command, to want to do of our own pleasure what we think we need no command to do. We stand under a *discipline* of reason, and in all our maxims must not forget our subjection to it or withdraw anything from it or by an egotistical illusion detract anything from the authority of the law (although our own reason gives it), so as to put the determining ground of our will, even though it conforms with the law, anywhere else than in the law itself and in respect for this law. Duty and what is owed[f] are the only names that we must give to our relation to the moral law. We are indeed lawgiving members of a kingdom of morals possible through freedom and represented to us by practical reason for our respect; but we are at the same time subjects in it, not its sovereign, and to fail to recognize our inferior position as creatures and to deny from self-conceit the authority of the holy law is already to defect from it in spirit, even though the letter of the law is fulfilled.

5:83

[d] *Zuneigung*
[e] *Ehrfurcht*
[f] *Schuldigkeit*

The possibility of such a commandment[g] as *Love God above all, and your neighbor as yourself* agrees with this very well.* For, as a commandment it requires respect for a law that *commands*[h] *love* and does not leave it to one's discretionary choice to make this one's principle. But love for God as inclination (pathological love) is impossible, for he is not an object of the senses. The same thing toward human beings is indeed possible but cannot be commanded, for it is not within the power of any human being to love someone merely on command.[i] It is, therefore, only *practical love* that is understood in that kernel of all laws. To love God means, in this sense, to do what He commands *gladly;* to love one's neighbor means to practice all duties toward him *gladly.* But the command that makes this a rule cannot command us to *have* this disposition in dutiful actions but only to *strive* for it. For, a command that one should do something gladly is in itself contradictory because if we already know of ourselves what it is incumbent upon us to do and, moreover, were conscious of liking to do it, a command about it would be quite unnecessary; and if we did it without liking to do it but only from respect for the law, a command that makes this respect the incentive of our maxim would directly counteract the disposition commanded. That law of all laws, therefore, like all the moral precepts of the Gospel, presents the moral disposition in its complete perfection, in such a way that as an ideal of holiness it is not attainable by any creature but is yet the archetype which we should strive to approach and resemble in an uninterrupted but endless progress. That is to say, if a rational creature could ever reach the stage of thoroughly *liking* to fulfill all moral laws, this would mean that there would not be in him even the possibility of a desire that would provoke him to deviate from them; for, to overcome such a desire always costs the subject some sacrifice and therefore requires self-constraint, that is, inner necessitation to what one does not altogether like to do. But no creature can ever reach this stage of moral disposition. For, being a creature and thus always dependent with regard to what he requires for complete satisfaction with his condition, he can never be altogether free from desires and inclinations which, because they rest on physical causes, do not of themselves accord with the moral law, which has quite different sources; and consequently, with reference to those desires, it is always necessary for him to base the disposition of his maxims on moral necessitation, not on ready fidelity but on respect, which *demands* compliance with the law even though this is done reluc-

5:84

---

*The principle of one's own happiness, which some would make the supreme principle of morality, is in striking contrast to this law. The former would go as follows: *Love yourself above all, but God and your neighbor for your own sake.*

[g] *Gebots*
[h] *befiehlt*
[i] *auf Befehl*

71

tantly; not on love, which is not anxious about any inner refusal of the will toward the law, even though it is necessary for him to make this latter – namely, mere love for the law (which would then cease to be a *command*, and morality, having passed subjectively into holiness, would cease to be *virtue*) – the constant though unattainable goal of his striving. For, in the case of what we highly esteem but yet dread (because of consciousness of our weakness), through increased facility in satisfying it the most reverential dread changes into liking and respect into love; at least this would be the consummate perfection of a disposition devoted to the law, if it were possible for a creature to attain it.

This consideration is intended not so much to bring to clear concepts the evangelical command just cited, in order to prevent *religious enthusiasm* in regard to love of God, but to determine accurately the moral disposition directly, in regard to our duties toward human beings as well, and to check, or where possible prevent, a *merely moral* enthusiasm which infects many people. The moral level on which a human being (and, as far as we can see, every rational creature as well) stands is respect for the moral law. The disposition incumbent upon him to have in observing it is to do so from duty, not from voluntary liking nor even from an endeavor he undertakes unbidden, gladly and of his own accord; and his proper moral condition, in which he can always be, is *virtue*, that is, moral disposition *in conflict*, and not *holiness* in the supposed *possession* of a complete *purity* of dispositions of the will. By exhortation to actions as noble, sublime, and magnanimous, minds are attuned to nothing but moral enthusiasm and exaggerated self-conceit; by such exhortations they are led into the delusion that it is not duty – that is, respect for the law whose yoke (though it is a mild one because reason itself imposes it on us) they must bear, even if reluctantly – which constitutes the determining ground of their actions, and which always humbles them inasmuch as they observe the law (*obey* it), but that it is as if those actions are expected from them, not from duty but as bare merit. For, when they imitate such deeds – namely, from such a principle – not only have they quite failed to fulfill the spirit of the law, which consists in the disposition subjecting itself to the law, not in the lawfulness of the action (whatever the principle may be); not only do they locate the incentive *pathologically* (in sympathy or self-love), not *morally* (in the law); but they produce in this way a frivolous, high-flown, fantastic cast of mind, flattering themselves with a spontaneous goodness of heart[j] that needs neither spur nor bridle and for which not even a command is necessary and thereby forgetting their obligation,[k] which they ought to think of rather than merit. Actions of others that are done with great sacrifice and for the sake of duty alone may indeed be praised by calling

[j] *freiwillige Gutartigkeit ihrer Gemüts*
[k] *Schuldigkeit*

them *noble* and *sublime* deeds, but only insofar as there are traces suggesting that they were done wholly from respect for duty and not from ebullitions of feeling. But if one wants to represent these to someone as examples to be imitated, respect for duty (which is the only genuine moral feeling) must be used as the incentive – this earnest, holy precept that does not leave it to our vain self-love to dally with pathological impulses (as far as they are analogous to morality) and to credit ourselves with *meritorious* worth. If only we search carefully we shall find for all actions that are praiseworthy a law of duty, which *commands* and does not leave it to our discretion to choose what may be agreeable to our propensity. This is the only way of representing them that educates the soul morally, because it alone is capable of firm and accurately determined principles.

If *enthusiasm* in the most general sense is an overstepping of the bounds of human reason undertaken on principles, then *moral enthusiasm* is such an overstepping of the bounds that practical pure reason sets to humanity, thereby forbidding us to place the subjective determining ground of dutiful actions – that is, their moral motive – anywhere else than in the law itself or to place the disposition which is thereby brought into the maxims anywhere else than in respect for this law, and so commanding us to make the thought of duty, which strikes down all *arrogance* as well as vain *self-love*, the supreme *life-principle* of all morality in human beings. 5:86

If this is so, then not only novelists and sentimental educators (even though they may be strongly opposed to sentimentalism) but sometimes even philosophers – and even the most austere of all, the Stoics – have ushered in *moral enthusiasm* instead of a sober but wise moral discipline, though the enthusiasm of the latter was more heroic while that of the former is of a more insipid and languishing character; and one can, without hypocrisy, say quite truly of the moral teaching of the Gospel that, by the purity of its moral principle but at the same time by the suitability of this principle to the limitations of finite beings, it first subjected all good conduct of man to the discipline of a duty laid before his eyes, which does not allow them to rove among fancied moral perfections, and set limits of humility (i.e., self-knowledge) to self-conceit as well as to self-love, both of which are ready to mistake their boundaries.

Duty! Sublime and mighty name that embraces nothing charming or insinuating but requires submission, and yet does not seek to move the will by threatening anything that would arouse natural aversion or terror in the mind but only holds forth a law that of itself finds entry into the mind and yet gains reluctant reverence (though not always obedience), a law before which all inclinations are dumb, even though they secretly work against it; what origin is there worthy of you, and where is to be found the root of your noble descent which proudly rejects all kinship with the inclinations, descent from which is the indispensable condition of that worth which human beings alone can give themselves?

It can be nothing less than what elevates a human being above himself (as a part of the sensible world), what connects him with an order of things that only the understanding can think and that at the same time has under it the whole sensible world and with it the empirically determinable exis-

5:87 tence of human beings in time and the whole of all ends (which is alone suitable to such unconditional practical laws as the moral). It is nothing other than *personality*, that is, freedom and independence from the mechanism of the whole of nature, regarded nevertheless as also a capacity of a being subject to special laws – namely pure practical laws given by his own reason, so that a person as belonging to the sensible world is subject to his own personality insofar as he also belongs to the intelligible world; for, it is then not to be wondered at that a human being, as belonging to both worlds, must regard his own nature in reference to his second and highest vocation only with reverence, and its laws with the highest respect.

On this origin are based many expressions that indicate the worth of objects according to moral ideas. The moral law is *holy* (inviolable). A human being is indeed unholy enough but the *humanity* in his person must be holy to him. In the whole of creation everything one wants and over which one has any power can also be used *merely as a means;* a human being alone, and with him every rational creature, is an *end in itself:* by virtue of the autonomy of his freedom he is the subject of the moral law, which is holy. Just because of this every will, even every person's own will directed to himself, is restricted to the condition of agreement with the *autonomy* of the rational being, that is to say, such a being is not to be subjected to any purpose that is not possible in accordance with a law that could arise from the will of the affected[1] subject himself; hence this subject is to be used never merely as a means but as at the same time an end. We rightly attribute this condition even to the divine will with respect to the rational beings in the world as its creatures, inasmuch as it rests on their *personality*, by which alone they are ends in themselves.

This idea of personality, awakening respect by setting before our eyes the sublimity of our nature (in its vocation) while at the same time showing us the lack of accord of our conduct with respect to it and thus striking down self-conceit, is natural even to the most common human reason and is easily observed. Has not every even moderately honorable man sometimes found that he has abstained from an otherwise harmless lie by which

5:88 he could either have extricated himself from a troublesome affair or even procured some advantage for a beloved and deserving friend, solely in order not to have to despise himself secretly in his own eyes? When an upright man is in the greatest distress, which he could have avoided if he could only have disregarded duty, is he not sustained by the consciousness that he has maintained humanity in its proper dignity in his own person

---

[1] *leidenden*

and honored it, that he has no cause to shame himself in his own eyes and to dread the inward view of self-examination? This consolation is not happiness, not even the smallest part of it. For, no one would wish the occasion for it on himself, or perhaps even a life in such circumstances. But he lives and cannot bear to be unworthy of life in his own eyes. This inner tranquility is therefore merely negative with respect to everything that can make life pleasant; it is, namely, only warding off the danger of sinking in personal worth, after he has given up completely the worth of his condition. It is the effect of a respect for something quite different from life, something in comparison and contrast with which life with all its agreeableness has no worth at all. He still lives only from duty, not because he has the least taste for living.

This is how the genuine moral incentive of pure practical reason is constituted; it is nothing other than the pure moral law itself insofar as it lets us discover the sublimity of our own supersensible existence and subjectively effects respect for their higher vocation in human beings, who are at the same time conscious of their sensible existence and of the dependence, connected with it, on their pathologically affected nature. Now, so many charms and attractions of life may well be connected with this incentive that even for their sake alone the most prudent choice of a reasonable Epicurean, reflecting on the greatest well-being of life, would declare itself for moral conduct; and it can even be advisable to connect this prospect of a cheerful enjoyment of life with that motive which is supreme and already sufficiently determining of itself; but this connection should be made only to counterbalance the allurements that vice does not fail to display on the opposite side, and not so as to place in this the proper moving force, not even the smallest part of it, when it is a question of duty. For that would be tantamount to wanting to taint the pure moral disposi- 5:89
tion in its source. The majesty of duty has nothing to do with the enjoyment of life; it has its own law and also its own court, and even though one might want to shake both of them together thoroughly, so as to give them blended, like medicine, to the sick soul, they soon separate of themselves; if they do not, the former will effect nothing at all, and though physical life might gain some force, the moral life would fade away irrecoverably.

CRITICAL ELUCIDATION OF THE ANALYTIC OF PURE PRACTICAL REASON

By the critical elucidation of a science, or of a portion of it that constitutes a system by itself, I understand the investigation and justification of why it must have precisely this and no other systematic form when it is compared with another system having a similar cognitive faculty as its basis. Now, practical reason has as its basis the same cognitive faculty as does speculative reason so far as both are *pure reason*. Therefore the difference in the systematic form of the one from that of the other must be determined by a comparison of the two, and the ground of this difference must be assigned.

The Analytic of pure theoretical reason had to do with cognition of such objects as could be given to the understanding; it thus had to begin from *intuition* and consequently (since this is always sensible) from sensibility, and only then progress to concepts (of the objects of this intuition), and could end with *principles* only after preparation by way of both these. Practical reason, on the contrary, since it does not have to do with objects for the sake of *cognizing* them but with its own ability *to make them real* (conformably with cognition of them), that is, with a *will* that is a causality inasmuch as reason contains its determining ground; since, accordingly, it does not have to provide an object of intuition but, as practical reason, *only a law* for such an object (because the concept of causality always contains reference to a law that determines the existence of a manifold in relation to one another); it follows that a critique of the Analytic of reason, insofar as it is to be a practical reason (and this is the real problem), must begin 5:90 from the *possibility of practical principles* a priori. Only from these could it proceed to *concepts* of objects of a practical reason, namely, to the concepts of the simply good and evil, in order first to give them in keeping with those principles (for, prior to those principles these cannot possibly be given as good and evil by any cognitive faculty), and only then could the last chapter conclude this part, namely the chapter about the relation of pure practical reason to sensibility and about its necessary influence upon sensibility to be cognized a priori, that is, about *moral feeling.* Thus the Analytic of practical pure reason divides the whole sphere of all the conditions of its use quite analogously with that of theoretical reason, but in reverse order. The Analytic of theoretical pure reason was divided into transcendental Aesthetic and transcendental Logic; that of practical reason, reversely, into Logic and Aesthetic of pure practical reason (if I may be allowed, merely by an analogy, to use these terms, which are not altogether suitable); the Logic in turn was there divided into Analytic of concepts and Analytic of principles, here into that of principles and concepts. The Aesthetic there had two parts, because of the twofold kind of sensible intuition; here sensibility is not regarded as a capacity for intuition at all but only as feeling (which can be a subjective ground of desire), and with respect to it pure practical reason admits no further division.

As to why this division into two parts with their subdivision was not actually undertaken here (as one might initially have been induced to attempt by the example of the first *Critique*), this is easily seen. For, since it is *pure reason* that is here considered in its practical use, and consequently as proceeding from a priori principles and not from empirical determining grounds, the division of the Analytic of pure practical reason must turn out like that of a syllogism, namely, proceeding from the universal in the *major premise* (the moral principle), through undertaking in a *minor premise* a subsumption of possible actions (as good or evil) under the former, to the *conclusion*, namely, the subjective determination of the will (an interest in the practically possible good and in the maxim based on it). For someone who has been able to convince himself of the propositions presented in the Analytic such comparisons will be gratifying; for they rightly occasion the expectation of perhaps being able some day to attain insight into the unity of the whole pure rational faculty (theoretical as well as practical) and to derive everything from one principle – the undeniable need of human reason, which finds complete satisfaction only in a complete systematic unity of its cognitions. 5:91

But if we now consider also the content of the cognition that we can have of a pure practical reason and by means of it, as the Analytic of pure practical reason presents this content, there is found, along with a remarkable analogy between it and the theoretical, no less remarkable differences. With respect to the theoretical, the *faculty of a pure rational cognition* a priori could be quite easily and evidently proved through examples from the sciences (in which, since they put their principles to the test in so many ways by methodic use, one need not fear so much as in common cognition a secret mixture of empirical grounds of cognition). But that pure reason, without the admixture of any empirical determining ground, is practical of itself alone: this one had to be able to show from the *most common practical use of reason,* by confirming the supreme practical principle as one that every natural human reason cognizes – a law completely a priori and independent of any sensible data – as the supreme law of its will. It was necessary first to establish and justify the purity of its origin even *in the judgment of this common reason* before science would take it in hand in order to make use of it, so to speak, as a fact that precedes all subtle reasoning about its possibility and all the consequences that may be drawn from it. But this circumstance can also be very well explained from what has just been said; it is because practical pure reason must necessarily begin from principles, which must therefore, as the first data, be put at the basis of all science and cannot first arise from it. But for this reason the justification of moral principles as principles of a pure reason could also be carried out very well and with sufficient certainty by a mere appeal to the judgment of common human understanding, because anything empirical that might slip into our maxims as a determining ground of the will *makes itself known* at once by the feeling of gratification or pain that necessarily attaches to it insofar as it arouses desire, whereas pure practical reason directly *opposes* taking this feeling into its principle as a condition. The dissimilarity of determining grounds (empirical and rational) is made known by this resistance of a practically lawgiving reason to every meddling inclination, by a special kind of *feeling,* which, however, does not precede the lawgiving of practical reason but is instead produced only by it and indeed as a constraint, namely, through the feeling of a respect such 5:92

as no human being has for inclinations of whatever kind but does have for the law; and it is made known so saliently and so prominently that no one, not even the most common human understanding, can fail to see at once, in an example presented to him, that he can indeed be advised by empirical grounds of volition to follow their charms but that he can never be expected to *obey* anything but the pure practical law of reason alone.

The distinction of the *doctrine of happiness* from the *doctrine of morals*, in the first of which empirical principles constitute the whole foundation whereas in the second they do not make even the smallest addition to it, is the first and most important business incumbent upon the Analytic of pure practical reason, in which it must proceed as *precisely* and, so to speak, as *scrupulously* as any geometer in his work. A philosopher, however, has greater difficulties to contend with here (as always in rational cognition through mere concepts without construction of them), because he cannot put any intuition (a pure noumenon) at its basis. He has, however, the advantage that, almost like a chemist, he can at any time set up an experiment with every human practical reason in order to distinguish the moral (pure) determining ground from the empirical, namely, by adding the moral law (as a determining ground) to the empirically affected will (e.g., that of someone who would gladly lie because he can gain something by it). When an analyst adds alkali to a solution of calcareous earth in hydrochloric acid, the acid at once releases[m] the lime and unites with the alkali, and the lime is precipitated. In just the same way, if a man who is otherwise honest (or who just this once puts himself only in

5:93   thought in the place of an honest man) is confronted with the moral law in which he cognizes the worthlessness of a liar, his practical reason (in its judgment of what he ought to do) at once abandons[n] the advantage, unites with what maintains in him respect for his own person (truthfulness), and the advantage, after it has been separated and washed from every particle of reason (which is altogether on the side of duty), is weighed by everyone, so that it can enter into combination with reason in other cases, only not where it could be opposed to the moral law, which reason never abandons but unites with most intimately.

But this *distinction* of the principle of happiness from that of morality is not, for this reason, at once an *opposition* between them, and pure practical reason does not require[o] that one should *renounce* claims to happiness but only that as soon as duty is in question one should *take no account* of them. It can even in certain respects be a duty to attend to one's happiness, partly because happiness (to which belong skill, health, wealth) contains means for the fulfillment of one's duty and partly because lack of it (e.g.,

[m] *verläßt*
[n] *verläßt*
[o] *will nicht*

poverty) contains temptations to transgress one's duty. However, it can never be a direct duty to promote one's happiness, still less can it be a principle of all duty. Now, because all determining grounds of the will except the one and only pure practical law of reason (the moral law) are without exception empirical and so, as such, belong to the principle of happiness, they must without exception be separated from the supreme moral principle and never be incorporated with it as a condition, since this would destroy all moral worth just as any empirical admixture to geometrical principles would destroy all mathematical evidence, which (in Plato's judgment) is the most excellent thing in mathematics, surpassing even its utility.

But instead of the deduction of the supreme principle of pure practical reason – that is, the explanation of the possibility of such a cognition a priori – nothing more could be adduced than that, if one had insight into the possibility of freedom of an efficient cause, one would also have insight into not merely the possibility but even the necessity of the moral law as the supreme practical law of rational beings, to whom one attributes freedom of the causality of their will; for, the two concepts are so inseparably connected that one could even define practical freedom through independence of the will from anything other than the moral law alone. But no insight can be had into the possibility of the freedom of an efficient cause, especially in the sensible world: we are fortunate if only we can be sufficiently assured that there is no proof of its impossibility, and are now forced to assume it and are thereby justified in doing so by the moral law, which postulates it. For, there are many who believe that they can nevertheless explain this freedom in accordance with empirical principles, like any other natural ability, and regard it as a *psychological* property, the explanation of which simply requires a more exact investigation of the *nature of the soul* and of the incentives of the will, and not as a *transcendental* predicate of the causality of a being that belongs to the sensible world (although this is all that is really at issue here); and they thus deprive us of the grand disclosure brought to us through practical reason by means of the moral law, the disclosure, namely of an intelligible world through realization of the otherwise transcendent concept of freedom, and with this deprive us of the moral law itself, which admits absolutely no empirical determining ground. It will therefore be necessary to add something here as a protection against this delusion, and to show *empiricism* in all its bare superficiality.

5:94

The concept of causality as *natural necessity*, as distinguished from the concept of causality as *freedom*, concerns only the existence of things insofar as it is *determinable in time* and hence as appearances, as opposed to their causality as things in themselves. Now, if one takes the determinations of the existence of things in time for determinations of things in themselves (which is the most usual way of representing them), then the necessity in the causal relation can in no way be united with freedom;

instead they are opposed to each other as contradictory. For, from the first it follows that every event, and consequently every action that takes place at a point of time, is necessary under the condition of what was in the preceding time. Now, since time past is no longer within my control, every action that I perform must be necessary by determining grounds *that are not within my control,* that is, I am never free at the point of time in which I act. Indeed, even if I assume that my whole existence is independent from any alien cause (such as God), so that the determining grounds of my causality and even of my whole existence are not outside me, this would not in the least transform that natural necessity into freedom. For, at every point of time I still stand under the necessity of being determined to action by *that which is not within my control,* and the series of events infinite a parte priori which I can only continue in accordance with a predetermined order would never begin of itself: it would be a continuous natural chain, and therefore my causality would never be freedom.

If, then, one wants to attribute freedom to a being whose existence is determined in time, one cannot, so far at least, except this being from the law of natural necessity as to all events in its existence and consequently as to its actions as well; for, that would be tantamount to handing it over to blind chance. But since this law unavoidably concerns all causality of things so far as *their existence in time* is determinable, if this were the way in which one had to represent also the *existence of these things in themselves* then freedom would have to be rejected as a null and impossible concept. Consequently, if one still wants to save it, no other path remains than to ascribe the existence of a thing so far as it is determinable in time, and so too its causality in accordance with the law of *natural necessity, only to appearance, and to ascribe freedom to the same being as a thing in itself.* This is certainly unavoidable if one wants to maintain both these mutually repellent concepts together; but in application, when one wants to explain them as united in one and the same action, and so to explain this union itself, great difficulties come forward, which seem to make such a unification unfeasible.[p]

If I say of a human being who commits a theft that this deed is, in accordance with the natural law of causality, a necessary result of determining grounds in preceding time, then it was impossible that it could have been left undone; how, then, can appraisal in accordance with the moral law make any change in it and suppose that it could have been omitted because the law says that it ought to have been omitted? That is, how can that man be called quite free at the same point of time and in regard to the same action in which and in regard to which he is nevertheless subject to an unavoidable natural necessity? It is a wretched subterfuge to seek to evade this by saying that the *kind* of determining grounds of his causality in accordance with

5:95

5:96

[p] *untunlich*

natural law agrees with a *comparative* concept of freedom (according to which that is sometimes called a free effect, the determining natural ground of which lies *within* the acting being, e.g., that which a projectile accomplishes when it is in free motion, in which case one uses the word "freedom" because while it is in flight it is not impelled from without; or as we also call the motion of a clock a free motion because it moves the hands itself, which therefore do not need to be pushed externally; in the same way the actions of the human being, although they are necessary by their determining grounds which preceded them in time, are yet called free because the actions are caused from within, by representations produced by our own powers, whereby desires are evoked on occasion of circumstances and hence actions are produced at our own discretion). Some still let themselves be put off by this subterfuge and so think they have solved, with a little quibbling about words, that difficult problem on the solution of which millennia have worked in vain and which can therefore hardly be found so completely on the surface. That is to say, in the question about that freedom which must be put at the basis of all moral laws and the imputation appropriate to them, it does not matter whether the causality determined in accordance with a natural law is necessary through determining grounds lying *within* the subject or *outside* him, or in the first case whether these determining grounds are instinctive or thought by reason; if, as is admitted by these men themselves, these determining representations have the ground of their existence in time and indeed in the *antecedent state,* and this in turn in a preceding state, and so forth, so that these determinations may be internal and they may have psychological instead of mechanical causality, that is, produce actions by means of representations and not by bodily movements: they are always *determining grounds* of the causality of a being insofar as its existence is determinable in time and therefore under the necessitating conditions of past time, which are thus, when the subject is to act, *no longer within his control* and which may therefore bring with them psychological freedom (if one wants to use this term for a merely internal chain of representations in the soul) but nevertheless natural necessity; and they therefore leave no *transcendental freedom,* which must be thought as independence from everything empirical and so from nature generally, whether it is regarded as an object of inner sense in time only or also of outer sense in both space and time; without this freedom (in the latter and proper sense), which alone is practical a priori, no moral law is possible and no imputation in accordance with it. Just for this reason, all necessity of events in time in accordance with the natural law of causality can be called the *mechanism* of nature, although it is not meant by this that the things which are subject to it must be really material *machines.* Here one looks only to the necessity of the connection of events in a time series as it develops in accordance with natural law, whether the subject in which this development takes place is called *automaton materiale,* when the machinery is driven by matter, or

5:97

81

with Leibniz *spirituale,* when it is driven by representations; and if the freedom of our will were none other than the latter (say, psychological and comparative but not also transcendental, i.e., absolute), then it would at bottom be nothing better than the freedom of a turnspit, which, when once it is wound up, also accomplishes its movements of itself.

Now, in order, in the case at hand, to remove the apparent contradiction between the mechanism of nature and freedom in one and the same action, one must recall what was said in the *Critique of Pure Reason* or follows from it: that the natural necessity which cannot coexist with the freedom of the subject attaches merely to the determinations of a thing which stands under conditions of time and so only to the determinations of the acting subject as appearance, and that, accordingly, the determining grounds of every action of the subject so far lie in what belongs to past time and *is no longer within his control* (in which must be counted his past deeds and the character as a phenomenon thereby determinable for him in his own eyes). But the very same subject, being on the other side conscious of himself as a thing in itself, also views his existence *insofar as it does not stand under conditions of time* and himself as determinable only through laws that he gives himself by reason; and in this existence of his nothing is, for him, antecedent to the determination of his will, but every action – and in general every determination of his existence changing conformably with inner sense, even the whole sequence of his existence as a sensible being – is to be regarded in the consciousness of his intelligible existence as nothing but the consequence and never as the determining ground of his causality as a *noumenon.* So considered, a rational being can now rightly say of every unlawful action he performed that he could have omitted it even though as appearance it is sufficiently determined in the past and, so far, is inevitably necessary; for this action, with all the past which determines it, belongs to a single phenomenon of his character, which he gives to himself and in accordance with which he imputes to himself, as a cause independent of all sensibility, the causality of those appearances.

5:98

The judicial sentences of that wonderful capacity in us which we call conscience are in perfect agreement with this. A human being may use what art he will to paint some unlawful conduct he remembers as an unintentional fault,*q* – as a mere oversight which one can never avoid altogether, and so as something in which he was carried away by the stream of natural necessity – and to declare himself innocent of it; he nevertheless finds that the advocate who speaks in his favor can by no means reduce to silence the prosecutor within him, if only he is aware that at the time he did this wrong he was in his senses, that is, had the use of his freedom; and while he *explains* his misconduct by certain bad habits,

q Versehen

which by gradual neglect of attention he has allowed to grow in him to such a degree that he can regard his misconduct as their natural consequence, yet this cannot protect him from the reproach and censure he casts upon himself. This is also the ground of repentance for a deed long past at every recollection of it, a painful feeling aroused by the moral disposition, which is empty in a practical way to the extent that it cannot serve to undo what has been done and would even be absurd (and Priestley,[10] a genuine *fatalist* proceeding consistently, declares it absurd; and for this candor he deserves more applause than those who, while maintaining the mechanism of the will in deeds' but its freedom in words, yet want it to be thought that they include it in their syncretistic system, though without making the possibility of such imputation comprehensible); but repentance, as pain, is still quite legitimate because reason, when it is a question of the law of our intelligible existence (the moral law), recognizes no distinction of time and asks only whether the event belongs to me as a deed and, if it does, then always connects the same feeling with it morally, whether it was done just now or long ago. For, the *sensible life* has, with respect to the *intelligible* consciousness of its existence (consciousness of freedom), the absolute unity of a phenomenon, which, so far as it contains merely appearances of the disposition that the moral law is concerned with (appearances of the character), must be appraised not in accordance with the natural necessity that belongs to it as appearance but in accordance with the absolute spontaneity of freedom. One can therefore grant that if it were possible for us to have such deep insight into a human being's cast of mind, as shown by inner as well as outer actions, that we would know every incentive to action, even the smallest, as well as all the external occasions affecting them, we could calculate a human being's conduct for the future with as much certainty as a lunar or solar eclipse and could nevertheless maintain that the human being's conduct is free. If, that is to say, we were capable of another view, namely an intellectual intuition of the same subject (which is certainly not given to us and in place of which we have only the rational concept), then we would become aware that this whole chain of appearances, with respect to all that the moral law is concerned with, depends upon the spontaneity of the subject as a thing in itself, for the determination of which no physical explanation can be given. In default of this intuition, the moral law assures us of this difference between the relation of our actions as appearances to the sensible being of our subject and relation by which this sensible being is itself referred to the intelligible substratum in us. From this perspective, which is natural to our reason though inexplicable, appraisals can be justified which, though made in all conscientiousness, yet seem at first glance quite contrary to all equity. There are cases in which human beings, even with

5:99

' *in der Tat.* For a definition of "deed" see *The Metaphysics of Morals* (6:224).

the same education that was profitable to others, yet show from childhood such early wickedness[s] and progress in it so continuously into their adulthood that they are taken to be born villains and quite incapable of improvement as far as their cast of mind is concerned; and nevertheless they are so judged for what they do or leave undone that they are censured as guilty of their crimes; indeed, they themselves (the children) find these censures as well founded as if, despite the hopeless natural constitution of mind[t] ascribed to them, they remained as accountable as any other human being. This could not happen if we did not suppose that whatever arises from one's choice (as every action intentionally performed undoubtedly does) has as its basis a free causality, which from early youth expresses its character in its appearances (actions); these actions, on account of the uniformity of conduct, make knowable a natural connection that does not, however, make the vicious[u] constitution of the will necessary but is instead the consequence of the evil and unchangeable principles freely[v] adopted, which make it only more culpable and deserving of punishment.

5:100

But a difficulty still awaits freedom insofar as it is to be united with the mechanism of nature in a being that belongs to the sensible world, a difficulty which, even after all the foregoing has been agreed to, still threatens freedom with complete destruction. In this danger there is at the same time, however, a circumstance that offers hope of an outcome still favorable to maintaining freedom, namely that the same difficulty presses much more strongly (in fact, as we shall presently see, presses only) upon the system in which existence determinable in time and space is held to be the existence of things in themselves; hence it does not force us to give up our main supposition of the ideality of time as a mere form of sensible intuition and so as merely a way of representing things that is proper to the subject as belonging to the sensible world; and thus the difficulty only requires us to unite this supposition with the idea of freedom.

That is to say: if it is granted us that the intelligible subject can still be free with respect to a given action, although as a subject also belonging to the sensible world, he is mechanically conditioned with respect to the same action, it nevertheless seems that, as soon as one admits that *God* as universal original being *is the cause also of the existence of substance* (a proposition that can never be given up without also giving up the concept of God as the being of all beings and with it his all-sufficiency, on which everything in theology depends), one must admit that a human being's actions have their determining ground in *something altogether beyond his control*, namely in the causality of a supreme being which is distinct from him and

5:101

---

[s] *Bosheit*
[t] *Naturbeschaffenheit ihres Gemüts*
[u] *arge*
[v] *freiwillig*

upon which his own existence and the entire determination of his causality absolutely depend. In fact, if a human being's actions insofar as they belong to his determinations in time were not merely determinations of him as appearance but as a thing in itself, freedom could not be saved. A human being would be a marionette or an automaton, like Vaucanson's,[11] built and wound up by the supreme artist; self-consciousness would indeed make him a thinking automaton, but the consciousness of his own spontaneity, if taken for freedom, would be mere delusion inasmuch as it deserves to be called freedom only comparatively, because the proximate determining causes of its motion and a long series of their determining causes are indeed internal but the last and highest is found entirely in an alien hand. Therefore I do not see how those who insist on regarding time and space as determinations belonging to the existence of things in themselves would avoid fatalism of actions; or if (like the otherwise acute Mendelssohn)[12] they flatly allow both to be conditions necessarily belonging only to the existence of finite and derived beings but not to that of the infinite original being, I do not see how they would justify themselves in making such a distinction, whence they get a warrant to do so, or even how they would avoid the contradiction they encounter when they regard existence in time as a determination attaching necessarily to finite things in themselves, while God is the cause of this existence but cannot be the cause of time (or space) itself (because this must be presupposed as a necessary a priori condition of the existence of things); and consequently his causality with respect to the existence of these things must be conditioned and even temporally conditioned; and this would unavoidably have to bring in all that is contradictory to the concept of his infinity and independence. On the other hand, it is quite easy for us to distinguish between the determination of the divine existence as independent of all temporal conditions and that of a being of the sensible world, the distinction being that between *the existence of a being in itself* and that of a *thing in appearance*. Hence, if this ideality of time and space is not adopted, nothing remains but Spinozism, in which space and time are essential determinations of the original being itself, while the things dependent upon it (ourselves, therefore, included) are not substances but merely accidents inhering in it; for, if these things exist merely as its effects *in time*, which would be the condition of their existence itself, then the actions of these beings would have to be merely its actions that it performs in any place and at any time. Thus Spinozism, despite the absurdity of its fundamental idea, argues more consistently than the creation theory can when beings assumed to be substances and *in themselves existing in time* are regarded as effects of a supreme cause and yet as not belonging to him and his action but as substances in themselves.

The difficulty mentioned above is resolved briefly and clearly as follows. If existence *in time* is only a sensible way of representing things which

5:102

85

belongs to thinking beings in the world and consequently does not apply to them as things in themselves, then the creation of these beings is a creation of things in themselves, since the concept of a creation does not belong to the sensible way of representing existence or causality but can only be referred to noumena. Consequently, if I say of beings in the sensible world that they are created, I so far regard them as noumena. Just as it would thus be a contradiction to say that God is a creator of appearances, so it is also a contradiction to say that as creator he is the cause of actions in the sensible world and thus of actions as appearances, even though he is the cause of the existence of the acting beings (as noumena). If it is now possible to affirm freedom without compromising the natural mechanism of actions as appearances (by taking existence in time to be something that holds only of appearances, not of things in themselves), then it cannot make the slightest difference that the acting beings are creatures, since creation has to do with their intelligible but not their sensible existence and therefore cannot be regarded as the determining ground of appearances; but it would turn out quite differently if the beings in the world as things in themselves existed *in time,* since the creator of substance would also be the author of the entire mechanism in this substance.

5:103   Of such great importance is the separation of time (as well as space) from the existence of things in themselves that was accomplished in the *Critique* of pure speculative reason.

It will be said that the solution to the difficulty given here involves even greater difficulty and is hardly susceptible of a lucid presentation. But is any other solution that has been attempted, or that may be attempted, easier and more apprehensible? One might rather say that the dogmatic teachers of metaphysics have shown more shrewdness than sincerity in keeping this difficult point out of sight as much as possible, in the hope that if they said nothing about it no one would be likely to think of it. If a science is to be advanced, all difficulties must be *exposed* and we must even *search* for those, however well hidden, that lie in its way; for, every difficulty calls forth a remedy that cannot be found without science gaining either in extent or in determinateness, so that even obstacles become means for promoting the thoroughness of science. On the contrary, if the difficulties are purposely concealed or removed merely through palliatives, then sooner or later they break out in incurable troubles that bring science to ruin in a complete skepticism.

. .
.

Since it is really the concept of freedom that, among all the ideas of pure speculative reason, alone provides such a great extension in the field of the supersensible, though only with respect to practical cognition, I ask myself *why it exclusively has such great fruitfulness* whereas the others indeed indicate the vacant place for possible beings of the pure understanding but cannot determine the concept of them by anything. I soon see that, since I can think nothing without a category, a category must first be sought in reason's idea of freedom with which I am now concerned, which is here the category of *causality;* and I see that, even though no corresponding intuition can be put under the *rational concept* of freedom, which is a transcendent concept, nevertheless a sensible intuition must first be given for the *concept of the understanding* (of causality) – for the synthesis of which the *rational concept of freedom* requires the unconditioned – by which   5:104 it is first assured objective reality. Now, all the categories are divided into two classes: the *mathematical,* which are directed merely to the unity of synthesis in the representation of objects, and the *dynamical,* which are directed to the unity of synthesis in the representation of the existence of objects. The former (those of quantity and quality) always contain a synthesis of the *homogeneous,* in which the unconditioned can never be found for the conditioned in space and time given in sensible intuition since it itself belongs in turn to space and time and must thus in turn always be conditioned; hence in the Dialectic of pure theoretical reason the two opposed ways of finding the unconditioned and the totality of the conditions for it were both false. The categories of the second class (those of the causality and of the necessity of a thing) did not at all require this homogeneity (of the conditioned and the condition in the synthesis) since what was to be represented here was not how the intuition is formed from a manifold within it but only how the existence of the conditioned object corresponding to it was to be added to the existence of the condition (added in the understanding, as connected with it), and there it was permitted to place in the intelligible world the unconditioned for the altogether conditioned in the sensible world (with regard to the causality as well as to the contingent existence of things themselves), although this unconditioned otherwise remained indeterminate, and permitted to make the synthesis transcendent; hence it was also found in the Dialectic of pure speculative reason that the two seemingly opposed ways of finding the unconditioned for the conditioned – in the synthesis of causality, for example, to think for the conditioned in the series of causes and effects of the sensible world a causality that is not further sensibly conditioned – did not in fact contradict each other, and that the same action which, as belonging to the sensible world, is always sensibly conditioned – that is, mechanically necessary – can at the same time, as belonging to the causality of an acting being so far as it belongs to the intelligible world, have as its basis a sensibly unconditioned causality and so be thought as free. Then, the only point at issue was whether this *can* be changed into *is,* that is, whether one could show in an actual case, as it were by a fact, that certain actions presuppose such a causality (intellectual, sensibly unconditioned causality), whether such actions are actual or only commanded, that is, objectively practically necessary. We could not hope to meet with

5:105   this connection in actions actually given in experience as events of the sensible world, since causality through freedom must always be sought outside the sensible world in the intelligible world. But other things, things outside the sensible world, are not given to perception and observation. Hence nothing remained but that there might be found an incontestable and indeed an objective principle of causality that excludes all sensible conditions from its determination, that is, a principle in which reason does not call upon something *else* as the determining ground with respect to its causality but already itself contains this determining ground by that principle, and in which it is therefore as *pure reason* itself practical. Now, this principle does not need to be searched for or devised; it has long been present in the reason of all human beings and incorporated in their being, and is the principle of *morality*. Therefore, that unconditioned causality and the capacity for it, freedom, and with it a being (I myself) that belongs to the sensible world but at the same time to the intelligible world, is not merely *thought* indeterminately and problematically (speculative reason could already find this feasible) but is even *determined with respect to the law* of its causality and *cognized* assertorically; and thus the reality of the intelligible world is given to us, and indeed as *determined* from a practical perspective, and this determination, which for theoretical purposes would be *transcendent* (extravagant), is for practical purposes *immanent*. We could not, however, take a similar step with respect to the second dynamical idea, namely that of a *necessary being*. We could not rise to it from the sensible world without the mediation of the first dynamical idea. For, if we wanted to attempt it we would have had to venture the leap of leaving all that is given to us and bounding into that of which nothing is given to us by which we could mediate the connection of such an intelligible being with the sensible world (because the necessary being is to be cognized as given *outside us*); on the other hand this is quite possible, as is now clear, with respect to *our own* subject inasmuch as we cognize ourselves *on the one side* as intelligible beings determined by the moral law (by virtue of freedom), and *on the other side* as active in the sensible world in accordance with this determination. The concept of freedom alone allows us to find the unconditioned and intelligible for the conditioned and sensible without going outside ourselves. For, it is our reason itself which by means of

5:106   the supreme and unconditional practical law cognizes itself and the being that is conscious of this law (our own person) as belonging to the pure world of understanding and even determines the way in which, as such, it can be active. In this way it can be understood why in the entire faculty of reason *only the practical* can provide us with the means for going beyond the sensible world and provide cognitions of a supersensible order and connection, which, however, just because of this can be extended only so far as is directly necessary for pure practical purposes.

On this occasion permit me to call attention to one thing, namely, that every step one takes with pure reason, even in the practical field where one does not take subtle speculation into consideration, nevertheless fits with all the moments*ⁿ* of the *Critique* of theoretical reason as closely, and indeed of itself, as if each step had been thought out with deliberate foresight merely to provide this confirmation. Such a precise agreement – in no way sought but offering itself (as anyone can convince himself if he will only carry moral considerations up to their principles) – of the most important propositions of practical reason with the remarks of the *Critique* of speculative reason, which often seemed overly subtle and unnecessary, occasions surprise and astonishment, and strengthens the maxim already cognized and praised by others: in every scientific investigation to pursue one's way with all possible exactness and candor, to pay no heed to offense that might be given outside its field but, as far as one can, to carry it through truly and completely by itself. Frequent observation has convinced me that when such an undertaking has been carried through to its end, that which, halfway through it, seemed to me at times very dubious in view of other, extraneous doctrines was at the end found to harmonize perfectly, in an unexpected way, with what had been discovered independently, without the least regard for those doctrines and without any partiality or prejudice for them, provided I left this dubiousness out of sight for a while and attended only to the business at hand until I had brought it to completion. Writers would save themselves many errors and much labor lost (because spent on a delusion) if they could only resolve to go to work with somewhat more candor.

ⁿ Momente

Book II
Dialectic of pure practical reason

Chapter I
On a dialectic of pure practical reason in general

Pure reason always has its dialectic, whether it is considered in its speculative or in its practical use; for it requires the absolute totality of conditions
for a given conditioned, and this can be found only in things in themselves.
Since, however, all concepts of things must be referred to intuitions which,
for us human beings cannot be other than sensible and hence do not let
objects be cognized as things in themselves but only as appearances, in
whose series of the conditioned and conditions the unconditioned can
never be found, an unavoidable illusion^x arises from the application of this
rational idea of the totality of conditions (and so of the unconditioned) to
appearances as if they were things in themselves (for, in the absence of a
warning critique they are always held to be such), an illusion which, however, would never be noticed as deceptive if it were not revealed by a *conflict*
of reason with itself in the application to appearance of its basic principle of
presupposing the unconditioned for everything conditioned. By this, however, reason is forced to investigate this illusion – whence it arises and how
it can be removed – and this can be done only through a complete critical
examination of the whole pure faculty of reason; thus the antinomy of pure
reason, which becomes evident in its dialectic, is in fact the most beneficial
error into which human reason could ever have fallen, inasmuch as it finally
drives us to search for the key to escape from this labyrinth; and when this
key is found, it further discovers what we did not seek and yet need, namely
a view into a higher, immutable order of things in which we already are and
in which we can henceforth be directed, by determinate precepts, to carry
on our existence in accordance with the highest vocation of reason.

    How that natural dialectic in the speculative use of pure reason is to be
resolved and how the error arising from an otherwise natural illusion is to
be avoided can be found in detail in the *Critique* of that faculty. But reason
in its practical use is no better off. As pure practical reason it likewise
seeks the unconditioned for the practically conditioned (which rests on
inclinations and natural needs), not indeed as the determining ground of
the will, but even when this is given (in the moral law), it seeks the

---

^{x} *Schein*

unconditioned totality of the object of pure practical reason, under the name of the *highest good.*

To determine this idea practically – that is, sufficiently for the maxims of our rational conduct – is the *doctrine of wisdom,* and this in turn, as a *science, is philosophy* in the sense in which the word was understood by the ancients, for whom it was a direction to the concept in which the highest good was to be placed and to the conduct by which it was to be acquired. We would do well to leave this word in its ancient sense, as a *doctrine of the highest good* so far as reason strives to bring it to *science.* For, on the one hand, the restrictive condition attached would suit the Greek expression (which signifies love of *wisdom*) while yet sufficing to embrace under the name of philosophy love of *science* and so of all speculative rational cognition insofar as it is serviceable to reason for that concept as well as for the practical determining ground, without letting us lose sight of the chief end on account of which alone it can be called doctrine of wisdom. On the other hand, it would do no harm to discourage the self-conceit of someone who ventures to claim the title of philosopher if one holds before him, in the very definition, a standard for self-estimation that would very much lower his pretension. For, to be a *teacher of wisdom* would mean something more than to be a student who has not yet come so far as to guide himself, and still less to guide others, with assured expectation of so high an end; it would mean to be a *master in the knowledge of wisdom,* which says more than a modest man would himself claim; and philosophy, as well as wisdom, would itself always remain an ideal, which objectively is represented completely only in reason alone, whereas subjectively, for a person, it is only the goal of his unceasing endeavors; and no one would be justified in professing to be in possession of it, so as to assume the name of philosopher, unless he could also show its infallible effect in his own person as an example (in mastery of himself and the unquestioned interest that he preeminently takes in the general good), which the ancients also required for deserving that honorable title.   5:109

We have only one further preliminary remark[y] to make with respect to the dialectic of pure practical reason in determining the concept *of the highest good* (a successful resolution of which would lead us to expect, as with the dialectic of theoretical reason, the most beneficial result, inasmuch as the self-contradictions of pure practical reason, honestly stated and not concealed), force us to undertake a complete critical examination of its own capacity.

The moral law is the sole determining ground of the pure will. But since this is merely formal (that is to say, it requires only that the form of a maxim be universally lawgiving), it abstracts as determining ground from all matter and so from every object of volition. Hence, though the highest

---

[y] Or "reminder," *Erinnerung*

good may be the whole *object* of a pure practical reason, that is, of a pure will, it is not on that account to be taken as its *determining ground,* and the moral law alone must be viewed as the ground for making the highest good and its realization or promotion the object. This reminder is important in so delicate a case as the determination of moral principles, where even the slightest misinterpretation corrupts dispositions. For, it will have been seen from the Analytic that if one assumes any object under the name of a good as a determining ground of the will prior to the moral law and then derives from it the supreme practical principle, this would always produce heteronomy and supplant the moral principle.

5:110   It is, however, evident that if the moral law is already included as supreme condition in the concept of the highest good, the highest good is then not merely *object:* the concept of it and the representation of its existence as possible by our practical reason are at the same time the *determining ground* of the pure will because in that case the moral law, already included and thought in this concept, and no other object, in fact determines the will in accordance with the principle of autonomy. This order of concepts of the determination of the will must not be lost sight of, since otherwise we misunderstand ourselves and believe that we are contradicting ourselves even where everything stands together in the most perfect harmony.

Chapter II
On the dialectic of pure reason in determining the concept of the highest good

The concept of the *highest* already contains an ambiguity² that, if not attended to, can occasion needless disputes. The highest can mean either the supreme *(supremum)* or the complete *(consummatum)*. The first is that condition which is itself unconditioned, that is, not subordinate to any other *(originarium);* the second is that whole which is not part of a still greater whole of the same kind *(perfectissimum).* That *virtue* (as worthiness to be happy) is the *supreme condition* of whatever can even seem to us desirable and hence of all our pursuit of happiness and that it is therefore the *supreme* good has been proved in the Analytic. But it is not yet, on that account, the whole and complete good as the object of the faculty of desire of rational finite beings; for this, *happiness* is also required, and that not merely in the partial eyes of a person who makes himself an end but even in the judgment of an impartial reason, which regards a person in the world generally as an end in itself. For, to need happiness, to be also

---

² *Zweideutigkeit*

worthy of it, and yet not to participate in it cannot be consistent with the perfect volition of a rational being that would at the same time have all power, even if we think of such a being only for the sake of the experiment. Now, inasmuch as virtue and happiness together constitute possession of the highest good in a person, and happiness distributed in exact proportion to morality (as the worth of a person and his worthiness to be happy) constitutes the *highest good* of a possible world, the latter means the whole, the complete good, in which, however, virtue as the condition is always the supreme good, since it has no further condition above it, whereas happiness is something that, though always pleasant to the possessor of it, is not of itself absolutely and in all respects good but always presupposes morally lawful conduct as its condition. 5:111

Two determinations *necessarily* combined in one concept must be connected as ground and consequent, and so connected that this *unity* is considered either as *analytic* (logical connection) or as synthetic (real *connection*), the former in accordance with the law of identity, the latter in accordance with the law of causality. The connection of virtue with happiness can therefore be understood in one of two ways: either the endeavor to be virtuous and the rational pursuit of happiness are not two different actions but quite identical, in which case no maxim need be made the ground of the former other than that which serves for the latter; or else that connection is found in virtue's producing happiness as something different from the consciousness of virtue, as a cause produces an effect.

Of the ancient Greek schools there were, strictly speaking, only two, which in determining the concept of the highest good followed one and the same method insofar as they did not let virtue and happiness hold as two different elements of the highest good and consequently sought the unity of the principle in accordance with the rule of identity; but they differed, in turn, in their choice of which of the two was to be the fundamental concept. The Epicurean said: to be conscious of one's maxim leading to happiness is virtue; the Stoic said: to be conscious of one's virtue is happiness. For the first, *prudence* was equivalent to morality; for the second, who chose a higher designation for virtue, *morality* alone was true wisdom.

One must regret that the acuteness of these men (whom one must, nevertheless, admire for having in such early times already tried all conceivable paths of philosophic conquest) was unfortunately applied in searching out identity between extremely heterogeneous concepts, that of happiness and that of virtue. But it was in keeping with the dialectical spirit of their times, which sometimes misleads subtle minds even now, to suppress essential and irreconcilable differences in principle by trying to change them into disputes about words and so to devise a specious unity of concept under merely different names; and this usually occurs in cases where the unification of heterogeneous grounds lies so deep or so high, or 5:112

would require so complete a transformation of the doctrines assumed in the rest of the philosophic system, that they are afraid to penetrate deeply into the real difference and prefer to treat it as a diversity merely in formulae.

While both schools tried to search out the sameness of the practical principles of virtue and happiness, they were not agreed as to how they would force this identity but separated infinitely from each other inasmuch as one put its principle on the aesthetic side*a* and the other on the logical side, the former in consciousness of sensible need, the other in the independence of practical reason from all sensible determining grounds. According to the Epicurean the concept of virtue was already present in the maxim of promoting one's own happiness; according to the Stoic, on the other hand, the feeling of happiness was already contained in consciousness of one's virtue. What is contained in another concept, however, is indeed identical with a part of the concept containing it but not identical with the whole, and two wholes can, moreover, be specifically different from each other although they consist of the same material,*b* if, namely, the two parts are combined into a whole in quite different ways. The Stoic maintained that virtue is the *whole highest good,* and happiness only the consciousness of this possession as belonging to the state of the subject. The Epicurean maintained that happiness is the *whole highest good,* and virtue only the form of the maxim for seeking to obtain it, namely, the rational use of means to it.

Now, it is clear from the Analytic that the maxims of virtue and those of one's own happiness are quite heterogeneous with respect to their supreme practical principle; and, even though they belong to one highest good, so as to make it possible, yet they are so far from coinciding that they greatly restrict and infringe upon each other in the same subject. Thus the question, *how is the highest good practically possible?* still remains an unsolved problem despite all the *attempts at coalition* that have hitherto been made. The Analytic has, however, shown what it is that makes the problem difficult to solve, namely that happiness and morality are two specifically quite *different elements* of the highest good and that, accordingly, their combination cannot be cognized *analytically* (as if someone who seeks his own happiness should find, by mere resolution*c* of his concepts, that in so acting he is virtuous, or as if someone who follows virtue should in the consciousness of such conduct find that he is already happy *ipso facto*); it must instead be a *synthesis* of concepts. But because this combination is cognized as a priori – thus as practically necessary and not as derived from experience –

5:113

---

a *ästhetischen . . . Seite,* i.e., on the side of feeling. See *The Metaphysics of Morals* (6:399–403,471).
b *Stoffe*
c *Auflösung*

and because the possibility of the highest good therefore does not rest on any empirical principles, it follows that the *deduction* of this concept must be *transcendental.* It is a priori (morally) necessary *to produce the highest good through the freedom of the will:* the condition of its possibility must therefore rest solely on a priori grounds of cognition.

I.
THE ANTINOMY OF PRACTICAL REASON

In the highest good which is practical for us, that is, to be made real through our will, virtue and happiness are thought as necessarily combined, so that the one cannot be assumed by pure practical reason without the other also belonging to it. Now, this combination is (like every other) either *analytic* or *synthetic.* Since, as has already been shown, the given combination cannot be analytic, it must be thought synthetically and, indeed, as the connection of cause and effect, because it concerns a practical good, that is, one that is possible through action. Consequently, either the desire for happiness must be the motive to maxims of virtue or the maxim of virtue must be the efficient cause of happiness. The first is *absolutely* impossible because (as was proved in the Analytic) maxims that put the determining ground of the will in the desire for one's happiness are not moral at all and can be the ground of no virtue. But the second is *also impossible* because any practical connection of causes and effects in the world, as a result of the determination of the will, does not depend upon the moral dispositions of the will but upon knowledge of the laws of nature and the physical ability to use them for one's purposes; consequently, no necessary connection of happiness with virtue in the world, adequate to the highest good, can be expected from the most meticulous observance of moral laws. Now, since the promotion of   5:114 the highest good, which contains this connection in its concept, is an a priori necessary object of our will and inseparably bound up with the moral law, the impossibility of the first must also prove the falsity of the second. If, therefore, the highest good is impossible in accordance with practical rules, then the moral law, which commands us to promote it, must be fantastic and directed to empty imaginary ends and must therefore in itself be false.

II.
CRITICAL RESOLUTION *d* OF THE ANTINOMY
OF PRACTICAL REASON

In the antinomy of pure speculative reason there is a similar conflict between natural necessity and freedom in the causality of events in the world. It was resolved by showing that there is no true conflict if the

---

d *Aufhebung*

events and even the world in which they occur are regarded (and they should also be so regarded) merely as appearances; for, one and the same acting being as *appearance* (even to his own inner sense) has a causality in the world of sense that always conforms to the mechanism of nature, but with respect to the same event, insofar as the acting person regards himself at the same time as *noumenon* (as pure intelligence, in his existence that cannot be temporally determined), he can contain a determining ground of that causality in accordance with laws of nature which is itself free from all laws of nature.

It is just the same with the foregoing antinomy of pure practical reason. The first of the two propositions, that the endeavor after happiness produces a ground for a virtuous disposition, is *absolutely false;* but the second, that a virtuous disposition necessarily produces happiness, is false *not absolutely* but only insofar as this disposition is regarded as the form of causality in the sensible world, and consequently false only if I assume existence in the sensible world to be the only kind of existence of a rational being; it is thus only *conditionally false.* But since I am not only warranted in thinking of my existence also as a noumenon in a world of

5:115 the understanding but even have in the moral law a purely intellectual determining ground of my causality (in the sensible world), it is not impossible that morality of disposition should have a connection, and indeed a necessary connection,*ᵉ* as cause with happiness as effect in the sensible world, if not immediately yet mediately (by means of an intelligible author of nature), a connection which, in a nature that is merely an object of the senses, can never occur except contingently and cannot suffice for the highest good.

Thus, despite this seeming conflict of a practical reason with itself, the highest good is the necessary highest end of a morally determined will and is a true object of that will; for it is practically possible, and the maxims of such a will, which refer to it as regards their matter, have objective reality, which at first was threatened by that antinomy in the combination of morality with happiness in accordance with a universal law, but only from a misinterpretation, because the relation between appearances was held to be a relation of things in themselves to those appearances.

When we find ourselves compelled to go so far, namely to the connection with an intelligible world, to seek the possibility of the highest good which reason points out to all rational beings as the goal of all their moral wishes, it must seem strange that philosophers both of ancient and modern times could nevertheless have found happiness in precise proportion to virtue already in *this life* (in the sensible world), or persuaded themselves that they were conscious of it. For, Epicurus as well as the Stoics extolled above all the happiness that arises from consciousness of living

ᵉ einen . . . Zusammenhang . . . habe

96

virtuously; and the former was not so base in his practical precepts as one might infer from the principles of his theory, which he used for explanation and not for action, or as they were interpreted by many who were misled by his use of the expression "pleasure"[f] for "contentment";[g] on the contrary, he reckoned the most disinterested practice of the good among the ways of enjoying the most intimate delight[h] and included in his scheme of pleasure[i] (by which he meant a constantly cheerful heart)[j] such moderation and control of the inclinations as the strictest moral philosopher might require; his chief divergence from the Stoics consisted only in his placing the motive in this pleasure, which they quite rightly refused to do. For, on the one hand, the virtuous Epicurus – like many morally well-disposed men of this day who nevertheless do not reflect deeply enough on their principles – fell into the error of presupposing the virtuous *disposition* in the persons for whom he wanted first of all to provide the incentive to virtue (and in fact an upright man cannot be happy if he is not first conscious of his uprightness; for, with such a disposition, the censure that his own cast of mind would force him to bring against himself in case of a transgression, and his moral self-condemnation would deprive him of all enjoyment of the agreeableness that his state might otherwise contain). But the question is, how is such a disposition and cast of mind in estimating the worth of one's existence possible in the first place, since prior to this no feeling at all for moral worth as such would be found in the subject? If a human being is virtuous he will certainly not enjoy life unless he is conscious of his uprightness in every action, however fortune may favor him in the physical state of life; but in order to make him virtuous in the first place, and so before he esteems the moral worth of his existence so highly, can one commend to him the peace of mind that would arise from consciousness of an uprightness for which he as yet has no sense?

5:116

But on the other hand, there is always present here the ground of an error of subreption *(vitium subreptionis)* and, as it were, of an optical illusion in the self-consciousness of what one *does* as distinguished from what one *feels* – an illusion that even the most practiced cannot altogether avoid. The moral disposition is necessarily connected with consciousness of the determination of the will *directly by the law.* Now, consciousness of a determination of the faculty of desire is always the ground of a satisfaction[k] in the action produced by it; but this pleasure, this satisfaction with oneself, is not the determining ground of the action: instead, the determi-

---

[f] *Wollust*

[g] *Zufriedenheit.* See *Groundwork of the Metaphysics of Morals* (4:393 note v) and *The Metaphysics of Morals* (6:375).

[h] *mit zu den Genußarten der innigste Freude*

[i] *Vergnügens*

[j] Compare *The Metaphysics of Morals* (6:485)

[k] *Wohlgefallens*

nation of the will directly by reason alone is the ground of the feeling of pleasure, and this remains a pure practical, not aesthetic, determination of the faculty of desire. Now, since this determination has exactly the same inward effect, that of an impulse to activity, as a feeling of the agreeableness expected from the desired action would have produced, we easily

5:117 look upon what we ourselves do as something that we merely passively feel and take the moral incentive for a sensible impulse, just as always happens in so-called illusion of the senses (in this case, inner sense). It is something very sublime in human nature to be determined to actions directly by a pure rational law, and even the illusion that takes the subjective side of this intellectual determinability of the will as something aesthetic and the effect of a special sensible feeling (for an intellectual feeling would be a contradiction) is sublime. It is also of great importance to take notice of this property of our personality and to cultivate as much as possible the effect of reason on this feeling. But one must also be on guard against demeaning and deforming the real and genuine incentive, the law itself – as it were, by means of a false foil – by such spurious praise of the moral determining ground as incentive as would base it on feelings of particular joys (which are nevertheless only results). Respect, and not the gratification or enjoyment of happiness, is thus something for which there can be no feeling *antecedent* to reason and underlying it (for this would always be aesthetic and pathological): respect as consciousness of direct necessitation of the will by the law is hardly an analogue of the feeling of pleasure, although in relation to the faculty of desire it does the same thing but from different sources; only by this way of representing things, however, can one attain what one seeks, namely that actions be done not merely in conformity with duty (as a result of pleasant feelings) but from duty, which must be the true end of all moral cultivation.

Have we not, however, a word that does not denote enjoyment, as the word happiness does, but that nevertheless indicates a satisfaction with one's existence, an analogue of happiness that must necessarily accompany consciousness of virtue? Yes! This word is *contentment with oneself,*[1] which in its strict meaning always designates only a negative satisfaction with one's existence, in which one is conscious of needing nothing. Freedom, and the consciousness of freedom as an ability to follow the moral law with an unyielding disposition, is *independence from the inclinations,* at least as motives determining (even if not as *affecting*) our desire, and so far as I am conscious of this freedom in following my moral maxims, it is the sole source of an unchangeable contentment, necessarily combined with it

5:118 and resting on no special feeling, and this can be called intellectual contentment. Aesthetic contentment (improperly so called), which rests on satisfaction of the inclinations, however refined they may be made out to

[1] *Selbstzufriedenheit*

be, can never be adequate to what is thought about contentment. For the inclinations change, grow with the indulgence one allows them, and always leave behind a still greater void than one had thought to fill. Hence they are always *burdensome* to a rational being, and though he cannot lay them aside, they wrest from him the wish to be rid of them. Even an inclination to what conforms with duty (e.g., to beneficence) can indeed greatly facilitate the effectiveness of *moral* maxims but cannot produce any. For in these everything must be directed to the representation of the law as determining ground if the action is to contain not merely *legality* but also *morality*. Inclination is blind and servile, whether it is kindly or not; and when morality is in question, reason must not play the part of mere guardian to inclination but, disregarding it altogether, must attend solely to its own interest as pure practical reason. Even this feeling of compassion and tender sympathy,*ᵐ* if it precedes consideration of what is duty and becomes the determining ground, is itself burdensome to right-thinking persons, brings their considered maxims into confusion, and produces the wish to be freed from them and subject to lawgiving reason alone.

From this we can understand how consciousness of this ability of a pure practical reason (virtue)*ⁿ* can in fact produce consciousness of mastery over one's inclinations, hence of independence from them and so too from the discontent that always accompanies them, and thus can produce a negative satisfaction with one's state, that is, *contentment*, which in its source is contentment with one's person. Freedom itself becomes in this way (namely indirectly) capable of an enjoyment, which cannot be called happiness because it does not depend upon the positive concurrence of a feeling; nor is it, strictly speaking, *beatitude*, since it does not include complete independence from inclinations and needs; but it nevertheless resembles the latter, at least insofar as one's determination of one's will can be held free from their influence and so, at least in its origin, it is analogous to the self-sufficiency that can be ascribed only to the supreme being.

From this resolution of the antinomy of practical pure reason it follows   5:119
that in practical principles a natural and necessary connection between the consciousness of morality and the expectation of a happiness proportionate to it as its result can at least be thought as possible (though certainly not, on this account, cognized and understood);*ᵒ* that, on the other hand, principles of the pursuit of happiness cannot possibly produce morality;

ᵐ *der Mitleids und der weichherzigen Teilnehmung.* See *The Metaphysics of Morals* (6:456–7).
ⁿ *wie das Bewußtsein dieses Vermögens . . . durch Tat (die Tugend);* perhaps "how consciousness of this ability of a pure practical reason through a deed (virtue)." According to *The Metaphysics of Morals* (6:394), virtue is a *Vermögen.* Although it would be inaccurate to call virtue a deed (see 6:224), this sentence allows that construal. Compare AK 5:3 note b, and 5:98, note b.
ᵒ *einsehen*

that, accordingly, the *supreme* good (as the first condition of the highest good) is morality, whereas happiness constitutes its second element but in such a way that it is only the morally conditioned yet necessary result of the former. Only with this subordination is the *highest good* the whole object of pure practical reason, which must necessarily represent it as possible since it commands us to contribute everything possible to its production. But since the possibility of such a connection of the conditioned with its condition belongs wholly to the supersensible relation of things and cannot be given in accordance with the laws of the sensible world, although the practical results of this idea – namely actions that aim at realizing the highest good – belong to the sensible world, we shall try to set forth the grounds of that possibility, first with respect to what is *immediately* within our power and then, secondly, in that which is not in our power but which reason presents to us, as the supplement to our inability, for the possibility of the highest good (which is necessary in accordance with practical principles).

III.
ON THE PRIMACY OF PURE PRACTICAL REASON IN ITS CONNECTION WITH SPECULATIVE REASON

By primacy among two or more things connected by reason I understand the prerogative of one to be the first determining ground of the connection with all the rest. In a narrower practical sense it signifies the prerogative of the interest of one insofar as the interest of the others is subordinated to it (and it cannot be inferior to any other). To every faculty of the mind one can attribute an *interest*, that is, a principle that contains the condition under which alone its exercise is promoted. Reason, as the

5:120   faculty of principles, determines the interest of all the powers of the mind but itself determines its own. The interest of its speculative use consists in the *cognition* of the object up to the highest a priori principles; that of its practical use consists in the determination of the *will* with respect to the final and complete end. That which is required for the possibility of any use of reason as such, namely, that its principles and affirmations must not contradict one another, constitutes no part of its interest but is instead the condition of having reason at all; only its extension, not mere consistency with itself, is reckoned as its interest.

If practical reason may not assume and think as given anything further than what *speculative* reason of itself could offer it from its insight, the latter has primacy. Supposing, however, that practical reason has of itself original a priori principles with which certain theoretical positions are inseparably connected, while these are withdrawn from any possible insight of speculative reason (although they must not contradict it): then the question is, which interest is supreme (not, which must give way, for one does not necessarily conflict with the other)? Whether speculative reason, which knows nothing about all that which practical reason offers for its acceptance, must accept these propositions and, although they are transcendent for it, try to unite them, as a foreign possession handed over to it, with its own concepts, or whether it is justified in obstinately following its own separate interest and, in accordance with the canon of Epicurus, rejecting as empty subtle reasoning everything that cannot accredit its objective reality by manifest examples to be shown in experience, however much it might be interwoven with the interest of the practical (pure) use of reason and in itself not contradict the theoretical, merely because it actually infringes upon the interest of speculative reason to the extent that it removes the bounds which the latter has set itself and hands it over to every nonsense or delusion of imagination?

In fact, to the extent that practical reason is taken as dependent upon pathological conditions, that is, as merely regulating the inclinations by the sensible principle of happiness, this demand could not be made on speculative reason. Mohammed's paradise or the fusion with the Deity of the theosophists and mystics would obtrude their monstrosities on reason according to the taste[p] of each, and one might as well have no reason at all as surrender it in such a way to all sorts of dreams. But if pure reason of itself can be and really is practical, as the consciousness of the moral law proves it to be, it is still only one and the same reason which, whether from a theoretical or a practical perspective, judges according to a priori principles; and then it is clear that, even if from the first perspective its capacity does not extend to establishing certain propositions affirmatively, although they do not contradict it, *as soon as these same propositions belong inseparably to the practical interest* of pure reason it must accept them – indeed as something offered to it from another source, which has not grown on its own land but yet is sufficiently authenticated – and try to compare and connect them with everything that it has within its power as speculative reason, being mindful, however, that these are not its insights but are yet extensions of its use from another, namely a practical perspective; and this is not in the least opposed to its interest, which consists in the restriction of speculative mischief.

5:121

Thus, in the union of pure speculative with pure practical reason in one cognition,[q] the latter has primacy, assuming that this union is not *contingent* and discretionary but based a priori on reason itself and therefore *necessary*. For, without this subordination a conflict of reason with itself would arise, since if they were merely juxtaposed (coordinate), the first would of itself close its boundaries strictly and admit nothing from

[p] *Sinn*
[q] *Verbindung . . . zu einem Erkenntnisse*

101

the latter into its domain, while the latter would extend its boundaries over everything and, when its need required, would try to include the former within them. But one cannot require pure practical reason to be subordinate to speculative reason and so reverse the order, since all interest is ultimately practical and even that of speculative reason is only conditional and is complete in practical use alone.

IV.
THE IMMORTALITY OF THE SOUL AS A POSTULATE OF PURE PRACTICAL REASON

The production of the highest good in the world is the necessary object of a will determinable by the moral law. But in such a will the *complete conformity*[r] of dispositions with the moral law is the supreme condition of the highest good. This conformity must therefore be just as possible as its object is, since it is contained in the same command to promote the object. Complete conformity of the will with the moral law is, however, *holiness*, a perfection of which no rational being of the sensible world is capable at any moment[s] of his existence. Since it is nevertheless required as practically necessary, it can only be found in an *endless progress*[t] toward that complete conformity, and in accordance with principles of pure practical reason it is necessary to assume such a practical progress as the real object of our will.

This endless progress is, however, possible only on the presupposition of the *existence* and personality of the same rational being continuing *endlessly* (which is called the immortality of the soul). Hence the highest good is practically possible only on the presupposition of the immortality of the soul, so that this, as inseparably connected with the moral law, is a **postulate** of pure practical reason (by which I understand a *theoretical* proposition, though one not demonstrable as such, insofar as it is attached inseparably to an a priori unconditionally valid *practical* law).

The proposition about the moral vocation of our nature, that only in an endless progress can we attain complete conformity with the moral law, is of the greatest usefulness, not merely in regard to the present supplement to the incapacity of speculative reason but also with respect to religion. In default of it, one either quite degrades the moral law from its *holiness* by making it out to be *lenient* (indulgent) and thus conformed to our convenience, or else strains ones's calling as well as ones's expectation to an unattainable vocation, namely to a hoped-for full acquisition of holiness of

---

[r] or "fitness," *Angemessenheit*
[s] *Zeitpunkte*
[t] Or "a progress to infinity," *ins Unendliche gehend*

will, and so gets lost in enthusiastic *theosophical* dreams that quite contra-   5:123
dict self-knowledge;" in both cases, constant *effort* to observe precisely and
fully a strict and inflexible command of reason, which is yet not ideal but
true, is only hindered. For a rational but finite being only endless progress
from lower to higher stages of moral perfection is possible. *The eternal
being,*" to whom the temporal condition is nothing, sees in what is to us an
endless series the whole of conformity with the moral law, and the holiness that his command inflexibly requires in order to be commensurable
with his justice in the share he determines for each in the highest good is
to be found whole in a single intellectual intuition of the existence of
rational beings. All that a creature can have with respect to hope for this
share is consciousness of his tried disposition, so that, from the progress
he has already made from the worse to the morally better and from the
immutable resolution he has thereby come to know, he may hope for a
further uninterrupted continuance of this progress, however long his existence may last, even beyond this life;* and thus he cannot hope, either
here or in any foreseeable future moment of his existence, to be fully
adequate to God's will (without indulgence or dispensation, which do not
harmonize with justice); he can hope to be so only in the endlessness of   5:124
his duration (which God alone can survey).

V.

THE EXISTENCE OF GOD AS A POSTULATE
OF PURE PRACTICAL REASON

In the preceding analysis the moral law led to a practical task that is set by
pure reason alone and without the aid of any sensible incentives, namely
that of the necessary completeness of the first and principal part of the

---

*Conviction of the immutability of one's disposition in progress toward the good seems,
nevertheless, to be in itself impossible for a creature. Because of this the Christian religious
doctrine has it come only from the same spirit that works sanctification, i.e., this firm
resolution and with it consciousness of steadfastness in moral progress. But even in a natural
way, someone who is aware of having persisted through a long portion of his life up to its end
in progress to the better, and this from genuine moral motives, may very well have the
comforting hope, though not certitude, that even in an existence continuing beyond this life
he will persevere in these principles; and although he is never justified here in his own eyes,
and can never hope to be justified even given the future increase of natural perfection to
which he looks forward – but with it of his duties as well – nevertheless in this progress
which, though it has to do with a goal endlessly postponed, yet holds for God as possession,
he can have a prospect of a future of *beatitude;* for this is the expression that reason employs
to designate complete *well-being* independent of all contingent causes in the world, which,
like *holiness,* is an idea that can be contained only in an endless progress and its totality, and
hence is never fully attained by a creature.

" *Selbsterkenntniss*
" Or "The Infinite Being," *Der Unendliche*

highest good, **morality**; and, since this can be fully accomplished only in an eternity, it led to the postulate of *immortality*. The same law must also lead to the possibility of the second element of the highest good, namely **happiness** proportioned to that morality, and must do so as disinterestedly as before, solely from impartial reason; in other words, it must lead to the supposition of the existence of a cause adequate to this effect, that is, it must postulate the *existence of God* as belonging necessarily to the possibility of the highest good (which object of our will is necessarily connected with the moral lawgiving of pure reason). We shall present this connection in a convincing manner.

Happiness is the state of a rational being in the world in the whole of whose existence *everything goes according to his wish and will*, and rests, therefore, on the harmony of nature with his whole end as well as with the essential determining ground of his will. Now, the moral law as a law of freedom commands through determining grounds that are to be quite independent of nature and of its harmony with our faculty of desire (as incentives); the acting rational being in the world is, however, not also the cause of the world and of nature itself. Consequently, there is not the least ground in the moral law for a necessary connection*ᵂ* between the morality and the proportionate happiness of a being belonging to the world as part of it and hence dependent upon it, who for that reason cannot by his will be a cause of this nature and, as far as his happiness is concerned, cannot by his own powers make it harmonize thoroughly with his practical princi- 5:125 ples. Nevertheless, in the practical task of pure reason, that is, in the necessary pursuit of the highest good, such a connection is postulated as necessary: we *ought* to strive to promote the highest good (which must therefore be possible). Accordingly, the existence of a cause of all nature, distinct from nature, which contains the ground of this connection, namely of the exact correspondence of happiness with morality, is also *postulated.* However, this supreme cause is to contain the ground of the correspondence of nature not merely with a law of the will of rational beings but with the representation of this *law*, so far as they make it the *supreme determining ground of the will*, and consequently not merely with morals in their form but also with their morality as their determining ground, that is, with their moral disposition. Therefore, the highest good in the world is possible only insofar as a supreme cause of nature having a causality in keeping with the moral disposition is assumed. Now, a being capable of actions in accordance with the representation of laws is *an intelligence* (a rational being), and the causality of such a being in accordance with this representation of laws is his *will*. Therefore the supreme cause of nature, insofar as it must be presupposed for the highest good, is a being that is the cause of nature by *understanding* and *will* (hence its

ᵂ *Zusammenhang*

author), that is, **God**. Consequently, the postulate of the possibility of the *highest derived good* (the best world) is likewise the postulate of the reality of a *highest original good,* namely of the existence of God. Now, it was a duty for us to promote the highest good; hence there is in us not merely the warrant but also the necessity, as a need connected with duty, to presuppose the possibility of this highest good, which, since it is possible only under the condition of the existence of God, connects the presupposition of the existence of God inseparably with duty; that is, it is morally necessary to assume the existence of God.

It is well to note here that this moral necessity *is subjective,* that is, a need, and not *objective,* that is, itself a duty; for, there can be no duty to assume the existence of anything (since this concerns only the theoretical use of reason). Moreover, it is not to be understood by this that it is necessary to assume the existence of God *as a ground of all obligation in general* (for this rests, as has been sufficiently shown, solely on the auton-   5:126 omy of reason itself). What belongs to duty here is only the striving to produce and promote the highest good in the world, the possibility of which can therefore be postulated, while our reason finds this thinkable only on the presupposition of a supreme intelligence; to assume the existence of this supreme intelligence is thus connected with the consciousness of our duty, although this assumption itself belongs to theoretical reason; with respect to theoretical reason alone, as a ground of explanation, it can be called a *hypothesis;* but in relation to the intelligibility of an object given us by the moral law (the highest good), and consequently of a need for practical purposes, it can be called *belief*[x] and, indeed, a pure *rational belief* since pure reason alone (in its theoretical as well as in its practical use) is the source from which it springs.

From this *deduction* it now becomes comprehensible why the *Greek* schools could never solve their problem of the practical possibility of the highest good: it was because they made the rule of the use which the human will makes of its freedom the sole and sufficient ground of this possibility, without, as it seemed to them, needing the existence of God for it. They were indeed correct in establishing the principle of morals by itself, independently of this postulate and solely from the relation of reason to the will, so that they made it the *supreme* practical condition of the highest good; but this principle was not on this account the *whole* condition of its possibility. The Epicureans had indeed assumed an altogether false principle of morals as supreme, namely that of happiness, and had substituted for a law a maxim of each choosing as he pleased according to his inclination;[y] they proceeded, however, *consistently* enough in this by demeaning their highest good in the same way, namely in proportion to

---

[x] Or "faith," *Glaube*
[y] *der beliebigen Wahl nach jedes seiner Neigung*

the meanness of their principle, and expecting no greater happiness than can be acquired by human prudence (including temperance and moderation of the inclinations), which,^{z} as we know, has to be paltry enough and turn out very differently according to circumstances, not to mention the exceptions which their maxims had to constantly admit and which made them unfit for laws. The Stoics, on the contrary, had chosen their supreme practical principle quite correctly, namely virtue, as the condition of the highest good; but inasmuch as they represented the degree of virtue 5:127   required by its pure law as fully attainable in this life, they not only strained the moral capacity of the *human being*, under the name of a *sage*, far beyond all the limits of his nature and assumed something that contradicts all cognition of the human being, but also and above all they would not let the second *component* of the highest good, namely happiness, hold as a special object of the human faculty of desire but made their *sage*, like a divinity in his consciousness of the excellence of his person, quite independent of nature (with respect to his own contentment), exposing him indeed to the ills of life but not subjecting him to them (at the same time representing him as also free from evil); and thus they really left out the second element of the highest good, namely one's own happiness, placing it solely in acting and in contentment with one's personal worth and so including it in consciousness of one's moral cast of mind – though in this they could have been sufficiently refuted by the voice of their own nature.

The doctrine of Christianity,* even if it is not regarded as a religious

---

*It is commonly held that the Christian precept of morals has no advantage with respect to its purity over the moral concepts of the Stoics; but the difference between them is nonetheless very obvious. The Stoic system made consciousness of strength of soul the pivot on which all moral dispositions were to turn; and although its disciples spoke of duties and even determined them quite well, yet they put the incentive and proper determining ground of the will in an elevation of one's cast of mind above the lower incentives of the senses, which have power only through weakness of soul. With them therefore, virtue was a certain heroism of the *sage*, who, raising himself above the animal nature of the human being, is sufficient to himself, and through the discourses on duties to others is himself raised above them and is not subject to any temptation to transgress the moral law. All this, however, they could not have done if they had represented this law in all its purity and strictness, as the precept of the Gospel does. If I understand by an *idea* a perfection to which nothing adequate can be given in experience, the moral ideas are not, on that account, something transcendent, that is, something of which we cannot even determine the concept sufficiently or of which it is uncertain whether there is any object corresponding to it at all, as is the case with the ideas of speculative reason; instead, the moral ideas, as archetypes of practical perfection, serve as the indispensable rule of moral conduct and also as the *standard of comparison*. Now, if I consider *Christian morals* on their philosophic side, then, compared with the ideas of the Greek schools they would appear as follows: the ideas of the *Cynics*, the *Epicureans*, the *Stoics*, and the *Christians* are *natural simplicity, prudence, wisdom*, and *holiness*. With respect to the path for attaining them, what distinguished the Greek schools from one another was that the Cynics found *common human understanding* sufficient, the others the path of *science* alone; but
^{z} It is not clear whether *die* refers to "happiness" or to "prudence."

doctrine, gives on this point a concept of the highest good (of the kingdom   5:128
of God) which alone satisfies the strictest demand of practical reason. The
moral law is holy (inflexible) and demands holiness of morals, although all
the moral perfection that a human being can attain is still only virtue, that is,
a disposition conformed with law *from respect* for law, and thus consciousness of a continuing propensity to transgression or at least impurity, that is,
an admixture of many spurious (not moral) motives to observe the law,
hence a self-esteem combined with humility; and so, with respect to the
holiness that the Christian law demands, nothing remains for a creature but
endless progress, though for that very reason he is justified in hoping for his
endless duration. The *worth* of a disposition *completely* conformed with the
moral law is infinite, since all possible happiness in the judgment of a wise
and all-powerful distributor of it has no restriction other than rational
beings' lack of conformity with their duty. But the moral law of itself still
does not *promise* any happiness, since this is not necessarily connected with
observance of the law according to our concepts of a natural order as such.
The Christian doctrine of morals now supplements this lack (of the second
indispensable component of the highest good) by representing the world in
which rational beings devote themselves with their whole soul to the moral
law as a *kingdom of God*, in which nature and morals come into a harmony,
foreign to each of them of itself, through a holy author who makes the
derived highest good possible. *Holiness* of morals is prescribed to them as a   5:129
rule even in this life, while the well-being proportioned to it, namely *beati-*
tude, is represented as attainable only in an eternity; for, the *former* must
always be the archetype of their conduct in every state, and progress toward
it is already possible and necessary in this life, whereas the *latter,* under the
name of happiness, cannot be attained at all in this world (so far as our own
capacity is concerned) and is therefore made solely an object of hope.
Nevertheless, the Christian principle of *morals* itself is not theological (and
so heteronomy); it is instead autonomy of pure practical reason by itself,
since it does not make cognition of God and his will the basis of these laws
but only of the attainment of the highest good subject to the condition of
observing these laws, and since it places even the proper *incentive* to observing them not in the results wished for but in the representation of duty
alone, faithful observance of which alone constitutes worthiness to acquire
the latter.

In this way the moral law leads through the concept of the highest good,

---

both found the mere *use of natural powers* sufficient for it. Christian morals, because it frames
its precept so purely and inflexibly (as must be done), deprives the human being of confidence that he can be fully adequate to it, at least in this life, but again sets it up by enabling
us to hope that if we act as well as is within our *power*, then what is not within our power will
come to our aid from another source, whether or not we know in what way. Aristotle and
Plato differed only with respect to the *origin* of our moral concepts.

as the object and final end of pure practical reason, *to religion, that is, to the recognition*[a] *of all duties as divine commands, not as sanctions – that is, chosen and in themselves contingent ordinances of another's will* – but as essential *laws* of every free will in itself, which must nevertheless be regarded as commands of the supreme being because only from a will that is morally perfect (holy and beneficent[b]) and at the same time all-powerful, and so through harmony with this will, can we hope to attain the highest good, which the moral law makes it our duty to take as the object of our endeavors. Here again, then, everything remains disinterested and grounded only on duty, and there is no need to base it on incentives of fear and hope, which if they became principles would destroy the whole moral worth of actions. The moral law commands me to make the highest possible good in a world the final object of all my conduct. But I cannot hope to produce this except by the harmony of my will with that of a holy and beneficent author of the world; and although in the concept of the highest good, as that of a whole in which the greatest happiness is represented as connected in the most exact

5:130   proportion with the greatest degree of moral perfection (possible in creatures), *my own happiness* is included, this is nevertheless not the determining ground of the will that is directed to promote the highest good; it is instead the moral law (which, on the contrary, limits by strict conditions my unbounded craving for happiness).

For this reason, again, morals[c] is not properly the doctrine of how we are to *make* ourselves happy but of how we are to become *worthy* of happiness. Only if religion is added to it does there also enter the hope of some day participating in happiness to the degree that we have been intent upon not being unworthy of it.

Someone is *worthy* of possessing a thing or a state when it harmonizes with the highest good that he is in possession of it. It can now be readily seen that all worthiness depends upon moral conduct, since in the concept of the highest good this constitutes the condition of the rest (which belongs to one's state), namely, of one's share of happiness. Now, from this it follows that *morals* in itself must never be treated as a *doctrine of happiness*, that is, as instruction in how to become happy; for morals has to do solely with the rational condition *(conditio sine qua non)* of happiness and not with the means of acquiring it. But when morals (which merely imposes duties and does not provide rules for selfish wishes) has been set forth completely, then – after the moral wish, based on a law, to promote the highest good (to bring the kingdom of God to us) has been awakened, which could not previously have arisen in any selfish soul, and for the sake of this wish the step to religion has been taken – then for the first time can this

[a] *Erkenntnis*
[b] *gütigen*
[c] Or "moral philosophy," *die Moral*

ethical doctrine also be called a doctrine of happiness, because it is only with religion that the *hope* of happiness first arises.

From this it can also be seen that if one asks about *God's final end* in creating the world, one must not name the *happiness* of the rational beings in it but *the highest good*, which adds a condition to that wish of such beings, namely the condition of being worthy of happiness, that is, the *morality* of these same rational beings, which condition alone contains the standard in accordance with which they can hope to participate in the former at the hands of a *wise* author. For, since *wisdom* considered theoretically signifies *cognition of the highest good*, and practically *the fitness of the will for the highest good*, one cannot attribute to a highest independent wisdom an end that would be based merely on beneficence.[d] For one cannot conceive the effect of this beneficence (with respect to the happiness of rational beings) as befitting the highest original good except under the limiting conditions of harmony with the *holiness* of his will.* Hence those who put the end of creation in the glory[e] of God (provided this is not thought anthropomorphically, as inclination to be praised) perhaps hit upon the best expression. For, nothing glorifies God more than what is most estimable in the world, respect for his command, observance of the holy[f] duty that his law lays upon us, when there is added to this his magnificent plan of crowning such a beautiful order with corresponding happiness. If the latter (to speak humanly) makes him worthy of love, by the former he is an object of worship (adoration). Human beings themselves can acquire love by beneficence, but by it alone they can never acquire respect, so that the greatest beneficence procures them honor[g] only when it is exercised in accordance with worthiness.

It now follows of itself that in the order of ends the human being (and with him every rational being) is an *end in itself*, that is, can never be used merely as a means by anyone (not even by God) without being at the same time himself an end, and that humanity in our person must, accordingly,

5:131

---

*In passing, and to make what is proper to these concepts distinguishable, I add only this remark. Although one ascribes to God various attributes the quality of which is found appropriate to creatures as well except that in him they are raised to the highest degree, e.g., power, knowledge, presence, goodness, and so forth, calling them omnipotence, omniscience, omnipresence, all-goodness, and so forth, there are still three that are ascribed to God exclusively and yet without the addition of greatness, and all of them are moral: he is the *only holy*, the *only blessed*, the *only wise*, because these concepts already imply the absence of limitation. According to the order of these attributes he is also the *holy lawgiver* (and creator), the *beneficent governor* (and preserver), and the *just judge* – three attributes which include everything by which God is the object of religion and in conformity with which the metaphysical perfections are added of themselves in reason.

[d] *Gütigkeit*

[e] *Ehre*

[f] Or "sacred," *heiligen*

[g] *ihnen . . . Ehre macht*, perhaps "does them honor"

5:132 be *holy*[h] to ourselves: for he is the *subject of the moral law* and so of that which is holy in itself, on account of which and in agreement with which alone can anything be called holy. For, this moral law is based on the autonomy of his will, as a free will which, in accordance with its universal laws, must necessarily be able at the same time *to agree* to that to which it is to *subject* itself.

VI.
ON THE POSTULATES OF PURE PRACTICAL REASON IN GENERAL

All of them proceed from the principle of morality, which is not a postulate but a law by which reason determines the will immediately; and this will, just because it is so determined as a pure will, requires these necessary conditions for observance of its precept. These postulates are not theoretical dogmas but *presuppositions* having a necessarily practical reference[i] and thus, although they do not indeed extend speculative cognition, they give objective reality to the ideas of speculative reason in *general* (by means of their reference to what is practical) and justify its holding concepts even the possibility of which it could not otherwise presume to affirm.

These postulates are those of *immortality,* of *freedom* considered positively (as the causality of a being insofar as it belongs to the intelligible world), and of the *existence of God.* The *first* flows from the practically necessary condition of a duration befitting the complete fulfillment of the moral law; the *second* from the necessary presupposition of independence from the sensible world and of the capacity to determine one's will by the law of an intelligible world, that is, the law of freedom; the *third* from the necessity of the condition for such an intelligible world to be the highest good, through the presupposition of the highest independent good, that is, of the existence of God.

Aiming at the highest good, made necessary by respect for the moral law, and the presupposition flowing from this of its objective reality lead through the postulates of practical reason to concepts that speculative reason could indeed present as problems but could never solve. Thus it 5:133 leads to 1: the problem in the solution of which speculative reason could do nothing but commit *paralogisms* (namely, the problem of immortality) because it lacked the mark of permanence by which to supplement the psychological concept of an ultimate subject, necessarily ascribed to the soul in self-consciousness, so as to make it the real representation of a substance; this mark practical reason furnishes by the postulate of a duration required for conformity with the moral law in the highest good as the

[h] Or "sacred," *heilig*
[i] *in notwendig praktischer Rucksicht*

whole end of practical reason. 2. It leads to the concept with regard to which speculative reason contained nothing but an *antinomy*, the resolution of which it could base only on a concept that was indeed problematically thinkable but not demonstrable or determinable as to its objective reality, namely the *cosmological* idea of an intelligible world and consciousness of our existence in it; it leads to this by means of the postulate of freedom (the reality of which it lays down through the moral law and with it the law of an intelligible world as well, to which speculative reason could only point but could not determine its concept). 3. As for that which speculative reason had to think but to leave undetermined as mere transcendental *ideal*, the *theological* concept of the original being, it furnishes significance to this (for practical purposes, i.e., as a condition of the possibility of the object of a will determined by that law), as the supreme principle of the highest good in an intelligible world, by means of moral lawgiving accompanied by power*j* in it.

But is our cognition really extended in this way by pure practical reason, and is what was *transcendent* for speculative reason *immanent* in practical reason? Certainly, but only *for practical purposes*. For we thereby cognize neither the nature of our souls, nor the intelligible world, nor the supreme being as to what they are in themselves, but have merely unified the concepts of them in the *practical* concept *of the highest good* as the object of our will, and have done so altogether a priori through pure reason but only by means of the moral law and, moreover, only in reference to it, with respect to the object it commands. But how freedom is even possible and how this kind of causality has to be represented theoretically and positively is not thereby seen; that there is such a causality is only postulated by the moral law and for the sake of it. It is the same with the remaining ideas, the possibility of which no human understanding will ever fathom although no sophistry will ever convince even the most common human being that they are not true concepts. 5:134

VII.

HOW IS IT POSSIBLE TO THINK OF AN
EXTENSION OF PURE REASON FOR PRACTICAL
PURPOSES WITHOUT THEREBY ALSO
EXTENDING ITS COGNITION AS SPECULATIVE?

In order not to be too abstract, we are going to answer this question at once in its application to the present case. In order to extend a pure cognition *practically* there must be a *purpose* given a priori, that is, an end as object (of the will) that, independently of all theoretical principles, is represented as practically necessary by an imperative determining the will

j *durch gewalthabende moralische Gesetzgebung*

immediately (a categorical imperative), and in this case that is the *highest good*. This, however, is not possible without presupposing three theoretical concepts (for which, because they are only pure rational concepts, no corresponding intuition can be found and consequently, by the theoretical path, no objective reality): namely, freedom, immortality, and God. Thus by the practical law that commands the existence of the highest good possible in a world, the possibility of those objects of pure speculative reason, the objective reality which the latter could not assure them, is postulated; by this the theoretical cognition of pure reason certainly receives an increment, but it consists only in this: that those concepts, otherwise problematic (merely thinkable) for it, are now declared[k] assertorically to be concepts to which real objects belong, because practical reason unavoidably requires the existence of them for the possibility of its object, the highest good, which is absolutely necessary practically, and theoretical reason is thereby justified in assuming them. But this extension of theoretical reason is no extension of speculation, that is, no positive use can now be made of it for *theoretical purposes*. For, since nothing further is accomplished in this by practical reason than that those concepts are real and really have their (possible) objects, but nothing is thereby given us by way of intuition of them (which can also not be demanded), no synthetic proposition is possible by this reality granted them. Hence this disclosure does not help us in the least for speculative purposes, although with respect to the practical use of pure reason it does help us to extend this cognition of ours.[l] The above three ideas of speculative reason are in themselves still not cognitions; nevertheless they are (transcendent) *thoughts* in which there is nothing impossible. Now they receive objective reality through an apodictic practical law, as necessary conditions of the possibility of what it commands us *to make an object*, that is, we are instructed by it *that they have objects*, although we are not able to show how their concept refers to an object, and this is not yet cognition *of these objects;* for one cannot thereby judge synthetically about them at all or determine their application theoretically; hence one can make no theoretical rational use[m] of them at all, in which use all speculative cognition of reason properly consists. Nevertheless, theoretical cognition, *not indeed of these objects* but of reason in general, is extended by this insofar as *objects were given* to those ideas by the practical postulates, a merely problematic thought having by this means first received objective reality. There was therefore no extension of the cognition *of given supersensible objects*, but there was nevertheless an extension of theoretical reason and of its cognition with respect to the supersensible in general, inasmuch as theoretical

---

[k] *erklärt werden*
[l] It is not clear from the text whether the phrase *zur Erweiterung dieses unseres Erkenntnisses* should be placed here or after *in speculativer Absicht*.
[m] *keinen theoretischen Gebrauch der Vernunft machen*

reason was forced to grant *that there are such objects*, though it cannot determine them more closely and so cannot itself extend this cognition of the objects (which have now been given to it on practical grounds and, moreover, only for practical use); for this increment, then, pure theoretical reason, for which all those ideas are transcendent and without objects, has to thank its practical capacity only. In this they become *immanent* and *constitutive* inasmuch as they are grounds of the possibility of *making real the necessary object* of pure practical reason (the highest good), whereas apart from this they are *transcendent* and merely *regulative* principles of speculative reason, which do not require it to assume a new object beyond experience but only to bring its use in experience nearer to completeness. But when once reason is in possession of this increment, it will, as speculative reason, go to work with these ideas in a negative way (really, only to secure its practical use), that is, not extending but purifying, so as on one side to ward off *anthropomorphism* as the source of *superstition* or specious 5:136 extension of those concepts by supposed experience, and on the other side *fanaticism*, which promises such an extension by means of supersensible intuition or feelings – all of which are hindrances to the practical use of pure reason, so that the removal of them certainly belongs to an extension of our cognition for practical purposes, without contradicting the admission that for speculative purposes reason has not in the least gained by this.

Every use of reason with respect to an object requires pure concepts of the understanding *(categories)*, without which no object can be thought. These can be applied for the theoretical use of reason, that is, for cognition of that kind, only insofar as intuition (which is always sensible) is also put under them, and therefore merely in order to represent by means of them an object of possible experience. But here *ideas* of reason, which cannot be given in any experience at all, are what I would have to think by means of categories in order to cognize an object. Here, however, our concern with these ideas is not for the sake of theoretical cognition of their objects but only with whether they have objects at all. Pure practical reason provides this reality, and theoretical reason has nothing further to do in this than merely *to think* those objects through categories, and this, as we have elsewhere clearly shown, can be done quite well without needing intuition (whether sensible or supersensible) because the categories have their seat and origin in the pure understanding solely as the faculty of thinking, independently of and prior to any intuition, and they always signify only an object in general, *in whatever way it may be given to us*. Now, insofar as the categories are to be applied to these ideas, it is not possible to give them any object in intuition; but *that an object really exists*, so that a category as a mere form of thought is here not empty but has significance, is sufficiently assured them by an object that practical reason presents beyond doubt in the concept of the highest good, namely the *reality of the concepts* that are required for the possibility of the highest good, without, however, effecting by this increment the least extension of cognition in accordance with theoretical principles.

5:137 If these ideas of God, of an intelligible world (the kingdom of God), and of immortality are determined more closely by predicates drawn from our own nature, this determination cannot be regarded as either a *sensualizing*" of those pure rational ideas (anthropomorphism) or as a transcendent cognition of *supersensible* objects; for these predicates are no others than understanding and will, considered moreover in the relation to each other in which they must be thought in the moral law, and hence only to the extent that a pure practical use is made of them. As for all the rest that is added to these concepts psychologically – that is, insofar as we observe these faculties of ours empirically *in their exercise* (for example, that human understanding is discursive so that its representations are not intuitions but thoughts, that these follow one another in time, that the human will is always dependent for its satisfaction upon the existence of its object, and so forth, which cannot be the case in the supreme being) – this is abstracted from in that case, and then what remains of the concepts by which we think of a pure intelligence*° is nothing more than what is required for the possibility of thinking of a moral law; thus there is indeed a cognition of God but only with practical reference, and if we attempt to extend it to a theoretical cognition we find an understanding that does not think but *intuits*, a will that is directed to objects upon the existence of which its satisfaction does not in the least depend (not to mention the transcendental predicates, as, e.g., a magnitude of existence, i.e., duration, which, however, is not in time, the only possible means we have of representing existence as magnitude). All of these are attributes of which we can form no concept fit for *cognition* of the object, and we learn from this that they can never be used for a *theory* of supersensible beings, so that on this side they are quite unable to ground a speculative cognition and their use is, instead, limited solely to the practice of the moral law.

This last is so obvious, and can be proved so clearly by fact, that one can confidently challenge all supposed *natural theologians*° (a singular name)* to cite (over and above the merely ontological predicates) even

---

*Learning*⁹ is, strictly speaking, only the sum total of the *historical* sciences. Consequently only the teacher of revealed theology can be called a theologian. If, however, one wants to call someone who is in possession of the rational sciences (mathematics and philosophy) *learned*, even though this could conflict with the meaning of the word (which always counts as learning only that which must be *taught*' and which, therefore, one cannot of oneself discover by reason), the philosopher, with his cognition of God as a positive science, would cut too poor a figure to let himself be called on that account a *learned* man.

" *Versinnlichung*
° *Verstandeswesen*
ᵖ *Gottesgelehrten*
⁹ *Gelehrsamkeit*
ʳ *gelehrt*

one property, say of the understanding or the will, determining this object   5:138
of theirs, of which it could not be shown incontestably that if everything
anthropomorphic is separated from it nothing would remain to us but the
mere word, without our being able to combine with it the least concept by
which we could hope for an extension of theoretical cognition. But with
respect to the practical there still remains to us, of the properties of
understanding and will, the concept of a relation to which the practical law
(which precisely determines a priori this relation of the understanding to
the will) furnishes objective reality. Once this is done, reality is given to
the concept of the object of a morally determined will (that of the highest
good) and with it to the conditions of its possibility, the ideas of God,
freedom, and immortality, but always only with reference to the practice of
the moral law (not for any speculative purpose).

After these reminders*ᵉ it is now easy to find the answer to the important question: *whether the concept of God is a concept belonging to physics* (and
therefore also to the metaphysics, which only contains the pure a priori
principles of the former in their universal meaning) *or to morals*. If, in
order to *explain* the arrangements of nature or their changes, one has
recourse to God as the author of all things, this is at least no physical
explanation and is a complete confession that one has come to an end of
one's philosophy; for, one is forced to assume something of which in itself
one otherwise has no concept, in order to be able to frame a concept of the
possibility of what one sees before one's eyes. But it is impossible through
metaphysics to proceed *by sure inferences* from knowledge of this world to
the concept of God and to the proof of his existence, for this reason: that
in order to say that this world was possible only through a *God* (as we must
think this concept) we would have to cognize this world as the most
perfect whole possible and, in order to do so, cognize all possible worlds
as well (so as to be able to compare them with this one), and would   5:139
therefore have to be omniscient. Finally,*ᶠ however, it is absolutely impossible to cognize the existence of this being from mere concepts, because
every existential proposition – that is, every proposition that says, of a
being of which I frame a concept, that it exists – is a synthetic proposition,
that is, one by which I go beyond that concept and say more about it than
was thought in the concept, namely, that to this concept *in the understanding* there corresponds an object *outside the understanding*, which it is absolutely impossible to elicit by any inference. Thus there remains for reason
only one single procedure by which to arrive at this cognition, namely, as
pure reason to start from the supreme principle of its pure practical use
(inasmuch as this is always directed simply to the *existence* of something as
a result of reason) and determine its object. And then, in its unavoidable

*ᵉ Or "According to these remarks," *Nach diesen Erinnerungen*
*ᶠ *Vollends*, perhaps "to cognize completely"

115

problem, namely that of the necessary direction of the will to the highest good, there is shown not only the necessity of assuming such an original being in relation to the possibility of this good in the world but – what is most remarkable – something that was quite lacking in the progress of reason on the path of nature, *a precisely determined concept of this original being.* Since we can know only a small part of this world and can still less compare it with all possible worlds, we can well infer from its order, purposiveness, and magnitude a *wise, beneficent, powerful,* and so forth author of it, but not his *omniscience, all-beneficence, omnipotence,* and so forth. It may even very well be granted that one is authorized" to supplement this unavoidable defect by a permitted, quite reasonable hypothesis, namely, that when wisdom, beneficence and so forth are displayed in all the parts that offer themselves to our closer cognition, it is just the same in all the rest, and that it would therefore be reasonable to ascribe all possible perfection to the author of the world; but these are not *inferences* in which we can pride ourselves on our insight, but only liberties^v which can be overlooked but still need further recommendation before we can make use of them. Thus the concept of God always remains, on the path of empirical inquiry (physics), a concept of the perfection of the first being not determined precisely enough to be held adequate to the concept of a deity (but with metaphysics in its transcendental part nothing at all is to be accomplished.)

5:140   When I now try to bring this concept into relation with the object of practical reason, I find that the moral principle admits it as possible only on the presupposition of an author of the world possessed of the *highest perfection.* He must be *omniscient* in order to cognize my conduct even to my inmost disposition in all possible cases and throughout the future, *omnipotent* in order to bestow results appropriate to it, and so too *omnipresent, eternal,* and so forth. Thus the moral law, by means of the concept of the highest good as the object of a pure practical reason, determines the concept of the original being as the *supreme being,* something that the physical (and, pursued higher, the metaphysical) and so the whole speculative course of reason could not effect. The concept of God, then, is one belonging originally not to physics, that is, to speculative reason, but to morals, and the same can be said of the other concepts of reason which we treated above as postulates of reason in its practical use.

If in the history of Greek philosophy we find no clear traces of a pure rational theology earlier than Anaxagoras, the reason is not that the older philosophers had not enough understanding or insight to raise themselves to it by the path of speculation, at least with the aid of a quite reasonable

" *befugt*
^v *Befugnisse*

116

hypothesis; what could have been easier, what more natural, than the thought that occurs of itself to everyone, to assume a single rational cause of the world having *all perfection* in place of indeterminate degrees of perfection of several causes? But the ills in the world seemed to them to be much too important objections to consider themselves justified in such a hypothesis. Thus they showed understanding and insight precisely in not permitting themselves this hypothesis and instead looked about among natural causes to see if they could not find among them the character*ᵂ* and capacity required for original beings. But once this acute people had advanced so far in their investigations as to treat philosophically even moral objects, about which other peoples had never done more than prate, they then first found a new need, namely a practical one, which did not fail to give them the determined concept of the original being; and in this speculative reason had the role of a spectator, or at best had the merit of embellishing a concept that had not grown on its own land and of furthering, by a train of confirmations from the study of nature which now came forward for the first time, not indeed its authority (which was already established) but only its display, with a supposed theoretical insight of reason.   5:141

By these reminders the readers of the *Critique* of pure speculative reason will be perfectly convinced how extremely necessary, how salutary for theology and morals that laborious *deduction* of the categories was. For, if they are placed in the pure understanding it is only by this deduction that we can be prevented from taking them, with Plato, to be innate and basing on them extravagant pretensions and theories of the supersensible to which we can see no end, thereby making theology a magic lantern of chimeras; but if they are taken to be acquired, this deduction prevents us from restricting, with Epicurus, all and every use of them, even for practical purposes, merely to objects and determining grounds of the senses. But now that the *Critique* has shown by that deduction, *first* that they are not of empirical origin but have their seat and source a priori in the pure understanding, and *second* that, since they are referred *to objects in general* independently of intuition of these objects, they indeed bring about *theoretical cognition* only in application to *empirical* objects but still, applied to an object given by pure practical reason, also serve for a *determined thought of the supersensible*, yet only to the extent that this is determined merely through such predicates as necessarily belong to the pure *practical purpose* given a priori and to its possibility. Speculative restriction of pure reason and its practical extension first bring it into that *relation of equality* in which reason in general can be used purposively, and this example shows better than any other that the path *to wisdom*, if it is to be assured and not impassible or misleading, must for us human beings unavoidably pass

---

ᵂ Beschaffenheit

through science; but it is not till science is completed that we can be convinced that it leads to that goal.

5:142

VIII.
ON ASSENT[x] FROM A NEED OF PURE REASON

A need of pure reason in its speculative use leads only to hypotheses, that of pure practical reason, however, to postulates; for in the first case I ascend from the derived as high *as I will* in the series of grounds and do not need an original ground[y] in order to give objective reality to what is derived (e.g., to the causal connection of things and changes in the world), but only in order to satisfy completely my inquiring reason with respect to it. Thus I see before me order and purposiveness in nature, and need not proceed to speculation in order to assure myself of their *reality;* instead, it is only in order *to explain* them that I need *to presuppose a Deity* as their cause; but, since an inference from an effect to a determined cause, especially to a cause so precise and so completely determined as we have to think in God, is always uncertain and doubtful, such a presupposition cannot be brought further than the degree of being the most reasonable opinion for us human beings.* On the other hand, a need *of pure practical* reason is based on a *duty,* that of making something (the highest good) the object of my will so as to promote it with all my powers; and thus I must suppose its possibility and so too the conditions for this, namely God, freedom, and immortality, because I cannot prove these by my speculative reason, although I can also not refute them. This duty is based on something that is indeed quite independent of these suppositions and of itself apodictically certain, namely the moral law; and so far it needs no further

5:143
support by theoretical opinions as to the inner character of things, the secret aim of the order of the world,[z] or a ruler presiding over it, in order to bind us most perfectly to actions unconditionally conformed to the law. But the subjective effect of this law, namely the disposition conformed with it and also made necessary by it to promote the practically possible highest good, nevertheless presupposes at least that the latter is *possible;* in the contrary case it would be practically impossible to strive for the object

---

*But even here we could not allege a need *of reason* if we had not before our eyes a problematic but yet unavoidable concept of reason, namely that of an absolutely necessary being. This concept now wants to be determined, and this, when the drive toward extension is added, is the objective ground of a need of speculative reason, namely, to determine more closely the concept of a necessary being that is to serve as the original ground of others and so to make this recognizable by some means. Without such prior necessary problems there are no *needs,* at least *not of pure reason;* the rest are needs of inclination.

[x] *Fürwahrhalten,* literally "holding to be true"

[y] *Urgrund*

[z] *Abzweckung der Weltordnung*

of a concept that would be, at bottom, empty and without an object. Now, the above-mentioned postulates concern only the physical or metaphysical conditions – in a word, those which lie in the nature of things – of the *possibility* of the highest good, not, however, for the sake of a discretionary speculative purpose but of a practically necessary end of a pure rational will, which does not here *choose;* instead, it *obeys* an inflexible command of reason that has its ground *objectively* in the character of things as they must be appraised universally by pure reason and is not based upon, say, *inclination,* which is by no means justified in at once assuming, for the sake of what we *wish* on merely *subjective* grounds, that the means to it are possible or that its object is real. This is, accordingly, a *need from an absolutely necessary point of view* and justifies its presupposition not merely as a permitted hypothesis but as a postulate from a practical point of view; and, granted that the pure moral law inflexibly binds everyone as a command (not as a rule of prudence), the upright man may well say: I *will* that there be a God, that my existence in this world be also an existence in a pure world of the understanding beyond natural connections, and finally that my duration be endless; I stand by this, without paying attention to rationalizations, however little I may be able to answer them or to oppose them with others more plausible, and I will not let this belief be taken from me; for this is the only case in which my interest, because I *may* not give up anything of it, unavoidably determines my judgment.*

. .

In order to prevent misinterpretations in the use of a concept as yet so   5:144
unusual as that of a pure practical rational belief, I may add one more remark. It might almost seem as if this rational belief is here announced as itself a *command,* namely to assume the highest good as possible. But a belief that is commanded is an absurdity. If, however, one recalls from the

---

*In the *Deutsches Museum,* February 1787, there is a treatise by a very subtle and clear-headed man, the late Wizenmann,[13] whose early death is to be lamented, in which he disputes the authorization to conclude from a need to the objective reality of its object and illustrates the point by the example of a *man in love,* who, having fooled himself into an idea of beauty that is merely a chimera of his own brain, would like to conclude that such an object really exists somewhere. I grant that he is perfectly correct in this, in all cases where the need is based upon *inclination,* which cannot necessarily postulate the existence of its object even for the one affected by it, much less can it contain a requirement valid for everyone, and therefore it is a *merely subjective* ground of the wish. But in the present case it is a *need of reason* arising from an *objective* determining ground of the will, namely the moral law, which necessarily binds every rational being and therefore justifies him a priori in presupposing in nature the conditions befitting it and makes the latter inseparable from the complete practical use of reason. It is a duty to realize the highest good to the utmost of our capacity; therefore it must be possible; hence it is also unavoidable for every rational being in the world to assume what is necessary for its objective possibility. The assumption is as necessary as the moral law, in relation to which alone it is valid.

preceding explanation what is required to be assumed in the concept of the highest good, one will become aware that the assumption of this possibility cannot be commanded, and that no practical disposition requires one to *grant* it but that speculative reason must concede it without being asked, since no one can want to maintain that a worthiness of rational beings in the world to be happy in conformity with the moral law combined with a possession of this happiness proportioned to it is *impossible* in itself. Now, with respect to the first element of the highest good, namely that which concerns morality, the moral law gives merely a command, and to doubt that possibility of that component would be tantamount to calling in question the moral law itself. But as for what concerns the second part of that object, namely happiness in thorough conformity with that worthiness, there is no need of a command to grant its possibility in general, since theoretical reason has nothing to say against it; but *the*
5:145 *way* in which *we* are to think such a harmony of the laws of nature with those of freedom has in it something with respect to which we have a *choice*, since theoretical reason decides nothing with apodictic certainty about it, and with respect to this there can be a moral interest which turns the scale.

I said above that in accordance with a mere course of nature in the world happiness in exact conformity with moral worth is not to be expected and is to be held impossible, and that therefore the possibility of the highest good on this side can be granted only on the presupposition of a moral author of the world. I deliberately postponed the restricting of this judgment to the subjective conditions of our reason so as not to make use of it until the manner of its assent had been determined more closely. In fact, the impossibility referred to is *merely subjective*, that is, our reason finds it *impossible for it* to conceive, in the mere course of nature, a connection so exactly proportioned and so thoroughly purposive[a] between events occurring in the world in accordance with such different laws, although, as with everything else in nature that is purposive, it nevertheless cannot prove – that is, set forth sufficiently on objective grounds – the impossibility of it in accordance with universal laws of nature.

Now, however, a deciding ground of a different kind comes into play so as to turn the scale in this irresolution of speculative reason. The command to promote the highest good is based objectively (in practical reason); its possibility in general is likewise objectively based (in theoretical reason, which has nothing against it). But as for the way we are to represent this possibility, whether in accordance with universal laws of nature without a wise author presiding over nature or only on the supposition of such an author, reason cannot decide this objectively. Now a *subjective* condition of reason enters into this, the only way in which it is theoreti-

[a] *zweckmäßig*

cally possible for it to think the exact harmony of the realm[b] of nature with the realm of morals as the condition of the possibility of the highest good, and at the same time the only way that is conducive to morality (which is subject to an *objective* law of reason). Now, since the promotion of the highest good, and therefore the supposition of its possibility, is *objectively* necessary (though only as a consequence of practical reason), while at the same time the manner, the way in which we would think it as possible rests with our choice, in which a free interest of pure practical reason decides   5:146
for the assumption of a wise author of the world, it follows that the principle that determines our judgment about it, though it is *subjective* as a need, is yet, as the means of promoting what is *objectively* (practically) necessary, the ground of a maxim of assent for moral purposes, that is, *a pure practical rational belief.* This, then, is not commanded but – being a voluntary[c] determination of our judgment, conducive to the moral (commanded) purpose and moreover harmonizing with the theoretical need of reason to assume that existence and to make it the basis of the further use of reason – it has itself arisen from the moral disposition; it can therefore often waver even in the well-disposed but can never fall into unbelief.

IX.
ON THE WISE ADAPTATION OF THE HUMAN BEING'S COGNITIVE FACULTIES TO HIS PRACTICAL VOCATION

If human nature is called to strive for the highest good, it must also be assumed that the measure of its cognitive faculties, especially their relation to one another, is suitable to this end. Now, the *Critique* of pure *speculative* reason proves its utter insufficiency for solving, conformably with this end, the most important problems that are proposed to it, although the *Critique* does not fail to recognize the natural hints of this same reason, which are not to be overlooked, nor the great steps that it can take to approach this great goal that is set before it, which, however, it can never reach of itself, even with the aid of the greatest cognition of nature. Nature then seems here to have provided for us only in a stepmotherly fashion with the faculty needed for our end.

Assuming now that nature had here complied with our wish and given us that capacity for insight or that enlightenment[d] which we would like to possess or which some believe erroneously they actually do possess, what would, as far as we can tell, be the result of it? Unless our whole nature were at the same time changed, the *inclinations*, which always have the first   5:147

[b] *Reichs*
[c] *freiwillig*
[d] *Erleuchtung*

121

word, would first demand their satisfaction and, combined with reasonable reflection, their greatest possible and most lasting satisfaction under the name of *happiness;* the moral law would afterward speak, in order to keep them within their proper limits and even to subject them all to a higher end which has no regard to inclination. But instead of the conflict that the moral disposition now has to carry on with the inclinations, in which, though after some defeats, moral strength of soul is to be gradually acquired, *God and eternity with their awful majesty* would stand unceasingly *before our eyes* (for what we can prove perfectly holds as much certainty for us as what we are assured of by our sight). Transgression of the law would, no doubt, be avoided: what is commanded would be done; but because the *disposition* from which actions ought to be done cannot be instilled by any command, and because the spur to activity in this case would be promptly at hand and *external,* reason would have no need to work itself up so as to gather strength to resist the inclinations by a lively representation of the dignity of the law: hence most actions conforming to the law would be done from fear, only a few from hope, and none at all from duty, and the moral worth of actions, on which alone in the eyes of supreme wisdom the worth of the person and even that of the world depends, would not exist at all. As long as human nature remains as it is, human conduct would thus be changed into mere mechanism in which, as in a puppet show, everything would *gesticulate* well but there would be *no life* in the figures. Now, when it is quite otherwise with us; when with all the effort of our reason we have only a very obscure and ambiguous view into the future; when the governor of the world allows us only to conjecture his existence and his grandeur, not to behold them or prove them clearly; when, on the other hand, the moral law within us, without promising or threatening anything with certainty, demands of us disinterested respect; and when, finally, this respect alone, become active and ruling, first allows us a view into the realm of the supersensible, though only with weak glances; then there can be a truly moral disposition, devoted immediately to the moral law, and a rational creature can become worthy of the highest good in conformity with the moral worth of his person and not merely with his actions. Thus what the study of nature and of the human being teaches us sufficiently elsewhere may well be true here also: that the inscrutable wisdom by which we exist is not less worthy of veneration in what it has denied us than in what it has granted us.

5:148

The
critique of practical reason
Part two

Doctrine of the method
of
pure practical reason

The *doctrine of the method* of pure *practical* reason cannot be understood as the way to proceed (in reflection as well as in exposition) with pure practical principles with a view to scientific *cognition* of them, which alone is properly called method elsewhere, in the *theoretical* (for popular cognition needs a *manner*ᵉ but science a *method*, i.e., a procedure *in accordance with principles* of reason by which alone the manifold of a cognition can become a *system)*. Here the doctrine of method is understood, instead, as the way in which one can provide the laws of pure practical reason with *access* to the human mind and *influence* on its maxims, that is, the way in which one can make objectively practical reason *subjectively* practical as well.

It is now clear that those determining grounds of the will which alone make maxims properly moral and give them a moral worth – the immediate representation of the law and the objectively necessary observance of it as duty – must be represented as the proper incentives to action, since otherwise *legality* of actions would be produced but not *morality* of dispositions. But it is not so clear, and on the contrary must at first glance seem to everyone quite improbable, that even subjectively that presentation of pure virtue can have *more power* over the human mind and can provide a far stronger incentive to effect even that legality of actions and to bring forth stronger resolutions to prefer the law to every other consideration, from pure respect for it, than all the deceptive allurementsᶠ of enjoyment and, in general, everything that may be counted as happiness, or even all threats of pain and troubles can produce. But it is really so, and if human nature were not so constituted, no way of representing the law by circumlocutions and by means recommending itᵍ would ever bring forth morality of disposition. Everything would be sheer hypocrisy; the law would be hated or even despised, though still observed for the sake of one's own advantage. The letter of the law (legality) would be found in our actions, but the spirit of it in our dispositions (morality) would not be found at all; and since with all our efforts we could not altogether free ourselves from reason in our judgment, we would unavoidably have to appear worthless, depraved human beings in our own eyes, even if we sought to compensate ourselves for this mortification before the inner court by enjoying the pleasure that, in our delusion, we suppose a natural or divine law has connected with the machinery of its police, guided only by what was done without troubling itself about the motives from which it was done.

It certainly cannot be denied that in order to bring either a mind that is still uncultivated or one that is degraded onto the track of the morally good in the first place, some preparatory guidance is needed to attract it

ᵉ *Art*
ᶠ *Anlockungen aus Vorspiegelungen*
ᵍ *emfehlende Mittel*

by means of its own advantage or to alarm it by fear of harm; but as soon as this machinery, these leading strings have had even some effect, the pure moral motive must be brought to bear on the soul, the motive which – not only because it is the only one that can ground a character (a consistent practical cast of mind in accordance with unchangeable maxims) but also because it teaches the human being to feel his own dignity – gives his mind power, unexpected even by himself, to tear himself away from all sensible attachments so far as they want to rule over him and to find a rich compensation for the sacrifice he makes in the independence of his rational nature and the greatness of soul to which he sees that he is called. We will therefore show, by observations anyone can make, that this property of our minds, this receptivity to a pure moral interest and hence the moving force of the pure representation of virtue, when it is duly brought to bear on the human heart is the most powerful incentive to the good and the only one when an enduring and meticulous observance of

5:153 moral maxims is in question. It must, however, be remembered that if these observations show only the reality of such a feeling but not any moral improvement brought about by it, this takes nothing away from[h] the only method there is for making the objectively practical laws of pure reason subjectively practical merely through the pure representation of duty, as if it were an empty fantasy. For, since this method has never yet been widely practiced experience can say nothing of its result; instead one can only ask for proofs of the receptivity to such incentives, which I will now present briefly and then sketch in a few words the method of founding and cultivating genuine moral dispositions.

If one attends to the course of conversation in mixed companies consisting not merely of scholars and subtle reasoners but also of business people or women, one notices that their entertainment includes, besides storytelling and jesting, arguing; for storytelling, if it is to have novelty and with it interest, is soon exhausted and jesting easily becomes insipid. Now, of all arguments there are none that more excite the participation of persons who are otherwise soon bored with subtle reasoning and that bring a certain liveliness into the company than arguments about the *moral worth* of this or that action by which the character of some person is to be made out. Those for whom anything subtle and refined in theoretical questions is dry and irksome soon join in when it is a question of how to make out the moral import of a good or evil action that has been related, and to an extent one does not otherwise expect of them on any object of speculation they are precise, refined, and subtle in thinking out everything that could lesson or even just make suspect the purity of purpose and consequently the degree of virtue in it. In these appraisals one can often see revealed the character of the person himself who judges others: some, in exercising

[h] *keinen Abbruch tue*

126

their judicial office especially upon the dead, seem inclined chiefly to defend the goodness that is related of this or that deed against all injurious charges of impurity and ultimately to defend the whole moral worth of the person against the reproach of dissimulation and secret wickedness; others, on the contrary, are more prone to contest this worth by accusations and fault-finding. One cannot always, however, attribute to the latter the 5:154 intention of arguing away all virtue from examples of human beings in order to make it an empty name: often it is, instead, only well-meant strictness in determining genuine moral import in accordance with an uncompromising law, comparison with which, instead of with examples, greatly lowers self-conceit in moral matters, and humility is not only taught but felt by anyone when he examines himself strictly. Nevertheless, one can for the most part see, in those who defend the purity of intention in given examples, that where there is a presumption of uprightness they would like to remove even the least spot from the determining ground lest, if the truthfulness of all examples were disputed and the purity of all human virtue denied, human virtue might in the end be held a mere phantom, and so all striving toward it would be deprecated as vain affectation and delusive self-conceit.

I do not know why educators of young people have not long since made use of this propensity of reason to enter with pleasure upon even the most subtle examination of the practical questions put to them and why they have not, after first laying the foundation in a purely moral catechism, searched through the biographies of ancient and modern times in order to have at hand instances for the duties presented, in which, especially by comparison of similar actions under different circumstances, they could well activate their pupils' appraisal in marking the lesser or greater moral import of such actions; they would find that even someone very young, who is not yet ready for speculation, would soon become very acute and thereby not a little interested, since he would feel the progress of his faculty of judgment; and, what is most important, they could hope with confidence that frequent practice in knowing good conduct in all its purity and approving it and, on the other hand, marking with regret or contempt the least deviation from it, even though it is carried on only as a game of judgment in which children can compete with one another, yet will leave behind a lasting impression of esteem on the one hand and disgust on the other, which by mere habituation,[i] repeatedly looking on such actions as deserving approval or censure, would make a good foundation for uprightness in 5:155 the future conduct of life. But I do wish that educators would spare their pupils examples of so-called *noble* (supermeritorious) actions, with which our sentimental writings so abound, and would expose them all[j] only to

---

[i] *Gewohnheit*
[j] *alles ... auszusetzen*, perhaps "refer everything"

duty and to the worth that a human being can and must give himself in his own eyes by consciousness of not having transgressed it; for, whatever runs up into empty wishes and longings for inaccessible perfection produces mere heroes of romance who, while they pride themselves on their feeling for extravagant greatness, release themselves in return from the observance of common and everyday obligation,[k] which then seems to them insignificant and petty.*

But if one asks: What, then, really is *pure* morality, by which as a touchstone one must test the moral content of every action? I must admit that only philosophers can make the decision of this question doubtful, for it is long since decided in common human reason, not indeed by abstract general formulae but by habitual use, like the difference between the right and the left hand. We will, accordingly, first show in an example the mark by which pure virtue is tested and, representing it as set before, say, a ten-year-old boy for his appraisal, see whether he must necessarily judge so of himself, without being directed to it by a teacher. One tells him the story of an honest man whom someone wants to induce to join the calumniators of an innocent but otherwise powerless person (say, Anne Boleyn, accused by Henry VIII of England). He is offered gain, that is, great gifts or high rank; he rejects them. This will produce mere approval and applause in the listener's soul, because it is gain. Now threats of loss begin. Among these calumniators are his best friends, who now refuse him their friendship; close relatives, who threaten to disinherit him (he is not wealthy); powerful people, who can pursue and hurt him in all places and circumstances; a prince who threatens him with loss of freedom and even of life itself. But, so that the measure of suffering may be full and he may also feel the pain that only a morally good heart can feel very deeply, represent his family, threatened with extreme distress and poverty, as *imploring him to yield* and himself, though upright, yet with a heart not hard or insensible[m] either to compassion or to his own distress; represent him at a moment when he wishes that he had never lived to see the day that exposed him to such unutterable pain and yet remains firm in his resolu-

5:156

---

*It is quite advisable to praise actions in which a great, unselfish, sympathetic disposition or humanity is manifested. But in this case one must call attention not so much to the *elevation of soul*, which is very fleeting and transitory, as to the *subjection of the heart* to *duty*, from which a more lasting impression can be expected, because this brings principles with it (but the former, only ebullitions).[l] One need only reflect a little and one will always find a debt that he has somehow incurred with respect to the human race (even if it were only that, by the inequality of human beings in the civil constitution, one enjoys advantages on account of which others must all the more do without), which will prevent the self-complacent image of *merit* from supplanting the thought of *duty*.

[k] *Schuldigkeit*
[l] *Aufwallungen*
[m] *doch eben nicht von festen, unempfindlichen Organen das Gefühl*

tion to be truthful, without wavering or even doubting; then my young listener will be raised step by step from mere approval to admiration, from that to amazement, and finally to the greatest veneration and a lively wish that he himself could be such a man (though certainly not in such circumstances); and yet virtue is here worth so much only because it costs so much, not because it brings any profit. All the admiration, and even the endeavor to resemble this character, here rests wholly on the purity of the moral principle, which can be clearly represented only if one removes from the incentive to action everything that people may reckon only to happiness. Thus morality must have more power over the human heart the more purely it is presented. From this it follows that if the law of morals and the image of holiness and virtue are to exercise any influence at all on our soul, they can do so only insofar as they are laid to heart in their purity as incentives, unmixed with any view to one's welfare, for it is in suffering that they show themselves most excellently. But that which, by being removed strengthens the effect of a moving force must have been a hindrance. Consequently every admixture of incentives taken from one's own happiness is a hindrance to providing the moral law with influence on the human heart. I maintain, further, that even in that admired action, if the motive from which it was done was esteem for one's duty, then it is just this respect for the law that straightaway has the greatest force on the mind of a spectator, and not, say, any pretension to inner magnanimity and a noble cast of mind; consequently duty, not merit, must have not only the most determinate influence on the mind but, when it is represented in the correct light of its inviolability, the most penetrating influence as well. 5:157

In our times, when one hopes to have more influence on the mind through melting, tender feelings or high-flown, puffed-up pretensions, which make the heart languid instead of strengthening it, than by a dry and earnest representation of duty, which is more suited to human imperfection and to progress in goodness, it is more necessary than ever to direct attention to this method. It is altogether contrapurposive to set before children, as a model, actions as noble, magnanimous, meritorious, thinking that one can captivate them by inspiring enthusiasm for such actions. For, since they are still so backward in observance of the commonest duty and even in correct estimation of it, this is tantamount to soon making them fantasizers. But even with the instructed and experienced part of humankind this supposed incentive has, if not a prejudicial effect on the heart, at least no genuine moral one, though this is what one wanted to bring about by means of it.

All *feelings*, especially those that are to produce unusual exertions, must accomplish their effect at the moment they are at their height and before they calm down; otherwise they accomplish nothing because the heart naturally returns to its natural moderate vital motion and accordingly falls back into the languor that was proper to it before, since something was applied that indeed stimulated it but nothing that strengthened it. *Principles* must be built on concepts; on any other foundation there can be only seizures, which can give a person no moral worth and not even confidence in himself, without which the consciousness of one's moral disposition and of a character of this kind, the highest good in human beings, cannot come to exist. Now, if these concepts are to become subjectively practical they must stop short with objective laws or morality, to be admired and esteemed with reference to humanity: the representation of them must be considered in relation to human beings and to the individual human

5:158   being; for then this law appears in a form that, though indeed highly deserving of respect, is not so pleasing as if it belonged to the element to which he is naturally accustomed but instead as it constrains him to leave this element, often not without self-denial, and to go to a higher element in which he can maintain himself only with effort and with unceasing apprehension of relapsing. In a word, the moral law demands obedience from duty and not from a predilection that cannot and ought not to be presupposed at all.

Let us now see in an example whether there is more subjective moving force as an incentive if an action is represented as a noble and magnanimous one than if it is represented merely as duty in relation to the earnest moral law. The action by which someone tries with extreme danger to his life to rescue people from a shipwreck, finally losing his own life in the attempt, will indeed be reckoned, on one side, as duty but on the other and even for the most part as a meritorious action; but our esteem for it will be greatly weakened by the concept of *duty to himself,* which seems in this case to suffer some infringement. More decisive is someone's magnanimous sacrifice of his life for the preservation of his country; and yet there still remains some scruple as to whether it is so perfect a duty to devote oneself to this purpose of one's own accord and unbidden, and the action has not in itself the full force of a model and impulse to imitation. But if it is an essential[n] duty, transgression of which violates the moral law in itself and without regard to human welfare and, as it were, tramples on its holiness (such as are usually called duties to God because in him we think the ideal of holiness in a substance), then we give the most perfect esteem to compliance with it at the sacrifice of everything that could ever have value for our dearest inclinations, and we find our soul strengthened and elevated by such an example when we can convince ourselves, in it, that human nature is capable of so great an elevation above every incentive that nature can oppose to it. Juvenal presents such an example in a climax that makes the reader feel vividly the force of the incentive present in the pure law of duty, as duty:

[n] *unerlaßliche*

Esto bonus miles, tutor bonus, arbiter idem Integer; ambiguae si quando citabere testis Incertaeque rei, Phalaris licet imperet, ut sis Falsus, et admoto dictet periuria tauro, Summum crede nefas animam praeferre pudori, Et propter vitam vivendi perdere causas.[o]

When we can bring any flattering thought of merit into our action, then the incentive is already somewhat mixed with self-love and thus has some assistance from the side of sensibility. But to put everything below the holiness of duty alone and become aware that one *can* do it because our own reason recognizes this as its command and says that one *ought* to do it: this is, as it were, to raise oneself altogether above the sensible world,[p] and this consciousness of the law as also an incentive is inseparably combined with consciousness of a power *ruling over sensibility*, even if not always with effect; yet frequent engagement with it and the initially minor attempts at using it give hope of its effectiveness, so that gradually the greatest, but purely moral, interest in it may be produced in us.

Accordingly, the method takes the following course. *At first* it is only a question of making appraisal of actions by moral laws a natural occupation and, as it were, a habit accompanying all our own free actions as well as our observation of those of others, and of sharpening it by asking first whether the action objectively *conforms with the moral law*, and with which law; by this, attention to such law as provides merely a *ground* of obligation is distinguished from that which is in fact *obligatory (leges obligandi a legibus obligantibus)*[q] (e.g., the law of what the *need* of human beings requires of me as contrasted with what their *right* requires, the latter of which pre-scribes essential duties whereas the former prescribes only nonessential[r] duties), and thus one teaches how to distinguish different duties that come together in an action. The other point to which attention must be directed is the question whether the action was also done (subjectively) *for the sake of the moral law*, so that it has not only moral correctness as a deed but also moral worth as a disposition by its maxim. Now, there is no doubt that this exercise and the consciousness of a cultivation of our reason in judging merely about the practical, arising from this exercise, must gradu-ally produce a certain interest in reasons's law itself and hence in morally good actions. For, we finally come to like something the contemplation of which lets us feel a more extended use of our cognitive powers, which is especially furthered by that in which we find moral correctness, since only

---

[o] Be a good soldier, a good guardian, and an incorruptible judge; if summoned to bear witness in some dubious and uncertain cause, though Phalaris[14] himself should dictate that you perjure yourself and bring his bull to move you, count it the greatest of all iniquities to prefer life to honor and to lose, for the sake of living, all that makes life worth living. (Juvenal *Satire* 8.79–84).

[p] The remainder of this sentence is grammatically difficult.

[q] Compare *The Metaphysics of Morals* (6:224).

[r] *außerwesentliche*

in such an order of things can reason, with its capacity to determine a priori in accordance with principles what ought to be done, find satisfaction. Even an observer of nature finally comes to like objects that at first offended his senses when he discovers in them the great purposiveness of their organization, so that his reason delights in contemplating them, and Leibniz spared an insect that he had carefully examined with a microscope and replaced it on its leaf because he had found himself instructed by his view of it and had, as it were, received a benefit from it.

But this employment of the faculty of judgment, which lets us feel our own cognitive powers, is not yet interest in actions and in their morality itself. It merely brings someone to like to entertain himself with such an appraisal and gives to virtue or the cast of mind according to moral laws a form of beauty, which is admired but not yet on that account sought *(laudatur et alget);*[s] it is the same with everything whose contemplation produces subjectively a consciousness of the harmony of our powers of representation and in which we feel our entire cognitive faculty (understanding and imagination) strengthened: it produces a satisfaction that can also be communicated to others, while nevertheless the existence of the object remains indifferent to us, inasmuch as the object is viewed only as the occasion of our becoming aware of the tendency of talents[t] in us which are elevated above animality. Now, however, the *second* exercise begins its work, namely to draw attention, in the lively presentation of the moral disposition in examples, to the purity of will, first only as a negative perfection of the will insofar as in an action from duty no incentives of inclination have any influence on it as determining grounds; by this, however, the pupil's attention is fixed on the consciousness of his *freedom* and, although this renunciation excites an initial feeling of pain, nevertheless, by its withdrawing the pupil from the constraint of even true needs, there is made known to him at the same time a deliverance from the manifold dissatisfaction in which all those needs entangle him and his mind is made receptive to the feeling of satisfaction from other sources. The heart is freed and relieved of a burden that always secretly presses upon it, when in pure moral resolutions, examples of which are set before him, there is revealed to the human being an inner capacity not otherwise correctly known by himself, the *inner freedom* to release himself from the impetuous importunity of inclinations so that none of them, not even the dearest, has any influence on a resolution for which we are now to make use of our reason. In a case where *I alone* know that the wrong is on my side and, although a free confession of it and an offer of satisfaction are strongly opposed by vanity, selfishness, and even an otherwise not illegitimate antipathy to him whose right I have detracted from, I am neverthe-

5:161

---

[s] [Honesty] is praised and starves. (Juvenal *Satire* 1.74).
[t] *Anlage der Talente*

less able to disregard all these considerations; and this includes consciousness of an independence from inclinations and from circumstances and of the possibility of being sufficient to myself, which is salutary to me in general, in other respects as well. And now the law of duty, through the positive worth that observance of it lets us feel, finds easier access through the *respect for ourselves* in the consciousness of our freedom. When this is well established, when a human being dreads nothing more than to find, on self-examination, that he is worthless and contemptible in his own eyes, then every good moral disposition can be grafted onto it, because this is the best, and indeed the sole, guard to prevent ignoble and corrupting impulses from breaking into the mind.

I have intended, here, only to point out the most general maxims of the doctrine of the method of moral cultivation and exercise. Since the variety of duties requires further special determinations for each kind of duty and would thus constitute a lengthy affair, I shall be excused if in a work such as this, which is only preparatory, I go no further than these outlines.

Conclusion

Two things fill the mind with ever new and increasing admiration and reverence,[u] the more often and more steadily one reflects on them: *the starry heavens above me and the moral law within me.* I do not need to search for them and merely conjecture them as though they were veiled in obscurity or in the transcendent region[v] beyond my horizon; I see them before me and connect them immediately with the consciousness of my existence. The first begins from the place I occupy in the external world of sense and extends the connection in which I stand into an unbounded magnitude with worlds upon worlds and systems of systems, and moreover into the unbounded times of their periodic motion, their beginning and their duration. The second begins from my invisible self, my personality, and presents me in a world which has true infinity but which can be discovered only by the understanding, and I cognize that my connection with that world (and thereby with all those visible worlds as well) is not merely contingent, as in the first case, but universal and necessary. The first view of a countless multitude of worlds annihilates, as it were, my importance as an *animal creature*, which after it has been for a short time provided with vital force (one knows not how) must give back to the planet (a mere speck in the universe) the matter from which it came. The second, on the contrary, infinitely raises my worth as an *intelligence* by my

5:162

[u] *Ehrfurcht*
[v] *im Überschwenglichen*

133

personality, in which the moral law reveals to me a life independent of animality and even of the whole sensible world, at least so far as this may be inferred from the purposive determination*w* of my existence by this law, a determination not restricted to the conditions and boundaries of this life but reaching into the infinite.

But though admiration and respect can indeed excite to inquiry, they cannot supply the want of it. What, then, is to be done in order to enter upon inquiry in a way that is useful and befitting the sublimity of the object? Examples may serve in this for warning but also for imitation. Consideration of the world began from the noblest spectacle that can ever be presented to the human senses and that our understanding can bear to follow in its broad extent, and it ended – in astrology. Morals began with the noblest property of human nature, the development and cultivation of which looked to infinite use, and it ended – in enthusiasm or in superstition. So it is with all crude attempts in which the principal part of the business depends upon the use of reason, which does not come of itself,

5:163 like the use of the feet, by frequent exercise, especially when it has to do with properties that cannot be directly exhibited in common experience. But after there had come into vogue, though late, the maxim of carefully reflecting beforehand on all the steps that reason proposed to take and not letting it proceed otherwise than on the track of a previously well-considered method, then appraisal of the structure of the universe obtained quite a different direction and along with it an incomparably happier outcome. The fall of a stone, the motion of a sling, resolved into their elements and the forces manifested in them and treated mathematically, produced at last that clear and henceforth unchangeable insight into the structure of the world which, with continued observation, one can hope will always be extended while one need never fear having to retreat.

This example can recommend that we take the same path in treating of the moral predispositions*x* of our nature and can give us hope of a similarly good outcome. We have at hand examples of reason judging morally. We can analyze them into their elementary concepts and, in default of *mathematics*, adopt a procedure similar to that of *chemistry* – the *separation*, by repeated experiments on common human understanding, of the empirical from the rational that may be found in them – and come to know both of them *pure* and what each can accomplish of itself; and in this way we can prevent on the one hand the errors of a still *crude*, unpracticed appraisal and on the other hand (what is far more necessary) the *leaps of genius* by which, as happens with the adepts of the philosopher's stone, without any methodical study or knowledge of nature visionary treasures are promised and true ones are thrown away. In a word, science (critically

w *zweckmäßigen Bestimmung*
x *Anlagen*

sought and methodically directed) is the narrow gate that leads to the *doctrine of wisdom,* if by this is understood not merely what one ought *to do* but what ought to serve *teachers* as a guide to prepare well and clearly the path to wisdom which everyone should travel, and to secure others against taking the wrong way; philosophy must always remain the guardian of this science, and though the public need take no interest[y] in its subtle investigations it has to take an interest in the *doctrines*[z] which, after being worked up in this way, can first be quite clear to it.

[y] *keinen Anteil . . . zu nehmen hat*
[z] *Lehren*

Index

morality – *continued*
  principle of pure practical reason
    basis of, 30, 37; material principles of,
    36–37, 55–56 (*see also* heteronomy);
    justification of moral principles, 77
    (*see also* deduction of the moral law)
mysticism, 101
  of practical reason, 61

nature, 39, 59ff.
  as existence of things under laws, 38;
    sensible vs. supersensible nature,
    38ff.; intelligible author of, 96 (*see also*
    God as moral author of nature)
necessity
  moral necessity, 29, 70–71
  objective vs. subjective necessity (custom)
    in judgments, 10–11, 45ff.
  objective vs. subjective necessity of
    practical principles, 18, 23–24
  subjective necessity of interest in
    happiness, 23
  subjective necessity of postulates of
    practical reason, 4, 9n, 105, 120–121
need 23, 94, 131; in finite rational beings, 23,
  53
need of reason, *see* reason, need of
noumena, 6, 38, 43, 44, 47ff., 78, 82, 86, 96

object of practical reason, 50ff., 91–92, 102
  and determining grounds of will, 52,
    54–56, 65; highest good as object not
    determining ground of will, 92, 108
  see also the good
obligation, 29, 70, 131; ground of vs. actual,
  131
omission, category of, 58
ought and can, 27–28, 131

pain, 51, 52ff.
paralogisms of speculative reason, 110
perfection
  (material) moral principle of, 36, 56
  moral perfection, 9n, 71–72, 102ff.,
    unending progress towards as ideal
    for finite rational beings, 103, 103n,
    106n, 107; cf. 72
  theoretical vs. practical senses of, 36ff.
  transcendental vs. metaphysical senses of,
    36
permitted, category of, defined: 9n, 58
personality, 74, 133–134
  category of, 57
  as independence from mechanism of
    nature, subjection to moral laws, 74
persons, 63, 66; *see also* humanity
philosophy
  critical, 4–5, 8n; dogmatic, 8n; as doctrine

  of wisdom, 91, 135; and science, 91,
    114n, 134–135
Plato, 107n, 117
pleasure, defined: 7–8n, 19, 23–24, 63, 68ff.,
    97–98
  feelings of pleasure as determining
    ground of choice, 20–22, 50–51, 55;
    based on receptivity of subject, 20,
    50–51, 55; what is pleasurable known
    only empirically, 19–20, 23, 50ff.;
    pleasure from objects of senses and
    understanding of one and the same
    kind, 21ff.
possibility
  moral vs. physical possibility of objects of
    volition, 50; cf. also 40, 57; moral
    impossibility, 60
postulates of practical reason, 9n, 41, 79, 102,
    110–111, 118–119
  vs. mathematical postulates, 9n, of
    geometry, 28; vs. hypotheses, 105,
    118; defined as indemonstrable
    theoretical proposition connected to
    unconditional practical law, 102, 110;
    concern physical and metaphysical
    conditions of necessary practical end,
    119; immortality of soul as, 102–103;
    existence of God as, 103–110; extend
    cognition for practical purposes
    without extending theoretical
    cognition, 4–5, 110–115 (*see also*
    cognition, theoretical); necessity of
    subjective though unconditional, 9n,
    105; cf. 4; warranted by need of pure
    practical reason, 118–119; content of
    rational faith, 119–121
precepts, practical, 18, 23, 57, 58; precept of
    advantage, 66; *see also* counsel
predicates, transcendental and ontological,
    114
Priestly, 83
primacy, defined: 100; of practical reason in
    relation to speculative reason, 101–102
principles, practical, defined: 17
  subjective vs. objective, 17–19; empirical
    practical principles furnish no laws,
    18; material practical principles,
    defined: 19, 37; all material practical
    principles fall under principle of self-
    love or happiness, 19–20; formal, 20,
    29, 30, 31, 37, 56 (*see also* form of law,
    practical law)
principle of contradiction, 45
prudence, 32ff., 75, 93, 106, 106n
psychology, 8n
punishment, 34ff., 53, 84
purposiveness of nature [*Zweckmäßigkeit*],
    116, 120, 132

Cambridge texts in the history of philosophy

Titles published in the series thus far

Antoine Arnauld and Pierre Nicole *Logic or the Art of Thinking* (edited by Jill Vance Buroker)

Boyle *A Free Enquiry into the Vulgarly Received Notion of Nature* (edited by Edward B. Davis and Michael Hunter)

Conway *The Principles of the Most Ancient and Modern Philosophy* (edited by Allison P. Coudert and Taylor Corse)

Cudworth *A Treatise Concerning Eternal and Immutable Morality* with *A Treatise of Freewill* (edited by Sarah Hutton)

Descartes *Meditations on First Philosophy*, with selections from the *Objections and Replies* (edited with an introduction by John Cottingham)

Kant *Critique of Practical Reason* (edited by Mary Gregor with an introduction by Andrews Reath)

Kant *The Metaphysics of Morals* (edited by Mary Gregor with an introduction by Roger Sullivan)

Kant *Prolegomena to any Future Metaphysics* (edited by Gary Hatfield)

La Mettrie *Machine Man and Other Writings* (edited by Ann Thomson)

Leibniz *New Essays on Human Understanding* (edited by Peter Remnant and Jonathan Bennett)

Malebranche *Dialogues on Metaphysics and on Religion* (edited by Nicholas Jolley and David Scott)

Malebranche *The Search after Truth* (edited by Thomas M. Lennon and Paul J. Olscamp)

Mendelssohn *Philosophical Writings* (edited by Daniel O. Dahlstrom)

Nietzsche *Daybreak* (edited by Maudemarie Clark and Brian Leiter, translated by R. J. Hollingdale)

Nietzsche *Human, All Too Human* (translated by R. J. Hollingdale with an introduction by Richard Schacht)

Nietzsche *Untimely Meditations* (edited by Daniel Breazeale, translated by R. J. Hollingdale)

Schleiermacher *On Religion: Speeches to its Cultured Despisers* (edited by Richard Crouter)